When should I travel to get the best airfare?
Where do I go for answers to my travel questions?
What's the best and easiest way to plan and book my trip?

frommers.travelocity.com

Frommer's, the travel guide leader, has teamed up with **Travelocity.com**, the leader in online travel, to bring you an in-depth, easy-to-use resource designed to help you plan and book your trip online.

At **frommers.travelocity.com**, you'll find free online updates about your destination from the experts at Frommer's plus the outstanding travel planning and purchasing features of Travelocity.com. Travelocity.com provides reservations capabilities for 95 percent of all airline seats sold, more than 47,000 hotels, and over 50 car rental companies. In addition, Travelocity.com offers more than 2,000 exciting vacation and cruise packages. Travelocity.com puts you in complete control of your travel planning with these and other great features:

Expert travel guidance from Frommer's—over 150 writers reporting from around the world!

Best Fare Finder—an interactive calendar tells you when to travel to get the best airfare

Fare Watcher—we'll track airfare changes to your favorite destinations

Dream Maps—a mapping feature that suggests travel opportunities based on your budget

Shop Safe Guarantee—24 hours a day/7 days a week live customer service, and more!

Whether traveling on a tight budget, looking for a quick weekend getaway, or planning the trip of a lifetime, Frommer's guides and Travelocity.com will make your travel dreams a reality. You've bought the book, now book the trip!

Frommer's

irreverent guide to Rome

other titles in the

irreverent guide

series

Irreverent Amsterdam

Irreverent Boston

Irreverent Chicago

Irreverent Las Vegas

Irreverent Los Angeles

Irreverent London

Irreverent Manhattan

Irreverent New Orleans

Irreverent Paris

Irreverent San Francisco

Irreverent Seattle/Portland

Irreverent Vancouver

Irreverent Walt Disney World

Irreverent Washington, D.C.

Frommer's

irreverent guide to Rome

By
Melanie
Mize

HUNGRY MINDS, INC.

a disclaimer

Please note that prices fluctuate in the course of time, and travel information changes under the impact of the many factors that influence the travel industry. We therefore suggest that you write or call ahead for confirmation when making your travel plans. Every effort has been made to ensure the accuracy of information throughout this book and the contents of this publication are believed correct at the time of printing. Nevertheless, the publishers cannot accept responsibility for errors or omissions or for changes in details given in this guide or for the consequences of any reliance on the information provided by the same. Assessments of attractions and so forth are based upon the author's own experience and therefore, descriptions given in this guide necessarily contain an element of subjective opinion, which may not reflect the publisher's opinion or dictate a reader's own experience on another occasion. Readers are invited to write to the publisher with ideas, comments, and suggestions for future editions.

Your safety is important to us, however, so we encourage you to stay alert and be aware of your surroundings. Keep a close eye on cameras, purses, and wallets, all favorite targets of thieves and pickpockets.

Published by HUNGRY MINDS, INC.

909 Third Avenue,
New York, NY 10022

ISBN 0-7645-6225-8
ISSN 1534-908X

Interior design contributed to by Tsang Seymour Design Studio

special sales

For general information on Hungry Minds' products and services please contact our Customer Care Department within the U.S. at 800-762-2974, outside the U.S. at 317-572-3993 or fax 317-572-4002.

For sales inquiries and reseller information, including discounts, premium and bulk quantity sales, and foreign-language translations, please contact our Customer Care Department at 800-434-3422 or fax 317-572-4002.

Manufactured in the United States of America

what's so irreverent?

It's up to you.

You can buy a traditional guidebook with its fluff, its promotional hype, its let's-find-something-nice-to-say-about-everything point of view. Or you can buy an Irreverent guide.

What the Irreverents give you is the lowdown, the inside story. They have nothing to sell but the truth, which includes a balance of good and bad. They praise, they trash, they weigh, and leave the final decisions up to you. No tourist board, no chamber of commerce will ever recommend them.

Our writers are insiders, who feel passionate about the cities they live in, and have strong opinions they want to share with you. They take a special pleasure leading you where other guides fear to tread.

How irreverent are they? One of our authors insisted on writing under a pseudonym. "I couldn't show my face in town again if I used my own name," she told me. "My friends would never speak to me." Such is the price of honesty. She, like you, should know she'll always have a friend at Frommer's.

Warm regards,

Michael Spring

Michael Spring
Publisher

contents

introduction

Romans are completely jaded. Hey, you would be, too, if your daily routine consisted of commuting past the Colosseum, gulping an espresso a few paces from the Pantheon, and shopping in the shadow of St. Peter's dome. Besides seeing masterpieces from the eras of Caesar, Constantine, Trajan, and Michelangelo on a daily basis, Romans are confronted with priceless artwork in their churches and major archaeological sites in their backyards. This makes for some interesting juxtapositions. For instance, one of Rome's largest bus hubs is practically on top of ruins from Caesar's time. To outsiders, this kind of seemingly casual treatment of priceless artifacts may seem careless and arrogant. Not the case—Romans love their city. Residents of the "Eternal City" are fiercely proud of their home, and most would not even consider living anywhere else. But life must go on, even in a city with this much ancient history still hanging around.

There is no bigger understatement than to say that there's a lot to see in Rome. A familiar joke about the Eternal City goes something like this: A man brags to his friend that he plans to take his wife to Rome for their 40th wedding anniversary. "What will you do for your 50th?" the friend asks. "I'll go and get her" is the reply. The collections in the Vatican Museums alone could keep you occupied for the rest of your natural life. And when you're finished with the Church's collection, there are at least 50 other museums and galleries worth of a visit. Whatever your fancy—Etruscan relics, medieval lore, Renaissance painting, or sappy English literature—Rome has a museum for it. Even pasta gets its props, with a small but comprehensive museum around the bend from the Trevi Fountain. And there are enough churches, chapels, and cathedrals that you could bow down to a different one each day for a year and still have some to spare. Frequent fliers can even be blessed in Fiumicino Airport's new chapel.

Any kind of traveler can satisfy a fetish with a trip to Rome. Gastronomes and gluttons can gobble up what is arguably some of the best food and wine on the planet. Saints and sinners can feast their eyes on St. Peter's Basilica, the Sistine Chapel, and possibly the pope. Culture vultures and history buffs can tour the Colosseum, meander about the Forum, and ponder the dimensions of the Pantheon. And shoppers, beware—a trip to Rome could likely do a number on the wallet. Couturier Valentino has his headquarters here, and all the "in" names in Italian fashion—Gucci, Prada, Brioni—have a spot on the wealthy shopping street, Via Condotti. It is impossible to see all of the treasures of Rome in one trip, much less in one lifetime.

We've all heard that Rome wasn't built in a day—actually, it took a couple thousand years and incalculable political upheavals for Rome to become the multilayered metropolis that it is now. Romulus, a man who, along with his twin brother, was suckled by a she-wolf on the Palatine Hill, got things going when he offed his brother (who was also vying for control of the area) and raped the nearby Sabine women to further the flock. Roman history even pinpoints the exact date of the city's founding—April 21, 753 BC—a day that is celebrated each year with grand, government-subsidized bashes.

Over the years, self-righteous emperors, pontiffs, and dictators have added on to—or peeled away—Rome's layers. Pope Julius II plowed through who knows how many standing constructions to create the Via Giulia, a straight, pilgrim route from the Ponte Sisto to the Vatican. Rome's short-lived stint as an independent kingdom, ruled by the Savoia clan, lasted only 12 years, but even it managed to change the physical face of the city in the wake of its demise, inspiring the construction of one of Rome's most despised monuments, the mammoth Vittoriano. As this book was going to press, Roman officials were discussing whether to jackhammer Via Fori

Imperiali—Mussolini's brainchild and one of the city's main traffic arteries—because they're certain that significant remains from classical Rome are buried beneath it. And just last year, an ancient palace was sacrificed to make way for new car park, built so that the busloads of Jubilee tourists could enjoy expanded parking possibilites when they come to visit the Vatican.

What's the Jubilee, you ask? It's a Catholic Holy Year, a 365-day-long celebration that rolls around every 25 years. It attracts more than 25 million tourists to this city of roughly three million, and is one of the biggest catalysts urging Rome to clean up its act. In case you missed it, Rome threw its biggest party ever in 2000, celebrating, in tandem, the Jubilee and the new millennium. For the year or so before Y2K, Rome was one enormous construction site, as everyone, from hoteliers to taverna owners, was busy making capital improvements on his or her properties. Additionally, roads were widened, statues were polished, and works of art were dusted off in anticipation of millions of Catholic pilgrims and regular old tourists. The attitude in Rome hadn't been more upbeat in decades.

Sadly, the massive Jubilee party did nothing to mask some of Rome's current societal ills. Racism, especially towards immigrant Albanians, Eritreans, and Chinese, is inherent in certain circles, and rarely will you see a dark face in anything more than a low-wage job. Antiquated civil laws that make it okay for male workers to pat female coworkers on the behind, as long as the move isn't "premeditated," still exist in Rome (and throughout Italy), as do antigay sentiments, spurred on by the never-wavering purview of the Catholic church. And then there's the pollution: Exhaust from thousands of cars, mopeds, and buses have sullied building facades and polluted the air, causing Rome to be one of the smoggiest cities in Europe.

Despite these serious problems, and the many minor ones—bureaucracy, crowded public transport, and theft, for starters—Rome is a gorgeous, intoxicating city. The days are almost always sunny, the pasta is always *al dente,* and the pace is always frenetic. In the film *La Dolce Vita,* a Fellini classic, Marcello Mastroianni says, "I love Rome. It's a dank jungle." Romans have learned to love Rome for all of its beauty and its disorder—and certainly, you will, too. *Buon divertimento!*

Rome

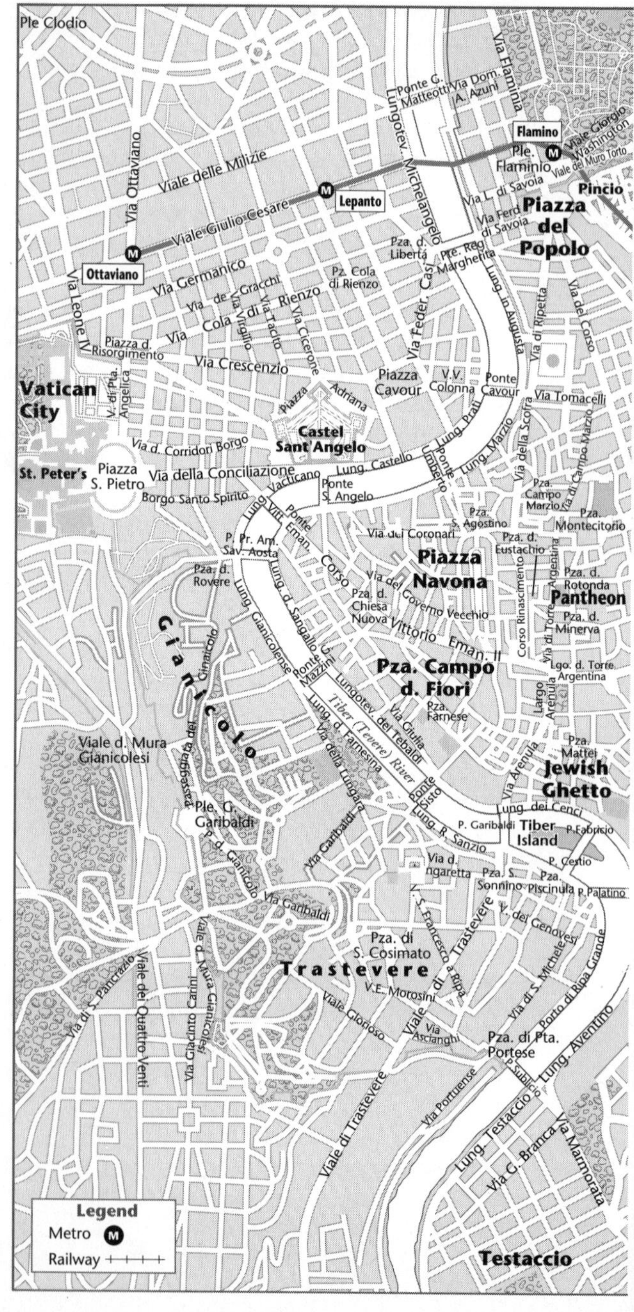

Ple Clodio
Via Ottaviano
Viale delle Milizie
Viale Giulio Cesare
Lepanto
Ottaviano
Via Germanico
Via Leone IV
Via de Gracchi
Via Virgilio
Via Cola di Rienzo
Via Tacito
Via Cicerone
Pz. Cola di Rienzo
Piazza d. Risorgimento
Via Crescenzio
Vatican City
V. di Pta. Angelica
Piazza Adriana
Castel Sant'Angelo
Via d. Corridori Borgo
St. Peter's
Piazza S. Pietro
Via della Conciliazione
Borgo Santo Spirito
Lungotev. Michelangelo
Ponte G. Matteotti
Via Dom. A. Azuni
Via Flaminia
Flamino
Ple. Flaminio
Viale Giorgio Washington
Viale del Muro Torto
Pincio
Via L. di Savoia
Via Ferd. di Savoia
Piazza del Popolo
Pza. d. Libertà
Pre. Reg. Margherita
Via Feder. Cesi
Lung. in Augusta
Via di Ripetta
Via del Corso
Piazza Cavour
V.V. Colonna
Ponte Cavour
Via Tomacelli
Lung. Prati
Ponte Umberto
Lung. Marzio
Via della Scrofa
Via di Campo Marzio
Lung. Castello
Lung. Vaticano
Ponte S. Angelo
Pza. Campo Marzio
Pza. Montecitorio
Pza. S. Agostino
Via dei Coronari
Lung. Vitt. Eman.
Ponte
P. Pr. Am. Sav. Aosta
Corso Vittorio Eman. II
Piazza Navona
Pza. d. Eustachio
Pza. d. Rotonda
Pantheon
Pza. d. Rovere
Via del Governo Vecchio
Pza. d. Chiesa Nuova
Corso Rinascimento
Via di Torre Argentina
Pza. d. Minerva
Lung. Gianicolense
Lung. d. Sangallo
Ponte G. Mazzini
Gianicolo
Pza. Campo d. Fiori
Lgo. d. Torre Argentina
Largo Arenula
Lungotev. dei Tebaldi
Via Giulia
Pza. Farnese
Tiber (Tevere) River
Lung. d. Farnesina
Via della Lungara
Viale d. Mura Gianicolesi
Passeggiata del Gianicolo
Pza. Mattei
Via Arenula
Jewish Ghetto
Ponte Sisto
Lung. dei Cenci
Ple. G. Garibaldi
P. Garibaldi
Tiber Island
P. Fabricio
Lung. R. Sanzio
P. d. Gianicolo
Via Garibaldi
Via d. Lungaretta
P. Cestio
Pza. S. Sonnino
Pza. Piscinula
P. Palatino
V. S. Francesco a Ripa
Viale di Trastevere
V. dei Genovesi
Via di S. Michele
Lung. Ripa Grande
Pza. di S. Cosimato
Trastevere
V.E. Morosini
Viale Glorioso
Via Asciangh
Porto di Ripa Grande
Pza. di Pta. Portese
P. Sublicio
Lung. Aventino
Via di S. Pancrazio
Viale dei Quattro Venti
Via Giacinto Carini
Viale d. Mura Gianicolesi
Via Portuense
Viale di Trastevere
Lung. Testaccio
Via G. Branca
Via Marmorata
Legend
Metro
Railway
Testaccio

0
1/4 Mi
0
1/4 Km
N
Giardino
Zoologico
Villa
Borghese
Piazza
di Siena
Spanish
Steps
Spagna
Via Veneto
Barberini
Pza.
Barberini
Termini
Piazza
Repubblica
Repubblica
Termini
Stazione
Termini
Castro
Pretorio
Piazza
Indipendenza
Ple. di
Porta Pia
Quirinale
Pza. d.
Quirinale
Pza.
Colonna
Pza.
Venezia
Pza.
dell'Esquilino
Via Cavour
Vittorio
Emanuele
Piazza
Vittorio
Eman. II
Ancient Rome
Roman
Forum
Colosseo
Pza. d.
Colosseo
Manzoni
Palatine
Hill
Circus Maximus
Aventine
Hill
Circo Massimo
Pza. di
Pta.
Capena
Piazza
Bocca
d. Verità
Piazza
Albania
Piramide
Pza. di
S. Giovanni
in Laterano
Pza. di
Pla. Metronia
Via Pinciana
Via Po
Via Isonzo
Via Tevere
Via Savoia
Margherita
Corso D'Italia
Via Campania
Via Sardegna
Via Sicilia
Via Boncompagni
Via Piave
Viale Castro
Pretorio
Via Vittorio Veneto
Via Ludovisi
Via di Porta Pinciana
Viale del Muro Torto
Via Sistina
Via Barberini
Via XX Settembre
Via Torino
Lgo. di
S. Susanna
Via Tritone
Lg. de
Tritone
Via del Quirinale
Via d.
Quattro Fontane
V. d. Viminale
Via Nazionale
Via Milano
Via XXIV Maggio
Via del Corso
Via d. Plebiscito
Via IV Nov.
Via dei Fori Imperiali
Via Cavour
Via Principe Amedeo
V. Carlo Alberto
Via Giovanni Giolitti
Via Marsala
Via Merulana
Via Leopardi
Via Macanate
Viale d. Domus Aurea
Via Labicana
Vle. Manzoni
Via. di S. Giovanni in Laterano
Via Claudia
Via di S. Gregorio
Via del Circo Massimo
Via della Navicella
Viale Aventino
Via D. Terme di Caracalla
Via Antonina
Via Druso
Via Sannio
Via Gallia
Via di S. Anselmo
Via D. Teatro di Marcello
Via Condotti
Pza. di Spagna
Via Fr. Crispi
Vle. della Trinità d. Monti
Viale dell'Uccelliera
Viale dei Cavalli Marini
Viale di Valle Giulia
Vle. dell'Aranciera
Vle. d. Magnolie
Viale P. Canonica
Pza.
Cinque-
cento
Staz. Termini

you probably didn't know

Don't believe—OK, believe—the hype... Rome has so many personalities, it's easy to understand why tourists pack a bag of misperceptions when they come here. On the one hand, it is the "Eternal City," a heap of crumbling ruins and traditions, where Caesar was murdered and where Nero played his flute. Then there's the myth of *La Dolce Vita,* tricking everyone into believing that all Romans scoot around on *motorini* in Gucci glasses and thousand-dollar suits. The Vatican, with all its history, and the Italian government, with all its notoriety, are located in Rome, bringing about notions of total piety and total corruption. High crime, high fashion, high art, and high-class snobbery have all been used to describe Rome, but none offer an accurate portrayal of the city. You'll notice from the offset that Rome is a city of contradictions, where you'll see massive traffic jams near the Colosseum, nuns window shopping, and respectable eateries offering *al fresco* dining within view of laundry lines. But, in many instances, Rome does live up to all the hype—and the clichés. The pope makes regular appearances, if not on television, then from his balcony overlooking St. Peter's Square. Ancient ruins are at every turn. Michelangelo's Sistine Chapel, with its brilliant hues and larger-than-life depictions of God, man, saints, and angels, really is one of the most spectacular sights you will ever lay your eyes on. Even romance—just like the kind that blossomed between Gregory Peck and Audrey Hepburn in *Roman Holiday*—really isn't such a cockamamie idea once you're in the Pincio Gardens, gazing out over the rooftops and domes. Of course, Rome does have its growing pains, from instances of petty crime to pollution, but you really can't blame a city that's been in business for more than 2,700 years.

Doin' the hand jive... The fact that Italians, in general, and Romans, in particular, talk with their hands is not overstated. In this respect, Romans tend to be parodies of themselves. Watch any interaction between a *barrista* (coffee barman) and a customer; between two drivers involved in a traffic accident; between a parent and a child; between a taxi driver and a passenger. A Roman indicates that a meal tastes good by rotating his thumb or forefinger on his cheek, as if there were a dimple. Ask a Roman for directions, and, if he doesn't know, he'll stick out both hands, palms upward, shrug his shoulders, and exclaim, "boh!" (meaning, roughly, "How should I know, you damn tourist?!"). However, if he does know, he may give you a variety of directions using both words and gestures to explain that you need to "turn left at the church with the large dome." There are thought to be at least 100 different hand gestures in Italy, each used to express different levels of anger, frustration, apathy, happiness, and a whole host of other emotions. In most cases, you should be able to tell from context what a Roman means when he talks with his hands. If not, you may want to move on to another person.

Do drink the water!... Rome is probably one of the last places in the world where it's okay to drink water from public fountains. Thanks to an ancient feat of engineering in the form of aqueducts (elaborately constructed devices that ferry water from far-away hills), Romans enjoy cold, clean *aqua*. And—what luck for tourists—it's perfectly acceptable to pull up to one of those running fountains known as *fontanelle* or *nasone* (literally, big noses) and take a sip of water. It's a bit *gauche* if you fill up your water bottle while you're there—but no one will blink an eye if you do it on a sweltering, summer day. Be on the lookout for signs that say *non potabile,* though. This means that you *can't* drink the water from a given fountain—unless you want to court a nasty case of Montezuma's revenge or worse.

Wackytabacchi... You just can't get more utilitarian than the tobacco shop, Italy's catch-all store for cigarettes, candy bars, phone cards, stamps, bus tickets, and more. These stores with a big "T" sign (usually white on a black background) are authorized to sell all of these items, and they usually offer other trinkets like postcards and provide services such as your morning *cappuccino* and *cornetto. Tabacchi* (the name means "tobaccos") are basically Italy's version of a convenience store, only grittier—and a hell of a lot more charming.

Minding your queues... To most Americans (New Yorkers are in a special category), cutting into line is considered the ultimate act of rudeness. In Rome, however, you'll find that it's almost *de rigeur.* "Why are all these people cutting in line, when I'm obviously next?" you'll wonder. Romans generally don't like to waste their precious *dolce vita* waiting in line, so queue-jumping is distressingly common—and politeness or meekness in the pecking order is definitely punished with a long, long wait. So if you find yourself in a situation when the line is not clearly defined—and you will, trust us—assert yourself. Assertively. How? Try giving a stern look and subtly muscling for position like an NBA player waiting for a rebound to come down. In other words, maneuver your body ever so carefully in front of the offender's path to the goal. They might roll their eyes—but the locals just might back off, too.

How to avoid becoming road kill... It never fails. You step out onto a Roman crosswalk, and the drivers just fail to stop. In fact, they usually speed up. It doesn't matter if you are in the crosswalk or if the walk signal's green: Drivers in Rome don't follow traffic rules, they take traffic *suggestions.* Driving fast, maneuvering from lane to lane, and being the first out of the blocks after a stop light is a Roman's way of expressing autonomy (just like line-jumping, as described above). Errant Vespa scooter drivers won't give you a break, either—they're usually the worst violators of the traffic rules. Thus, your best bet for getting across a busy street is just to step out and start walking. Drivers will ultimately slow down, though they may honk their horns at you until you're across. Scary? Sure. Alternatively, follow a nun, a priest or a *mamma* with children in a stroller onto a crosswalk. Few drivers will want to press their luck with *those* folks and risk eternal damnation.

Is there really a patron saint of motorists?... You betcha. Each year on March 9, Roman motorists drive up to the church of **Santa Francesca Romana** (near the Forum) for a chance to have their vehicles blessed. Apparently, early Roman drivers adopted Santa Francesca as the patron saint of motorists because of her ability to be in two places at one time, a feature that drivers felt cars also provided. Another equally amusing procession takes place at the church of Sant'Eusebio. Each year on January 17, Romans bring their cats, dogs, parakeets, and other pets to the church to be blessed, thus ensuring that their furry or feathered friends secure a spot in heaven.

Is that really Pope Pius X in there?!... Over the years, Roman Catholics have done their darnedest to collect relics to sanctify their churches and bring pilgrim dollars to their coffers. Walk around in just about any church in Rome and you're bound to find props better left to a haunted house. Check out St. Thomas's shriveled up "doubting finger," encased in a chapel behind the altar at **Santa Croce in Gerusalemme.** (If you recall, St. Thomas touched Christ's wound with this finger to see if it was real.) Another disturbing relic—that of St. John's beheaded melon—is kept at **San Silvestro in Capite.** Luckily, this is kept out of sight in a beautiful silver reliquary. Of course, **St. Peter's** has plenty to make your skin crawl. Perhaps the most disturbing is that of the body of Pope Pius X, who lies "in state" in a glass sarcophagus on the left-hand side of the church, not far from the entrance. A death mask covers his face and gloves cover his hands—but the body is real. Some say it's a miracle that his body has remained intact for so long; others say it's just very good embalming technique. By the way, when cardinals reopened the tomb of Pope John XXIII in spring 2001, after more than 38 years, they found that his body had not decomposed, either—and he, too, is now slated for a glass sarcophagus in St. Peter's.

Coping with *menefreghismo*... It's not your imagination. That waiter/museum attendant/policeman/fill-in-the-blank-public servant really couldn't care less about you or your problems. Romans have long felt relieved of any civic or social duties, basically assuming an "if it doesn't directly affect me, it isn't my problem" attitude. Roman shopkeepers, restaurateurs, and nightclub doormen routinely ignore customers—especially backpackers and frumpy dressers—if they don't like their looks, or for just about any other reason. Falling victim to the attitude of a *menefreghista* can be extremely frustrating, and there's really nothing you can do about it: Romans are not easily impressed by the almighty dollar (or lira or yen or Deutsch mark), and they enjoy the liberty of closing early, opening late, or just slacking off during the entire month of August—this in spite of the frenetic speed with which they drive and drink coffee. Frankly, they just don't give a damn about all the rest. Get used to it.

Why you should have paid attention in high school Latin class... While in the *urbs aeterna* (Eternal City), you'll no doubt discover that Latin still lives—on monuments, sewer lids, lampposts, garbage cans, and other unlikely places. You'll see the letters *SPQR* (Senatus Populusque Romanus) everywhere, as the city government has long attached this term—it means the "Roman Senate and People"—to anything having to do with public works. The pope rarely gives speeches in Latin these days, but at the end of most addresses, he usually proclaims *urbi et orbi,* meaning roughly, "Rome, the world, and the rest of humanity." See? You should have studied harder. During the 2000 Italian presidential campaign, one political poster even read "Roma: Caput Mundi? No! Penultima in Europa." It seems that the Romans are *still* bitter about the fall of the Empire and the loss of their *Caput Mundi* (capital of the world) status—and this is not even to mention Italy's lousy, last-minute defeat to France in the 2000 Euro soccer championships. So brush up on your Pig Latin; it just might come in handy.

No, really, he's hitting on me... Roman men have no shame when it comes to preying on female tourists, employing smooth moves and just enough English to hit on women at nightclubs, at bus stops, and even among the treasures at the Vatican. (A recent ruling handed down from Italy's Supreme Court even made it legal for male colleagues to pat female colleagues on the butt—so long as the pats were "occasional." No, we're not making this up.) A combination *ciao,* wink, and a smile is the usual *modus operandi,* sometimes innocent and sometimes leading to the touchy-feely business; most often you'll hear "bella!" (beautiful), "ragazza!" (girl), or "biondina!" (if you are blonde). Unless you're really interested—note: Murphy's Law states that only the goofiest-looking Italian guys will approach you—do as the *Romane* (Roman women) do and give these guys short shrift. A forceful *lasciami in pace* (leave me alone!) accompanied with an evil look will usually do the trick. If that doesn't work, a stern *vaffanculo* (take a guess what that one means) should get your point across.

Cat scratch fever... There is no "Romulus and Remus" story about how the Roman cat population began. But everyone knows that the *gatti* have been living in and around Roman ruins for centuries. In 1988, the Roman government passed a law allowing cats to live where they are born, resulting in a proliferation of cat colonies, especially around the **Colosseum,** the **Pantheon,** and the **Area Sacra** at Largo Argentina. Living the good life, the strays rely on *gattare* (feline caregivers, usually female) to bring them meals of leftover pasta, meat, and other scraps. The cats don't typically respond to tourist offerings of food or affection, so it's best just to admire them from afar. However, if you're intent on rescuing a kitty, contact the **Torre Argentina Cat Sanctuary** (tel 06/687 21 33; www.romancats.com), which allows cat lovers to adopt felines.

Smoking, the national pastime... You know it's bad when you arrive at the airport, see the *non fumare* signs and, simultaneously, see several smokers lighting up at the baggage claim. The majority of Romans smoke, and you'll be hard pressed to find a space that is reserved for non-smokers. Shop owners regularly smoke in their boutiques, museum guards sometimes puff away only a few feet from priceless artworks, and most restaurants lack adequate non-smoking sections. *Metropolitana* platforms seem to be the only places where Romans obey the no-smoking laws—but, then, you're already inhaling train fumes. It will be interesting to see how attitudes toward smoking change in 2002, when new European Union laws go into effect. In early 2002, all cigarette packs in Europe must display giant warnings, covering 30 percent of the front and back of each pack, and must do away with terms such as "light," "low tar," and "mild." By the end of the year, new graphic warnings, showing exactly what happens to a smoker's teeth or lungs, will appear on packs. If that's not a deterrent, then what is?

How to avoid eating brains, lungs, and tails... In case you didn't know, the traditional Roman meal consists of animal parts usually reserved to make hot dogs. If you're a vegetarian—or if the thought of eating innards makes you queasy—there are a few foods you should steer clear of. *Coda alla vaccinara* is oxtail braised in a broth of celery and tomato. *Pajata* is the glorified name of dish that is made from the intestines of an unweaned calf and is typically served with rigatoni. Avoid menu items that contain *cervello* (brain), *tripa* (tripe), *animelli* (pancreas and glands), or *lingua* (tongue). The terms *Offal* and *Quinto Quarto* (literally, fifth quarter) are used in general to describe this type of cuisine. If, on the other hand, you're they adventurous type, go to **Cecchino dal 1887** [see Dining] for the total *offal* experience.

Drinking without getting drunk... Forget that a glass of wine usually starts at a low 4,000L and that a very good bottle of *vino* can cost little more than five bucks. Also, ignore the little old man who orders a Campari while you're still sipping on your morning coffee. Alcohol is everywhere, and it's available at all times of the day. But, somehow, you'll rarely see a Roman rip-roaring drunk. Why? Moderation is one reason. Romans tend to drink lots of wine, but with meals, finishing off with an alcoholic *digestivo* like *amaro* (bitters) or *limoncello* (a strong lemon-flavored drink). Public drunkenness is especially frowned upon and can garner stiff fines from the police, if they see fit.

It's August; where the hell is everybody?... Depending on your point of view, Rome can be magical or miserable during the month of August. Most Romans take off for the beach or the mountains during this month, leaving tourists to contend with hundreds of closed shops and restaurants, irregular museum hours, and the God-forsaken heat. Even the pope tends to skip town during August, opting for the cool air at his summer retreat in Castelgandolfo. But, if you've got your heart set on a trip to Rome during August, don't fret. What you'll find are relatively empty *piazze* and galleries, manageable traffic, cheaper hotel prices, and a city that is, despite (or because of) its steamy temperatures, undeniably alluring.

accomm

1

odations

The recipe for the prototypical Roman hotel is wall-to-wall marble, God-awful frescoes of local landmarks, and tons of chintz. Five-star hotels are notorious for piling on the gilt and glitter, the result often being a jumbled mess of Baroque stylings and grandma-approved florals. Of course, in the case are made of the deluxe hotels, the marble is from Carrara, the chandeliers are made of Murano glass, and the period antiques are real. What's unfortunate is that the gaudy approach to decor has trickled down to the lesser hotels, and many of these two- and three-star inns are unable to pull off such ornate furnishings without looking a bit frumpy. However, the one good thing that came of the 2000 Jubilee was a practical overhaul of all the hotels in the city. Sure, many of the one-stars remain dodgy, and the five-stars remain palatial. But those in the middle have added cushy carpeting, gotten rid of (most of) those smoke-stained drapes, or put in new, springy mattresses. Sadly, despite all the renovations, many of Rome's accommodations remain inaccessible to the disabled. If you need a room equipped for wheelchairs, call, fax, or email ahead with your specs—and expect the worst anyway. You may have to travel up or down a flight of stairs to get to any elevator.

Winning the Reservations Game

Jubilee notwithstanding, Rome is extremely popular and always packed with pilgrims, history buffs, fashion mavens, gourmands, and busloads of foreigners. Rome actually has two high seasons, one ranging from Easter through summer, the other comprised of the temperate fall months and the Christmas season. The highest hotel rates are in June and July. Your best bet is to plan your trip during the short low seasons, which—generally speaking—include the months of November, January, February, and August. Even then, you may have trouble finding vacancies or reasonably priced rooms. Discounts, too, are hard to come by in Rome, though some hotels will offer 10 to 20-percent discounts if you book over the Internet. Make sure you print out a copy of the Web bargain. Before you go, you may want to check out the list put out by the **Azienda di Promozione Turistica di Roma** (also known as the APT or the Rome Tourism Promotion Bureau, www.romaturismo.com). Each year, this office classifies all of the city's hotels, awards them stars, and sets a minimum and maximum rate charge for each based on its classification. No hotel may charge you more than the maximum price listed in the agency's book *Roma Annuario: Hotels/Residences* or on its website. (Contact the APT with questions or complaints at Via

Parigi 11, 00185 Rome; tel 0/488 99 253, fax 06/488 99 238.) Once you're in Rome, finding a hotel can be difficult—but it's not impossible. **Enjoy Rome** (tel 06/445 18 43, open Mon–Fri 8:30am–2pm and 3:30–6pm, Sat 8:30–2), a free service run by amiable, English-speaking 20-somethings, can often locate you a room at the last minute, but note that its finds are often budget/hostel places. **Free Hotel Reservation Service** (tel 06/699 10 00, open daily 7am–10pm) has a multilingual staff and is also worth a shot. They also have desks at the Fiumicino airport and the Termini train station, the former being less stressful than the latter. Alternatives to the hotel hassle are bed and breakfast accommodations, which are springing up everywhere these days, and religious inns, which are run by disciplined holy men and women. Rome's B&Bs are handled by the **Bed and Breakfast Association** (Piazza del Teatro di Pompeo 2, tel 06/687 73 48, fax 06/687 48 81, www.bb.rm.it).

Is There a Right Address?

If you're really determined to stay in total luxury away from the real pulse of the city, look no farther than the **Via Veneto,** where the majority of Rome's five-star hotels are clustered—and where a heavy tourist population from the United States, Japan, and Germany reigns supreme. Other five-stars, such as the **Hassler Villa Medici** and the **St. Regis Grand,** are scattered throughout the city (in the Spanish Steps and Piazza Esedra areas, respectively), whereas the renowned **Cavalieri Hilton** is far on the outskirts near the Vatican. There are a number of lavish hotels in the **Centro Storico,** but mostly what you'll find is modest, comfortable lodging. The key is knowing what you want to do while you're visiting the Eternal City. History buffs can stay almost anywhere and be close to ruins. But the best areas are near **Piazza della Rotonda** (also known as **Piazza del Pantheon**) and **Campo de' Fiori.** There are, indeed, a few adequate hotels in the immediate vicinity of the **Colosseum,** but you'll find more bargains on the sometimes-loud, but centrally located **Via Cavour.** (This street's Metro station is also only one stop away on Linea B for those who can't—or simply choose not to—hoof it. St. Peter's and the Vatican Museums are at the top of most peoples' itineraries, and there are quite a few unassuming hotels in the **Borgo Pio** area immediately outside of Vatican City that afford full-frontal views of the basilica's dome or more intimate views of medieval alleyways. Admittedly, hotels in the Vatican area often feel isolated from the rest of the city, as it's quite a trek from here to center city *trattorie,* markets, and bars. A practical compromise is to stay in the **Prati** neighborhood, about halfway between the Vatican and **Piazza del Popolo.** Gastronomes can stay just about anywhere in Rome and feel satisfied. However, some of the best places to stay are near **Piazza Navona** and **Campo de' Fiori,** the latter abutting the Jewish **Ghetto.** Tons of restaurants ranging from the okay to the outstanding are scattered throughout these adjacent neighborhoods. So, you can pop down from your hotel for lunch, dine on authentic Roman cuisine, then lug yourself upstairs for a *siesta.* To avoid spending too much on cab fare, night owls are also advised to stay in the Navona and Campo areas, which are within walking distance to some great *enoteche* and *discoteche.* If you're a die-hard shopper, concentrate on the **Spanish Steps/Via Condotti** area, where a criss-crossing of small streets provides ample accommodation choices. For those who would rather sample the local flavor, lodging in **Trastevere** might be a good choice. Artisan boutiques and rustic *trattorie* abound in this neighborhood. And, if you're not afraid of public transportation or long walks, Trastevere is due south of the Vatican and just across the river from the *Centro Storico.*

The Lowdown

Now starring... Before you dive into the fray, know that you do have a few laws and guidelines on your side for a change. All hotels in Italy are rated on a five-star system (with five stars being the highest class), and, as ordered by the Italian Government and the Italian State Tourist Board, each hotel must prominently display the number of stars on its facade. The stars are directly proportional to the type of service and the amount of amenities you'll receive, though plenty of four-stars are as ritzy as five-stars and some two- and three-star establishments are extremely friendly or offer surprising views. Bottom line? If you arrive in Rome without a reservation, don't be put off by the number of stars you see staring back at you from the wall. Also remember that law requires all Italian hoteliers to show you their available rooms upon request.

When the company's paying... The century-old **St. Regis Grand** (a.k.a., L Grand Hotel) reopened in December 1999 after a 10-month, $35-million renovation, and the results are definitely cliché—but undeniably luxurious. The lobby was completely outfitted in the richest gold and crimson fabrics, Murano glass chandeliers, and Empire-style antiques. The guestrooms were given a palatial look, with sumptuous draping curtains, tasteful, one-of-a-kind, over-the-bed frescoes, and touches of marble and gilt. There's even a Bulgari Suite, created in conjunction with the famed jeweler: We're talking 24-hour butler service, dinner on Bulgari-designed china, and original artworks culled from the company's private collection. Needless to say, rack rates are stratospheric. Its sister hotel, **The Westin Excelsior,** is equally extravagant—but to the point of looking like a Versace fashion set gone wrong. Oriental rugs contrast with leopard-print chairs, antique furniture and crystal vases clutter the lobby, and absurd amounts of gilt (not to be confused with guilt; you'll find none of *that* here) from floor to ceiling are liable to blind you. But if that's your kind of thing, check out the two-story Villa La Cupola suite and its frescoed *cupola,* whirlpool, private gym, private media center (whatever that is), and terrace with bar. Also vying for attention on the Via Veneto are the **Majestic** and **Regina Hotel Baglioni,** both super-luxury hotels with a past. Built in 1889, the Majestic was one of the first hotels on the street, and it remains first choice for a bevy of celebrities like Springsteen, Barishnykov, and Pavarotti. The Regina Baglioni was once the home of Queen Margherita—probably the only queen in history to have a pizza named after her—and this seven-story *palazzo* is a city landmark. For a quieter sort of elegance, check out the **Hassler Villa Medici,** with its small but regal rooms and prime real estate at the top of the Spanish Steps. It's the only privately owned, five-star hotel in the city (and one of very few in Europe). The hotel is lavish without being brash, which is probably why celebs (Madonna, Cindy Crawford) and royal families come here when they need to avoid the spotlight.

Hanging out with the inn crowd... For the well-heeled traveler, a few hotels in Rome fit the bill. At first, the chic-suited, good-looking staff at the retooled **Hotel de Russie** seem quite snobby in the cold, gray marble lobby, but they're surprisingly warm and friendly. In one of the best locations in town, at the edge of Piazza del Popolo, this plush place features neutral decor, a deluxe spa, and a garden that will make you weep. Top models invade Rome at the end of July to take part in the "Donne Sotto le Stelle" fashion show at the Spanish Steps. Stay at **Gregoriana** down the street, and you may just get to room next to Naomi or Kate. Style mavens have long been attracted to the 19-room Gregoriana for its William Morris–style decor as well as its privacy. There are no public rooms here, so you'll just have to settle for room service—which is available 24 hours a day, of course. The **Ripa All Suites Hotel** impresses with an impossibly hip, minimalist look. Everything in this Trastevere hotel, from the red lacquer reception desk to the modern black-and-white bedrooms to the on-site DJ/sushi bar, adheres to a New York-meets-Asia concept. Okay—so the location isn't ideal for sightseeing. But it does remind you that Rome is a chic metropolis, not just an aging tourist mecca. On the other hand, if you want to feel like you're in a time warp, stay at the **Cardinal,** in a Bramante-built *palazzo* on the picturesque Via Giulia. The hotel interior, with cathedral ceilings, antique furnishings, and cardinal-red accents, has retained a sort of Renaissance sensibility; outdoors, the ivy-draped cobblestone street has the sort of charm that's sometimes difficult to find in Rome's urban jungle.

Oops, I'm almost at my credit limit... You wouldn't think so, but you can actually find decent budget beds in central Rome with a little work. The Termini area surrounding the city's main train station has loads of budget hotels, many of which are shoddy and a bit seedy. But the relatively new **Hotel des Artistes** is a friendly, family-run *pensione* where you can get a double room with a private bath. Opened in 1995 and refurbished in 1999, this popular hotel includes personal touches like fresh-cut flowers and original modern paintings in all the rooms—and, incredibly, the entire hotel is non-smoking. The *Hostel* des Artistes, which is actually the fifth floor of the hotel, has dorm-like and private rooms, all of which share bathrooms in the hall; if you're low on cash, you can get a bed for about 35,000L (around $18) per night. Not far from

Termini in the Piazza Esedra area, **Oceania** has a clean, cozy set-up despite its nondescript exterior. Besides sizable rooms, the hotel also has amenities like data ports and satellite television that you hardly ever find in a two-star. Surprisingly, there are also some budget hotels occupying some prime real estate in the historic center. The front rooms at **Abruzzi** get great views of the Pantheon (though also a heap of noise from the tourist hordes down below). Without the view, rooms are modest, and not much to write home about. With first-century A.D. ruins on the ground floor and a guest list that includes John Keats, you'd think that **Navona,** within walking distance of some of Rome's best dining and antique shopping, would be pricey. Yet its rooms start at around 16,000L per night. Run by a friendly Italian-Australian couple, the hotel has a quaint, grandmotherly feel, with pastel-hued furnishings, cutesy art prints, and frilly linens. Meanwhile, the accommodations at **Casa Kolbe,** at the base of the Palatine hill, are utilitarian—if not spartan—remnants of the hotel's days as an abbey. But the sparse rooms are comfy and many look out onto a pretty courtyard.

Shopper's paradise... Many boutique hotels are clustered around the Via Condotti/Spanish Steps area, providing you with a convenient home base for dropping off your shopping bags. **Condotti,** around the corner from the same-named street on Via Mario de' Fiori, lacks the sort of luxe look preferred by fashionistas, but it's ideal for shoppers. If you don't mind stepping over hordes of sunbathers on your way from shop to hotel and back, **Scalinata di Spagna** couldn't be a better choice. Wake up in the morning, walk out the front door, and the Spanish Steps and Via Condotti unfold before you. The **Carriage** is on one of the quieter streets in the shopping district (Via delle Carozze, the Street of the Carriages). Compared with other hotels in this prime location, this place is moderately priced—and some rooms even have patios. Collectors of early 20th–century antiques will flip when they see **Locarno,** one of the coolest hotels in Rome where decor is concerned. Art deco is the theme here, including an original wrought-iron cage elevator and etched glass, Tiffany-style lamps. Borrow a bike from the hotel concierge and window-shop on wheels.

Luscious love nests... If Jean Paul Sartre and Simone de Beauvoir were able to get existential at this inn while visiting Rome (or so goes the brochure literature), then why can't you? **Sole al Pantheon,** which has some rooms that look out onto the Pantheon, has a romantic feel without being overdone. Floors are of red brick tile, rooms are painted in muted greens, beiges, and neutrals, and coffered ceilings (which recall the one in the temple across the way) are hand-painted. The **Raphaël Hotel** is located in a quiet, ivy-draped corner a few alleys away from Piazza Navona and has a sultry luxe look with velvet couches in the foyer, original Renaissance art, and suffused lighting throughout. The house restaurant is Mediterranean with a French accent, with more than a few hedonistic meals on the menu. Convenient to shopping on Via del Corso, the rooms at the gracious **Valadier** look like James Bond's shag pads. The bedroom design is part Art deco and part 21st-century space age, all pulled together with blonde wood and black lacquer furniture, padded (soundproof) walls, and a mirrored ceiling.

A room with a view... Almost every room in Rome has a view of *something* interesting: a quiet, cobbled alley; a building with unusual architecture; or a dainty fountain. Throw open your windows at **Nerva** and you might be treated to up-close-and-personal views of the ruins of the Imperial Fora and Trajan's Markets. The rooms at the **Teatro di Pompeo** don't look out on any ruins at all, but the hotel boasts a breakfast nook that's built right into the ancient foundation of the theater where Julius Caesar got whacked. The intimate, 12-room hotel is fancy yet low-key, and located on a quiet side street near Campo de' Fiori; as such, it has developed quite a following. Book months in advance if you wanna stay here.

The upper floor, west-wing rooms of the **Delta Colosseo** will get you glimpses of the Colosseum, though none better than the ones you'll get from the hotel's rooftop pool. The only hotel that looks onto the Trevi Fountain is **Fontana.** Yes, the rushing water of the fountain can be soothing, but it's drowned out by the din of tourists from sun-up until after midnight. A trio of hotels have rooms facing the Pantheon: the upscale **Sole al Pantheon,** the affordable **Albergo del**

Senato, and **Abruzzi,** a dirt-cheap *pensione* within spitting distance of the ancient temple. If you're willing to splurge—and the timing is right—you can book a room at the **Hassler Villa Medici.** Every room here is named after what it looks out upon, be it the Villa Medici, Trinità de'Monti, or St. Peter's. Many of the hotel's regular guests have standing reservations for these rooms, but you might get lucky and hit a cancellation.

Where to sleep when you've got a 5am flight or train ticket... The only hotel located at Rome's Fiumicino Airport is the all-new **Hilton Rome Airport,** accessible from any terminal. As you would expect, the hotel has tons of conference space, a business center, a health club, and an indoor pool. And, you can take the train or a complimentary shuttle into town. Also new, the **Sol Melia Aurelia Antica** is an anomaly in Rome. All rooms offer views of rolling fields, some peppered with sheep and cattle; amenities are almost overdone (like the extra toothbrush, toothpaste, and cotton swabs in the bathrooms); and nary an American voice breaks the silence in the breakfast room. A free shuttle bus will transport you to the bustle of the airport or downtown to the Via Veneto if you get tired of the tranquillity. The recently refurbished **Sheraton Hotel Roma,** with a whopping 650 guestrooms, is one of the original chains near Fiumicino, and has few surprises. Here you'll find your typically bland business hotel; rooms (and, yes, many of the guests) have little to no character. This place is also really popular with the tour-bus crowd. Even though it's within view of Termini Station, **Mediterraneo** has a lazy air that belies the pure chaos unfolding outside. Doormen are discreet, elevators open to a dull chime, and the walls are soundproof. Mediterraneo's spacious rooms are a little worn around the edges, but all boast relatively sizable private bathrooms, perfect if you're constantly in and out. Though few opera enthusiasts really come to Rome to see the opera (Milan and Venice are better choices), they might be persuaded to take in *Tosca* if they stay in the **Quirinale.** Largely a business hotel, but equally suitable for couples, Quirinale has direct access to the Teatro dell'Opera and is only blocks from Termini. **Hotel des Artistes,** a funky hotel-cum-hostel to the northern side of the station, is just 10 minutes away and invites a quirky, youthful mix of people, all of whom tend to mingle at night on the rooftop deck. Convenient Internet access in the lobby also makes it worthwhile for the visitor just breezing through.

For those seeking a normal hotel room... Face it: Sometimes, you're just plain sick of quaint European-style hotels; nobody said Europe had to be an endless progression of weird walk-in showers and closet-sized bathrooms down the hall. If you're feeling that way, Rome offers a handful of American-style chain hotels in which you can take a break and trade character for a little comfort. The **Marriott Grand Hotel Flora** sits right at the top of the Via Veneto and caters to a largely American crowd. It's got the sort of lavish lobby one would expect in Rome, but the rest is rather uninteresting—you might as well be in Kansas City. Views over the Borghese Gardens, however, are quite nice. In a fantastic location right behind the Pantheon, the **Crowne Plaza Minerva,** run by the Holiday Inn group, has all the typical amenities of a chain hotel, including satellite televisions, a business center, and a friendly, English-speaking staff. And, unlike other chains in the city, the hotel is housed in a 17th-century *palazzo* that still retains a unique look despite renovations in 1990. Conversely, the **Cavalieri Hilton,** built in the suburbs near the Vatican, is far from the tourist attractions. Because of this, the hotel offers discounts during the low season—rooms sometimes can be had for as "little" as $150 per night. Of course, staying out here may mean that your only dinner choice is La Pergola [see Dining], one of Rome's most outrageously priced restaurants.

Closer to God are thee... Since the pilgrim route is virtually a toll road, many hotels have lined up around Catholic pilgrimage sites to cash in. The result is a glut of cheap-looking yet overpriced hotels, among them a few clean, honest souls. No doubt the most pious accommodations are near the Vatican. **Bramante,** located in a 16th-century building designed by Domenico Fontana, is one of the original pilgrim hotels. It was converted into an inn for visiting Catholics during the 1870s, then into a regular hotel in 1960. Sandwiched in a small corner of Borgo Pio, just blocks from St. Peter's, the hotel has 16 small but cozy rooms, some of which look out onto Il Passetto, the pope's escape corridor to Castel Sant'Angelo. Not content to look like a grandmother's dressing gown (which is typical of a number of hotels in the Vatican area), **Spring House,** just around the corner from the entrance of the Vatican Museums, has red leather seating in the lobby, bright, color-washed guestrooms, and a cozy bar—which can be hard to come by in this neighborhood of bishops and other do-gooders. It's no coincidence that the **Columbus** on the grand Via della Conciliazione (the same road that leads to St. Peter's Square) gives off a holier-than-thou air. The hotel is housed in a 15th-century *palazzo* that was once the home of Julius II, the pope responsible for the construction of St. Peter's Basilica (and Michelangelo's back problems). Because the Santa Maria Maggiore church is not far from Termini station, there are quite a few decent hotels in this area, too. **Gallia,** a classy four-star, was given a complete makeover in 1999. Its rooms, now sporting a sort of dull, business-hotel look, are still not up to snuff; then again, you're paying for the view from the terrace and the feeling that you could almost reach out and touch the dome of the basilica. Also renovated in 1999, **Verona** is a quaint, family-run inn with a gorgeous interior courtyard; small, rather sparse doubles; and a few triples and quads suitable for families or pilgrim groups. **Santa Prassede,** named after the other important church in the neighborhood, is a simple two-star hotel with wood-beamed ceilings, parquet floors, and ascetic but comfortable rooms. Once you get over the fact that, from the outside, the **Bled** looks slightly like the house in the *Amityville Horror* (don't even get me started on the name), you should have a good night's sleep. In a quiet, residential neighborhood just down the street from Santa Croce in Gerusalemme and several blocks from San Giovanni in Laterano, the place is run by the Italian Leonardi chain (who also run Gallia). Expect friendly service and rooms that are cozy, if a bit worn.

Sisters are doing it for themselves... Now here's something different. If you want a simple, clean room at a good price—and don't mind getting back in for a curfew—you might want to consider one of the hotels around Rome run by nuns and monks. Only blocks from the banks of the Tiber and a stroll from Trastevere, the **Casa di Santa Francesca Romana** offers ascetic accommodations in a 15th-century convent. Unlike the majority of religious inns, the Casa di Santa Francesca Romana has a reasonable 1am curfew. (Still, don't expect to sleep in—the nuns begin singing promptly at 8 each morning.) Run by a group of stern sisters, the 25-room **Casa San Giuseppe** is also on Rome's left bank, just a couple blocks from the Botanical Gardens and Trastevere's funky eateries. Rooms are, of course, spartan, but most look out onto a charming courtyard and the Tiber River. Finding a room near the Spanish Steps for less than $300 per night, never mind under $100 per night, is virtually impossible—unless you stay at **Nostra Signora di Lourdes.** So what if you have to be in by 10:30 each night? The location is incredible.

Family values... For the most part, hotel rooms in Rome tend to be on the small side. So, if you're traveling with the family, you may have trouble finding ample accommodations. Merely a block from the Colosseum, **Lancelot** has some serious decorating issues, pairing ugly florals with more ugly florals. But the location, spacious rooms, and friendly staff tend to make up for any design mistakes. **Ponte Sisto,** which recently underwent complete renovations, has some great views of the Tiber from its picture windows. There's plenty of room for kids here, and six of the 106 guest rooms have been configured for disabled access—still fairly uncommon in this city of uneven cobblestones. Across the river, in the safe Prati neighborhood, the **Arcangelo** is another good choice. Located in the shadow of the medieval fortress of Castel Sant'Angelo and a 10-minute walk to the Vatican, the Arcangelo has triples that start at 320,000L. **Gallia** and **Mediterraneo** also have affordable, family-sized accommodations, but watch out for the busy streets—both are located in heavy traffic areas.

Come on, block the noise... While the majority of rooms in Rome have been soundproofed to dull out the awful buzzing of cars, *motorini,* and tourists, it's still often hard to find respite from the din. Located on a hard-to-get-to-by Vespa alley around the corner from Piazza Navona, **Due Torri** is one of the quieter hotels in the *Centro Storico.* And why shouldn't it be? The hotel was originally built in 1518 as a residence for a number of cardinals and bishops, who couldn't afford to lose a good night's sleep. On a side street just off the bustling Via Fori dei Imperiali, the **Fori Imperiali Cavalieri** is well situated near the Colosseum and the Roman Forum, but is mostly void of tourists and traffic. Unfortunately, none of the rooms here have views of the ruins, but that's probably what keeps the loud tour groups away from this tidy hotel. **Sant'Anselmo,** on the other hand, owes its tranquillity to its location atop the ritzy, residential Aventine hill across from a Benedictine monastery. Resembling more of a palace in the countryside than an urban hotel, Sant'Anselmo has a mirrored hall à la Versailles, tasteful reproductions of Louis XVI furniture, and hand-detailed artwork on the bedroom walls and crown moldings. A real find in Trastevere is the **Santa Maria,** built on the site of a 15th-century cloister and housed within its own private courtyard. If you don't mind staying across the Tiber from the city center, this is perhaps the loveliest hotel in town. And, to boot, it was completely refurbished in 2000.

Where the towels say *His* and *His*... Surprisingly, gay-friendly hotels abound in this Catholic town. Yes, its rooms are hardly bigger than a walk-in closet, but you really can't beat the location of **Scalinata di Spagna,** a 15-room luxury hotel at the top and to the right of the Spanish Steps. Don't come looking for great views, though, unless you like to people-watch: Only the rooftop terrace—and pricey rooms 10 and 12—afford you a glimpse of St. Peter's. About halfway between Campo de' Fiori and Piazza Navona is the **Residenza San Pantaleo,** with bargain rates sometimes less than $100 per night. If you're aiming to hit the gay club circuit, you may want to try the **Pyramid**'s ordinary but comfortable rooms. Staying here means you're a stone's throw from all the major bars and discos in the Testaccio and Ostiense neighborhoods and just a Metro ride away from the major tourist sites. Be alert for the freeloaders and pimps that invade the area by night. For accommodations fit for a queen—and not the regal kind—check out the swank **Westin Excelsior** or the deluxe **Majestic** on the Via Veneto. Both hotels are gay-friendly, attracting a mixed crowd of fashion designers, movie stars, and other fabulous people.

Cheap sleeps... Romans don't really "do" breakfast, so it's not all that surprising to discover that B&B's are thin on the ground. However, they're slowly catching on. Located on the second floor of a 16th-century building, **Casa Banzo** is an exceptional bed and breakfast near Campo de' Fiori with black-and-white marble floors, vaulted ceilings, and large picture windows. Rooms have minimal decorations, but at least they're comfortable. The ochre-washed courtyard at the **B&B ai Musei Vaticani** is the most outstanding feature; otherwise, rooms are ordinary and cramped. But, given the inn's position no more than two blocks from the entrance of the Vatican Museums, it's a steal. **Nicolini B&B** looks more like your friend's apartment, and is just as comfortable. Big windows look out onto a quiet Trastevere side street and the common area is decorated with modern art prints and comfy chairs. Not far from Santa Maria Maggiore, you can stay at the quirky **Vacanze Romane,** which resembles more of a Parisian holiday than a Roman one. Vintage toys and retro French posters are on display throughout, and the B&B has quite a following among French tourists. Don't worry, though—the owners speak English, too.

The Index

$$$$$	500,000L and up
$$$$	350,000–500,000L
$$$	250,000–350,000L
$$	150,000–250,000L
$	150,000L and less

Abruzzi. Budget hotel with views of the Pantheon. Back rooms are cheaper and quieter.... *Tel 06/679 20 21, no fax. Piazza della Rotonda 69, buses 64, 70, 75, 116. $.* **(see pp. 21, 23)**

Albergo del Senato. Within spitting distance of the Pantheon; Senior Suites have the best views. A rooftop garden is in the works.... *Tel 06/678 43 43, fax 06/699 40 297. Piazza della Rotonda 73, buses 64, 70, 75, 116. $$$.* **(see p. 22)**

Arcangelo. Quiet, modest hotel located in the residential Prati neighborhood. Close to the Vatican. Buffet breakfast included.... *Tel 06/687 41 43, fax 06/689 30 50, arcangelo@travel.it. Via Boezio 15, Metro Ottaviano. 33 rooms. $$–$$$.* **(see p. 26)**

B&B ai Musei Vaticani. On a quiet street near the Vatican Museums. The B&B has 3 rooms, 2 of which are doubles, 1 master. 1 private bath. Self-serve breakfast, courtyard. Minimum 3-night stay. No credit cards. Closed Jan, Feb, and Aug.... *Tel 06/682 10 776, fax 06/682 15 9921. Via Sebastiano Veniero 78, Metro Ottaviano. 3 rooms. $.* **(see p. 28)**

Bled. Odd-looking, stand-alone hotel in a lazy, residential area. Rooms are a bit cramped, but pretty. Breakfast, which is included in the price, is served in a cozy nook with vinyl banquettes.... *Tel 06/702 78 08, fax 06/702 79 35, leonardi@travel.it. Via Santa Croce in Gerusalemme 40, Metro Manzoni. 47 rooms. $–$$$.* **(see p. 25)**

Bramante. Small pilgrim hotel in the Borgo Pio (Vatican) area. Breakfast included.... *Tel 06/688 06 426, fax 06/687 98 81,* *www.hotelbramante.com. Vicolo delle Palline 24, Metro Ottaviano. 16 rooms. $$$–$$$$.* **(see p. 24)**

Cardinal. Close to the center, but in a world of its own. Airy inn with a wealthy clientele. Breakfast, inclusive in price, is served in the garden.... *Tel 06/688 02 719, fax 06/678 63 76. Via Giulia 62. 70 rooms. $$$$–$$$$$.* **(see p. 20)**

Carriage. Named for the horse-drawn carriages that used to line the streets here; elegant and tranquil despite its center-city location. Rooms are furnished with antiques, and 2 rooms have private terraces.... *Tel 06/699 01 24, fax 06/678 82 79, hotel.carriage@alfanet.it. Via delle Carrozze 36, Metro Spagna. $$$–$$$$.* **(see p. 21)**

Casa Banzo. Rooms in this B&B have vaulted ceilings, are decorated with antiques, and all have private bathrooms. Two rooms have balconies. Continental breakfast. Two-night minimum stay. No credit cards. Closed Feb, July, and Aug.... *Tel 06/683 39 09, fax 06/686 45 75. Piazza Monte di Pieta 30, buses 46, 64, 70, 81, 492. 3 rooms. $–$$* **(see p. 28)**

Casa di Santa Francesca Romana. Sparse accommodations in a 15th-century convent. Breakfast included. Curfew at 1am.... *Tel 06/581 21 25, fax 06/583 57 97. Via del Vascellari 61, tram 8. $* **(see p. 26)**

Casa Kolbe. Quiet, two-star inn on one of Rome's lovely, untrodden streets near the Palatine. *Prix-fixe* meals are served at the hotel for an extra 25,000L.... *Tel 06/679 88 66, fax 06/699 41 550. Via di San Teodoro 44, buses 95, 175, 181. 63 rooms. $* **(see p. 21)**

Casa San Giuseppe. Views of a small garden and the Tiber make up for the sober surroundings. Breakfast included. Curfew at 1am.... *Tel 06/583 33 490, fax 06/581 32 50. Vicolo Moroni 22, tram 8. $* **(see p. 26)**

Cavalieri Hilton. On the northern outskirts of the city with great panoramic views of St. Peter's. Home of the famous La Pergola restaurant. Other amenities include on-site tennis courts, a gym, and a pool.... *Tel 06/350 91, fax 06/350 92 241, www.cavalieri-hilton.it. Via Cadlolo 101. 375 rooms. $$$$$* **(see pp. 17, 24)**

Columbus. The Columbus was a monastery before it was transformed into tourist lodging and much of the original woodwork and many of the frescoes still remain. St. Peter's is at the end of the street.... *Tel 06/686 54 35, fax 06/686 48 74, www.hotelcolumbus.net. Via della Conciliazione 33, bus 64, Metro Ottaviano. 92 rooms. $$$$$* **(see p. 25)**

Condotti. Classy, Piazza di Spagna hotel with elegant public areas and somewhat frumpy rooms. Elevator is reached by climbing 10 steps.... *Tel 06/679 46 61, fax 06/679 04 57, www.hotelcondotti.com. Via Mario de' Fiori 37, Metro Spagna. 16 rooms. $$–$$$$* **(see p. 21)**

Crowne Plaza Minerva. Pricier than Holiday Inns in the States, the Crowne Plaza Minerva looks out onto the Gothic-style Santa Maria Sopra Minerva church and the backside of the Pantheon. The hotel was completely refurbished in 1990 by Italy's star architect and interior designer, Paolo Portoghesi.... *Tel 06/695 201, fax 06/679 41 65, www.crowneplaza.com. Piazza della Minerva 69, buses 64, 70, 75, 116. 134 rooms. $$$$$* **(see p. 24)**

Delta Colosseo. One of the biggest hotels near the Colosseum, right at the base of the Colle Oppio park and the Domus Aurea. Cookie-cutter rooms and an occasionally distant staff, but the rooftop pool makes up for everything.... *Tel 06/770 021, fax 06/700 57 81, www.accor-hotels.it. Via Labicana 144, buses 81, 85, 87, tram 30, Metro Manzoni. 160 rooms. $$$$–$$$$$* **(see p. 22)**

Due Torri. Once the residence of clergymen, this quiet inn retains an old-world charm (i.e., some rooms are cramped). Tucked into an alley a few blocks from Piazza Navona.... *Tel 06/687 69 83, fax 06/686 54 42, www.hotelduetorriroma.com. Vicolo del Leonetto 23, buses 46, 64, 70, 81, 492. $$$–$$$$* **(see p. 27)**

Fontana. Roll out of bed and look down on the massive Trevi Fountain. Crowd noise often drowns out the sound of the water; you can drown out both with soundproof windows. Charge for A/C in the summer. No elevator.... *Tel 06/678 61 13, fax 06/679 00 24, www.fontanahotel.com. Piazza di Trevi 96. 24 rooms. $$–$$$* **(see p. 22)**

Fori Imperiali Cavalieri. Pretty, quiet hotel a few blocks from the ancient city. Extremely helpful, English-speaking staff. Breakfast included.... *Tel 06/679 62 46, fax 06/679 72 03. Via Frangipane 34, Forum routes. 24 rooms. $$$* **(see p. 27)**

Gallia. Upgraded to a four-star after 1999 renovations, the hotel has new linens and carpeting in all the guestrooms, plus electronic locks and a safe. The breezy, rooftop terrace affords great views of Santa Maria Maggiore and its obelisk. Breakfast included.... *Tel 06/478 24 769, fax 06/481 80 77, leonardi@travel.it. Via di Santa Maria Maggiore 143, buses 16, 27, 70, 71, J2, J3, J6. 33 rooms. $$–$$$$* **(see pp. 25, 26)**

Gregoriana. Robert Morris florals and leopard prints dominate the decor at this simple, modish inn. Breakfast is served in the bedrooms.... *Tel 06/679 42 69, fax 06/678 42 58. Via Gregoriana 18, Metro Spagna or Barberini. 19 rooms. $$$–$$$$* **(see p. 20)**

Hassler Villa Medici. A privately owned five-star hotel in the best location in town (facing the Spanish Steps). Service is discreet and rooms are small, but incredibly luxurious.... *Tel 06/699 340, fax 06/678 99 91, www.hotelhasslerroma.com. Piazza Trinità dei Monti 6, Metro Spagna. 100 rooms. $$$$$* **(see pp. 17, 19, 23)**

Hilton Rome Airport. Massive new 517-room hotel connected by covered overpass to Fiumicino Airport. All modern amenities, and children under 12 stay free.... *Tel 06/652 58, fax 06/652 56 525, rm_rome-apt@hilton.com. Via Arturo Ferrarin 2. $$$–$$$$* **(see p. 23)**

Hotel de Russie. From its stark, marble lobby, to its fashionable spa, to its private, Mediterranean-style terrace/garden, the Hotel de Russie has got it all. Throw in the location, right on Piazza del Popolo, and fuhgeddaboutit.... *Tel 06/328 881, fax 06/328 88 888, www.rfhotels.com. Via del Babuino 9, Metro Spagna, Flaminio. 129 rooms. $$$$$* **(see p. 19)**

Hotel des Artistes. Three brothers run this very nice, very informal hotel/hostel on the north side of Termini. Rooms are unique, modern, inexpensive, and completely nonsmoking. Breakfast is included only for the rooms with private baths.... *Tel 06/445 43 65, fax 06/446 23 68,* *www.hoteldesartistes.com. Via Villafranca 20, Metro Castro Pretorio. 32 rooms.$–$$* **(see pp. 20, 23)**

Lancelot. Congenial Colosseum-area hotel ideal for business travelers or families. Free parking available. Breakfast included.... *Tel 06/704 50 615, fax 06/704 50 640, www.lancelothotel.com. Via Capo d'Africa 47, tram 30, Metro Colosseo. 61 rooms. $$$* **(see p. 26)**

Locarno. Art-deco style accommodations in the middle of the *Centro Storico.* A small, attractive patio is in the back.... *Tel 06/361 08 41, fax 06/321 52 49, www.hotel locarno.com. Via della Penna 22, Metro Flaminio. 48 rooms. $$$* **(see p. 21)**

Majestic. One of the first hotels on the Via Veneto still attracts a chi-chi crowd. Rates start at around $400 per night, breakfast not included.... *Tel 06/421 441, fax 06/488 09 84, www.hotelmajesticroma.com. Via Veneto 50, buses 52, 53, 56, 58,116, 490, Metro Barberini. 95 rooms. $$$$$* **(see pp. 19, 28)**

Marriott Grand Hotel Flora. Luxurious rooms overlooking the Villa Borghese and the Via Veneto make up for a somewhat stuffy atmosphere. Once a *Dolce Vita* hangout, now a favorite with business travelers.... *Tel 06/489 929, fax 06/482 03 59, www.marriott.com. Via Veneto 191, buses 52, 53, 56, 58, 116, 490, Metro Spagna (Villa Borghese exit). 156 rooms. $$$$$* **(see p. 24)**

Mediterraneo. One of the tallest hotels in town, built during Mussolini's time when height regulations weren't a consideration. The 10-story hotel has an institutional air, but the rooms are large and quiet. Ideal for families or tour groups, and right near Termini.... *Tel 06/488 40 51, fax 06/475 09 76, www.bettojahotels.it. Via Cavour 15, Metro Termini or Repubblica. 267 rooms. $$$* **(see pp. 23, 26)**

Navona. Hard to believe this is only a one-star hotel. Keats and Shelley were once boarders on the upper floors, and ancient ruins are in the basement. Bright, spacious rooms, many of which have showers. No doubt, the hotel is extremely popular with returning visitors, so book months in advance.... *Tel 06/686 42 03, fax 06/688 03 802, navona@posta2000.com. Via dei Sediari 8, buses 46, 64, 70, 81, 492. 21 rooms. $–$$* **(see p. 21)**

Nerva. Family-run three-star near the Forum. Rooms are on the small side but clean, and some have views of the ancient city; recommended for history buffs.... *Tel 06/678 18 35, fax 06/699 22 204, hotelnerva@libero.it. Via Tor de'Conti 3, buses 44, 46, 56, 60, 62, 64. 19 rooms. $$–$$$* **(see p. 22)**

Nicolini B&B. Ideal for friends or small families. Staying at Nicolini B&B is like staying in an apartment. One master bedroom, 1 double room, and 2 baths. Breakfast is served in a private garden. Located between Trastevere and the Botanical Gardens. Three-night minimum stay. No credit cards. Closed Aug, Oct, and Feb.... *Tel 06/699 24 722, fax 06/697 87 084. Vicolo della Penitenza 19, Lungotevere routes. 2 rooms. $* **(see p. 28)**

Nostra Signora di Lourdes. If you don't mind going indoors when everyone else is stepping out, then try this convent a few blocks from the Spanish Steps. Women and married couples allowed. 10:30pm curfew.... *Tel 06/474 53 24, no fax. Via Sistina 113, Metro Spagna. $* **(see p. 26)**

Oceania. The central location and the low *pensione* rates draw in the tourists. Cozy decor and super-friendly service keep them coming back. Very handsome two-star.... *Tel 06/482 46 96, fax 06/488 55 86, www.hoteloceania.it. Via Firenze 38, Metro Repubblica. 9 rooms. $–$$* **(see p. 21)**

Ponte Sisto. Views of the Tibe and Ponte Sisto and walking distance to Trastevere, the Ghetto, and Campo de' Fiori, plus breakfast served in an interior courtyard.... *Tel 06/686 311, fax 06/686 31 801. Via dei Pettinari 64, buses 23, 57, 92, 95, 716. 106 rooms. $$$–$$$$* **(see p. 26)**

Pyramid. Gay-friendly hotel near nighttime hot-spots. Dull, but clean rooms.... *Tel 06/578 00 09, fax 06/575 82 61, info@chc.it. Via Magazzini Generali 4, Metro Piramide. 38 rooms. $–$$* **(see p. 27)**

Quirinale. An oasis off Via Nazionale with a large private courtyard on the backside of the hotel. Special feature is its private entrance into the Teatro dell'Opera.... *Tel 06/47 07, fax 06/482 00 99, www.hotelquirinale.it. Via Nazionale 7, Metro Repubblica. 200 rooms. $$$$$* **(see p. 23)**

Raphaël. Romantic inside and out. An ivy-draped *palazzo* gives way to a gorgeous lobby filled with antiques and a small collection of Picasso treasures. Parquet floors, 18th-century–style furnishings, and paisley curtains accent the bedrooms.... *Tel 06/682 831, fax 06/687 89 93, www.raphaelhotel.com. Largo Febo 2, buses 46, 64, 70, 81, 492. 70 rooms. $$$$$* **(see p. 22)**

Regina Hotel Baglioni. The former home of Italy's Queen Margherita is now a luxe lodging.... *Tel 06/421 11 11, fax 06/420 12 130, www.baglionihotels.com. Via Veneto 72, buses 52, 53, 56, 58, 116, 490, Metro Barberini. 129 rooms. $$$$$* **(see p. 19)**

Residenza San Pantaleo. Affordable inn near Piazza Navona is a welcome mat for gay and lesbian travelers. Bright, clean rooms include AC, TV, and breakfast.... *Tel 06/683 23 45, fax 06/686 80 73. Piazza San Pantaleo 3, buses 46, 64, 70, 81, 492. $$–$$$* **(see p. 27)**

Ripa All Suites Hotel. Winner of many design awards, the Ripa has an East-meets-West flair and a chic, international clientele. The on-site sushi bar and nightclub are worth checking out. Breakfast included.... *Tel 06/58 611, fax 06/581 45 50, www.ripahotel.com. Via Luigi Gianniti 21, trams 8, 30. 170 rooms. $$$$$* **(see p. 20)**

Santa Maria. Quiet Trastevere hotel situated on the site of a former cloister. Recently remodeled rooms are small, but very charming. The staff is exceptionally congenial. Breakfast included.... *Tel 06/589 46 26, fax 06/589 48 15, www.htlsantamaria.com. Vicolo del Piede 2, Trastevere routes. $$–$$$* **(see p. 27)**

Sant'Anselmo. Attractive and serene hotel located in former villa on the Aventine hill near orange groves and rose gardens. Breakfast served in a covered courtyard.... *Tel 06/574 35 47, fax 06/578 36 04, frpiroli@tin.it. Piazza Sant'Anselmo 2, bus 94. $$$–$$$$* **(see p. 27)**

Santa Prassede. Very affordable given its location a few paces from Santa Maria Maggiore. No televisions in rooms—but there's a TV lounge. Breakfast included.... *Tel 06/481 48 50, fax 06/474 68 59, santaprassede@italyhotel.com. Via Santa Prassede 25, buses 16, 27, 70, 71, J2, J3, J6. 25 rooms. $–$$* **(see p. 25)**

Scalinata di Spagna. There's no getting closer to the Spanish Steps. The rooftop terrace has some of the best views in Rome. Stylish and gay-friendly.... *Tel 06/679 30 06, fax 06/699 40 598, www.hotelscalinata.com. Piazza Trinità dei Monti 17, Metro Spagna. 16 rooms. $$$$–$$$$$* **(see pp. 21, 27)**

Sheraton Hotel Roma. Enormous hotel near Fiumicino Airport attracts a large conventioneer crowd. Cookie-cutter rooms. Runs a free shuttle to the airport and the city center.... *Tel 06/54 531, fax 06/594 06 89, www.sheraton.com/roma. Viale del Pattinaggio 100. 650 rooms. $$$$$* **(see p. 23)**

Sole al Pantheon. In operation as an inn since the 15th century, the Sole al Pantheon is quaint, but fully modern. Choose a room with a view of the Pantheon (and lots of noise) or one overlooking the inner courtyard.... *Tel 06/678 04 41, fax 06/69 94 06 89, hotsole@flashnet.it. Piazza della Rotonda 63, buses 64, 70, 75, 116. 25 rooms. $$$$–$$$$$* **(see p. 22)**

Sol Melia Aurelia Antica. New hotel in idyllic surroundings. Free shuttle will get you to the city center or the airport in a jiffy. Otherwise, amuse yourself in the pool or fitness center. Spanish-style buffet breakfast included.... *Tel 06/665 441, fax 06/664 15 878, www.solmelia.com. Via degli Aldobrandeschi 223. $$$$–$$$$$* **(see p. 23)**

Spring House. A three-star with a modern look, near the Vatican Museums.... *Tel 06/397 20 948, fax 06/397 21 047, www.hotelspringhouse.com. Via Mocenigo 7, Metro Ottaviano. 35 rooms. $–$$$* **(see p. 25)**

St. Regis Grand. More luxury than you can stand. Grand, ballroom-sized lobby has a 1-ton chandelier of Murano glass, marble floors have been retrofitted with warming controls, and there's even a private wine cellar. Service is also at your beck-and-call, with "personal butler" services on floors two and three. Rates start at around $900 per night, breakfast not included.... *Tel 06/470 91, fax 06/474 73 07, www.stregis.com/grandrome. Via Vittorio Emanuele Orlando 3, Metro Repubblica. 170 rooms. $$$$$* **(see pp. 17, 19)**

Teatro di Pompeo. A must for history buffs, as this hotel is built atop the ruins of the Pompeii Theater, where Caesar was assassinated. Quiet, individually styled rooms. Close to Campo de' Fiori.... *Tel 06/683 00 170, fax 06/688 055 31, hotel.teatrodipompeo@tiscalinet.it. Largo del Pallaro 8.[TK buses?] 13 rooms. $$–$$$* **(see p. 22)**

Vacanze Romane. Located on the 4th floor of a building near Santa Maria Maggiore, this unique B&B is decorated with antique toys and retro French posters. Three double rooms, 2 communal bathrooms. No minimum stay required. No credit cards. Closed Jan, Feb 1–15, Aug, and Dec 1–15.... *Tel and fax 06/444 10 79. Via Carlo Alberto 26, buses 16, 27, 70, 71, J2, J3, J6. 3 rooms. $* **(see p. 28)**

Valadier. Probably the only convent-turned-brothel-turned-hotel in Rome. Sexy inn boasts tasteful decor (with the exception of the mirrored ceilings), a rooftop garden, and a piano lounge. Breakfast included.... *Tel 06/361 19 98, fax 06/320 15 58, www.hotelvaladier.com. Via della Fontanella 15, Metro Spagna. 48 rooms. $$$–$$$$$* **(see p. 22)**

Verona. Refurbished in 1999, the Verona has very basic rooms and a lovely courtyard. Right in front of Santa Maria Maggiore. Breakfast and parking included.... *Tel 06/487 12 44, fax 06/488 42 12, www.hotelverona-roma.com. Via Santa Maria Maggiore 154, buses 16, 27, 70, 71, J2, J3, J6. 33 rooms. $$–$$$* **(see p. 25)**

Westin Excelsior. Sister hotel of the St. Regis Grand, the Excelsior is the most ornate of the Via Veneto hotels, boasting scads of statues, wall-to-wall marble, and silk-paneled corridors. A piano bar and restaurant are also on-site.... *Tel 06/470 81, fax 06/482 62 05, www.westin.com/excelsior-roma. Via Veneto 125, buses 52, 53, 56, 58, 116, 490, Metro Barberini. 327 rooms. $$$$$* **(see pp. 19, 27)**

Spanish Steps Accommodations

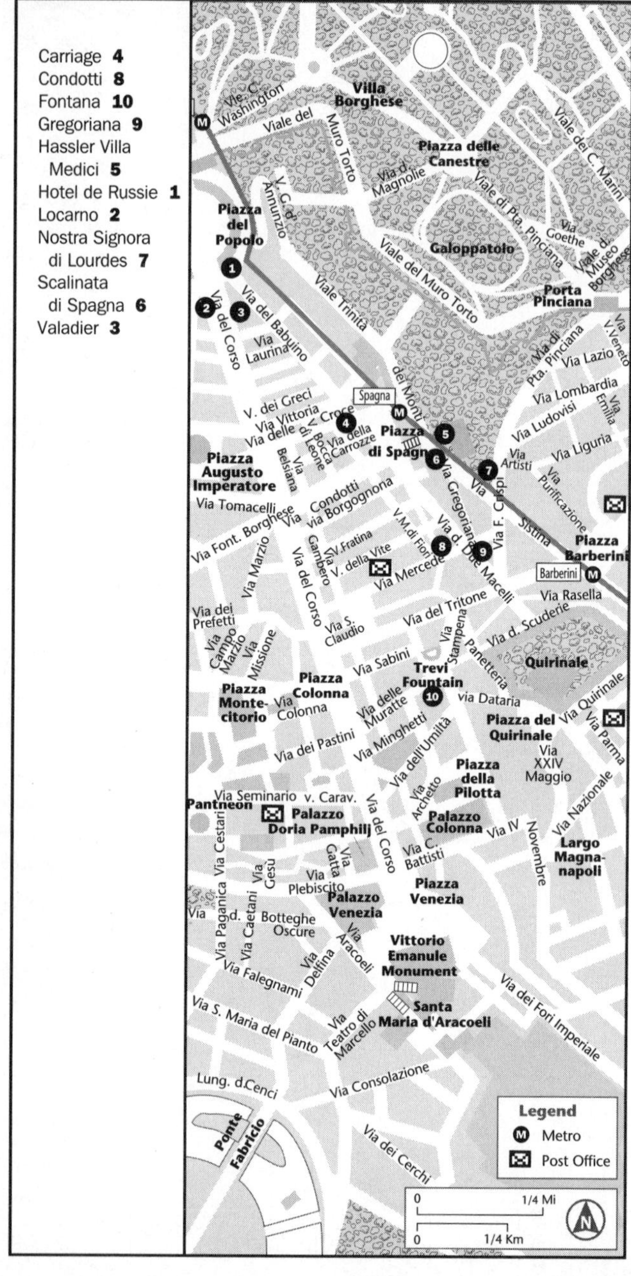

Via Veneto & Termini Accommodations

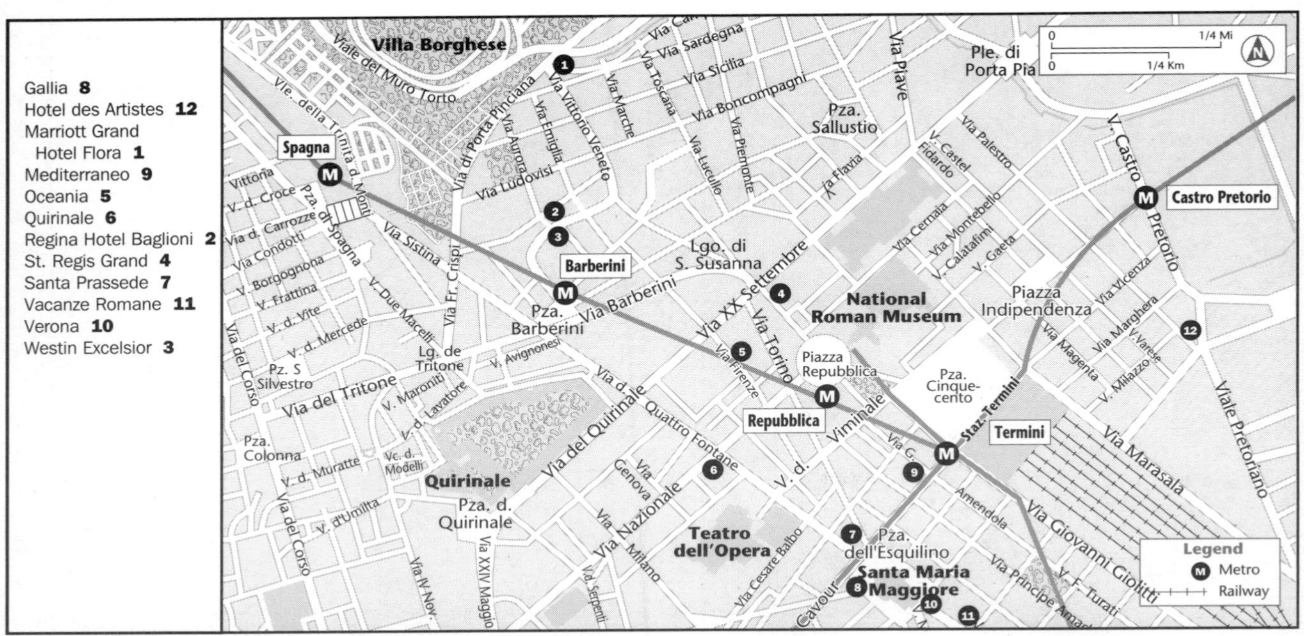

Campo de' Fiori & Piazza Navona Accommodations

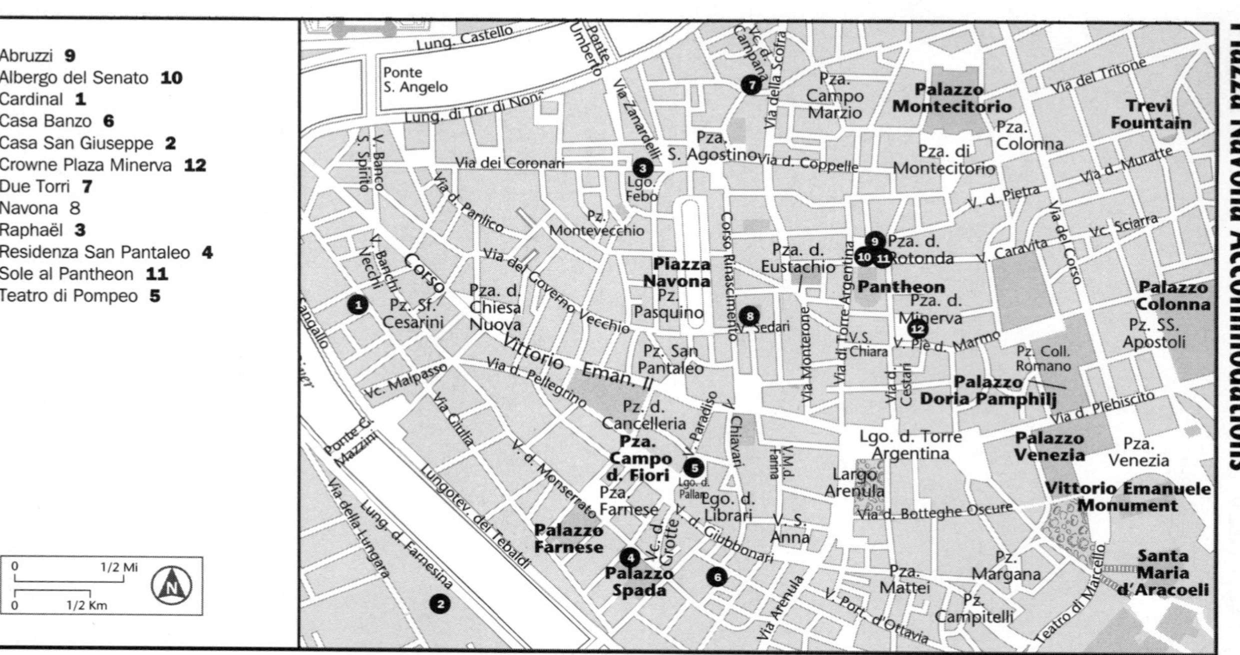

Vatican City Area Accommodations

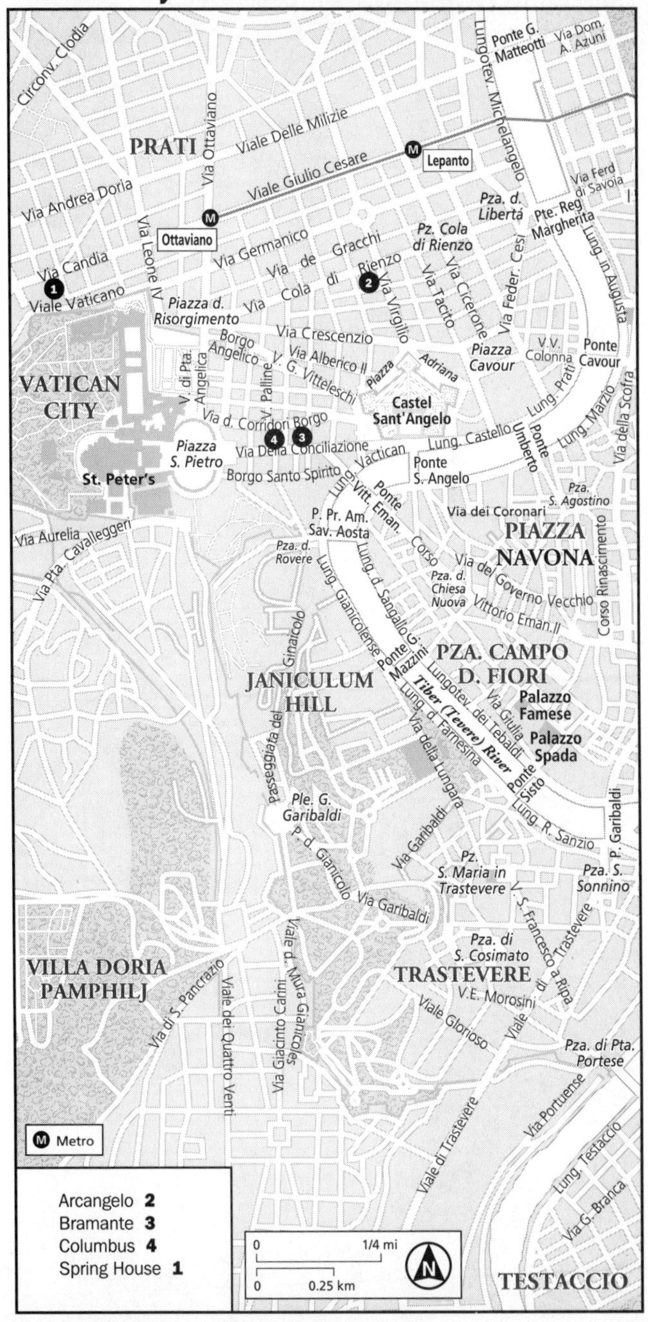

Rome Accommodations

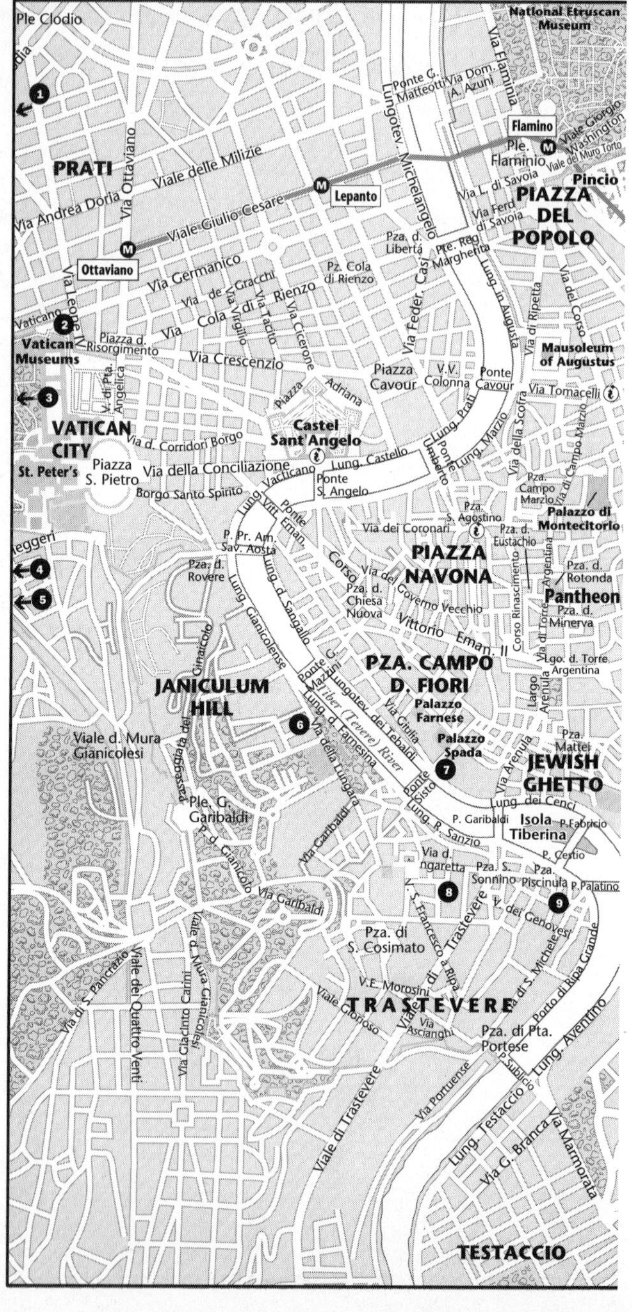

B&B ai Musei Vaticani 2
Bied 14
Casa di Santa Francesca Romana 9
Cavalieri Hilton 1
Delta Colosseo 13
Hilton Rome Airport 4
Lancelot 12
Nicolini B&B 6
Ponte Sisto 7
Pyramid 10
Santa Maria 8
Sant'Anselmo 11
Sheraton Hotel Roma 5
Sol Melia Aurelia Antica 3
National Gallery of Modern Art
Galleria Borghese
VILLA BORGHESE
Piazza di Siena
SPANISH STEPS
Spagna
VIA VENETO
Barberini
PZA. BARBERINI
Keats-Shelley Memorial
National Roman Museum
National Gallery of Ancient Art
TERMINI
Stazione Termini
Castro Pretorio
Piazza Indipendenza
Piazza Repubblica
Repubblica
Termini
Palazzo del Quirinale
Trevi Fountain
Teatro dell'Opera
Santa Maria Maggiore
Palazzo Colonna
Palazzo Doria Pamphilj
Palazzo Venezia
Vittorio Emanuele Monument
Via Cavour
Vittorio Emanuele
Piazza Vittorio Eman. II
CAMPIDOGLIO
Capitoline Museums
San Pietro in Vincoli
Golden House of Nero
Colosseo
Roman Forum
Colosseum
ANCIENT ROME
Manzoni
PALATINE HILL
Circus Maximus
AVENTINE HILL
Circo Massimo
San Giovanni in Laterano
Baths of Caracalla
Piramide
Legend
Information
Metro
Railway
1/4 Mi
1/4 Km

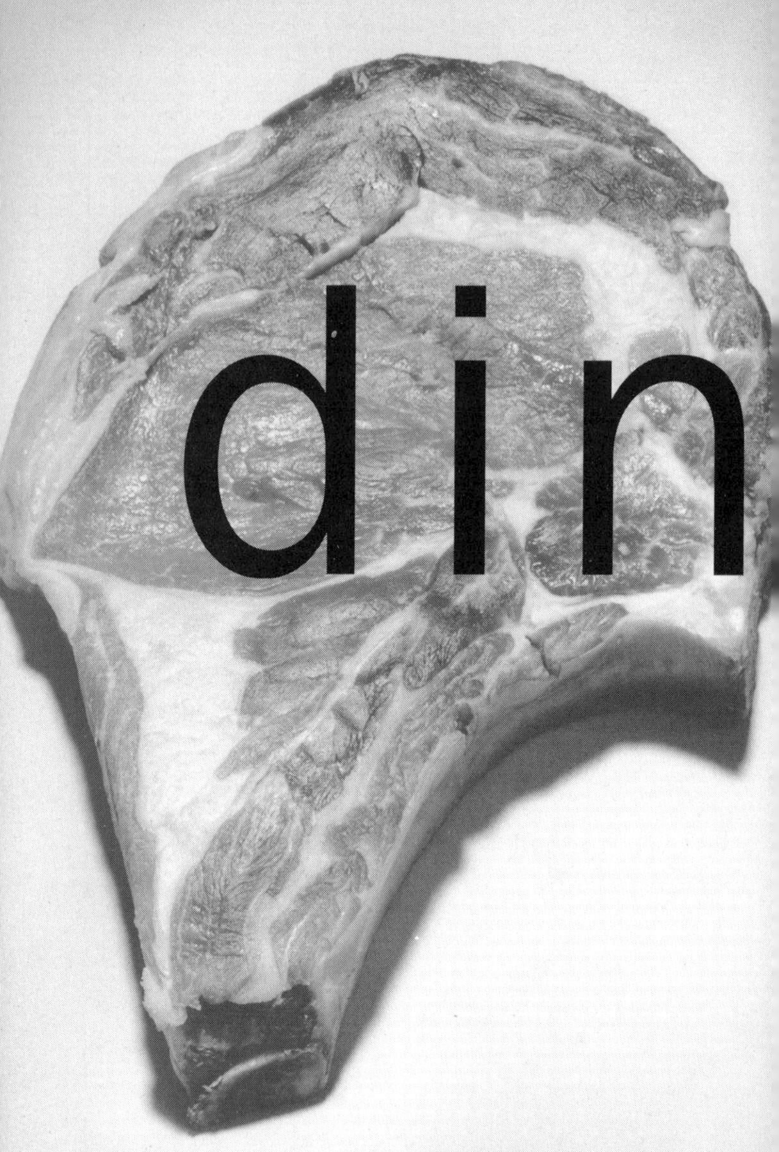
din

ing 2

The restaurant scene in Rome is more like what you'd find in a village than in a cosmopolitan city of more than three million. There are scads of traditional Roman eateries serving hearty fare—heavy on meat and rich pastas—and a number of old-time, rustic *trattorie* that still don't accept credit cards. Where you don't find Roman restaurants, you'll more than likely find places that rely on regional Italian recipes, especially those from Emilia-Romagna (Bologna), Tuscany, Campania (Naples), and Sicily. If you're the type that likes a lot of variety in your meals, though, you're out of luck: Rome is decidedly lacking in international dining options. And, despite the city's reputation as a mecca for style, there are relatively few modern restaurants experimenting with fusion of Italian and international cuisines. However, this is changing slowly, thanks to an influx of immigrants from Asia, Northern Africa, and elsewhere. Chic, minimalist bistros with casual service are also popping up everywhere, for better or for worse, edging out the traditional trats. Unfortunately, a glut of McDonald's and other fast food chains have also invaded once-idyllic squares. Avoid these unless you're really homesick, and avoid any restaurant's posted *menu turistico*—at all costs: More often than not, the food will be substandard and overpriced.

Only in Rome

All of those unpleasant parts of the animal that Europeans are notorious for eating—brains, lungs, intestines, and so forth—are the guts, so to speak, of traditional Roman cuisine. Much of it is taken from the *quinto quarto*, the fifth quarter—or, if you will, hot dog ingredients, parts of an animal that were historically given to Rome's down-at-heel slaughterhouse workers. Over the years, they developed specialty dishes based on these ingredients that persist today, including *rigatoni alla pajata* (intestines from an unweaned calf), *coda alla vaccinara* (braised oxtail in ragù), *trippa* (tripe), and the city specialty *bucatini all'amatriciana*—long hollow pasta in a spicy sauce of tomatoes and *guanciale* (bacon)—have garnered local fans and sent others running in the other direction. Rome's time-honored Jewish cuisine is related, heavy on the offal but also including deep-fried treats like *filetti di baccalà, carciofi alla giudia* (Jewish-style artichokes), and *fiori di zucca* (zucchini flowers stuffed with cheese and slivers of anchovies). Vegetarians need not shy away from the city, however: When it comes to fruit and vegetables, Romans are particular about variety and freshness. You can see evidence of this each day at any of the produce markets, including in Campo de' Fiori. Chefs from around the city raid the markets in the early hours for eggplant, artichokes, asparagus, tomatoes, mushrooms, zucchini, and more, all of which inevitably wind up as *contorni* (vegetable side dishes) or as the focus of a pasta or risotto dish. Meat-free *primi,* such as *tagliolini con cacio e pepe* (pasta with sheep's cheese and pepper) or even a simple *spaghetti al pomodoro* (spaghetti with marinara sauce) are extremely common, even at the priciest establishments. It's not at all unusual to order a first course and a side of vegetables. However, if you're vegan, you may want to check out Rome's growing number of vegetarian restaurants.

When to Eat—and Drink

Prima colazione (breakfast) is usually just a cappuccino and a *cornetto,* a croissant or jam-filled pasty, which can be taken up until 11am; the single easiest way to quickly identify yourself as a tourist in Rome is to order a cappuccino any time after 11am. For Italians, this foamy coffee drink is for breakfast *only*—not after dinner, and not as a late-day treat. Sure, the *barrista* will serve you one whenever you like, but that doesn't mean he'll approve (though he'll still be happy to take your money). More common in the afternoon is a shot of espresso or a *macchiato*—espresso with a splash of steamed milk. Lunch starts at around noon and can often last until 3:30pm. Because breakfast is so small, lunches are traditionally the main meal of the day, when workers head home for a *primo,* a *secondo,* and a nap. (Note that nearly all shops will be closed during this time for this reason.) However, lazy, long lunches are becoming a thing of the past, as more and more businesses conform to an American-style workday. Either way, Romans don't start showing up for dinner until after 8:30pm, so smart travelers may want to book for 8pm to beat the crowd but also revel in its charming chaos.

Getting the Right Table

In the past, *prenotazioni* (reservations) were made only for the most exclusive restaurants. But today you'd be wise to book even at the local pizza joint, just in case. Romans like to eat out at least once a week, and tourist throngs are never-ending, even at restaurants that seem out of the way. To make sure you don't end up at a cramped corner table or wedged between the restrooms and the kitchen, call several days (or, for some places, weeks or months) in advance. Better yet, have your hotel concierge or a Roman friend make a reservation for you. *Maitre d's* are generally hospitable, but reservations have been known to fly out the window, especially when an important friend or celebrity shows up. If you decide to wing it instead, know that you may not be able to get in, even if a restaurant looks empty. *Riservato* cards are usually laid on tables at opening time, even if a reservation is hours away. Also be aware that, even if you reserve a non-smoking table, you may end up sitting right next to a smoker. Many restaurants rely on smoke-eating machines to rid their establishments of clouds of thick smoke—but in smaller eateries, the non-smoking areas basically abut the smoking tables (if they exist at all).

The Lowdown

Starbucks could learn a thing or two... Coffee shops are a dime a dozen in Rome, and while the coffee is nearly always great, pricing and atmosphere are highly variable. **Antico Caffé Greco,** once the haunt of Casanova and Goethe, is by all accounts a tourist trap and has the prices to match. Sitting down at one of the cafe's marble-top tables (perhaps under an autographed photo of Marcello Mastroianni) will cost you about six times more than standing at the bar. However, the establishment's *granità di caffe* (a coffee-flavored Italian ice) is one of the finest summer treats around. Locals line up morning, noon, and night for the pre-sweetened espresso served at **Bar Sant'Eustachio,** around the corner from the Pantheon. This is one of the few places where Romans will indulge in a *caffè grande* rather than the traditional espresso shot. The side streets off of Piazza della Rotonda also boast **Tazza D'Oro,** a larger, less amicable bar where you can jolt and bolt in a matter of seconds. Avoid getting scolded by paying for your coffee before you order it. Meanwhile, cappuccino Communists like to linger beneath the red flags and left-wing memorabilia at **Da Vezio,** a Ghetto mainstay. Sick of java? **Babington's Tea Room,** an upscale slice of England on Piazza di Spagna, is the place for a scone and a spot of tea. Expect high prices, but genteel service.

Local heroes... It's hard to understand how **Checchino dal 1887,** Rome's quintessential *quinto quarto* restaurant, can get away with charging such steep prices for what was once peasant food. Still, this is the place to go if you want to splash out on a traditional Roman meal. Located across the Monte Testaccio square from a former slaughterhouse, Checchino charges an arm and a leg (90,000L per person, about $45) for *offal* delights like rigatoni con pajata (veal intestines engorged with cow's milk) and fried brains. **La Campana,** which has been around since 1528 (and perhaps as early as 1450), once served Goethe and continues to be the old standby for journalists and politicians. Here, you can get a hearty *primo* of *bucatini all'amatriciana* and a *secondo* of *saltimbocca* (veal topped with sage and prosciutto) at prices that won't make you faint. Conversely, the trattoria **Sora Lella** has been operating at its location on the Isola Tiberina since 1993 (previous stints were in Campo de' Fiori). Founded by Elena "Lella" Fabrizi—an Italian film and television star who regularly starred as a sympathetic *nonna* (grandmother)—this eatery is legendary for its rustic Roman cuisine. Son Aldo runs the place now, basing the many pasta and rice dishes on his mother's homegrown recipes. Denizens of (and visitors to) the "Dolce Vita street" Via Veneto are again flocking to **Harry's Bar,** now restored to its former stuffiness. If you're craving a "real" Martini (not the aperitif of the same name), then head to the restaurant's American bar—a $15 cocktail never tasted so good. **Sabatini,** prominently located on Trastevere's main square, looks like a tourist trap—and it *is* a tourist trap to some extent. But a taste of the friendly restaurant's patented *spaghetti alle vongole* (spaghetti and clam sauce) is splurge-worthy nevertheless. Likewise, **Alfredo alla Scrofa** (yes, of *fettuccine Alfredo* fame) has a decidedly American clientele who comes to see photos and memorabilia of old Hollywood stars and former patrons, like Douglas Fairbanks and Ava Gardner, and savor the classic, fattening, triple-butter dish. It's basically Hollywood on the Tiber.

Hip, trendy—and the food's good, too... If you go to **'Gusto,** don't bother looking for red-checkered tablecloths. This airy restaurant/pizzeria/bar looks like it was pulled together with several runs to IKEA. It conforms to a modern yuppie restaurant ethic, with unfinished wood accents, white paper table liners, and a photogenic staff. Nevertheless, the atmosphere is friendly, the pizzas and pastas are delectable, and the prices are reasonable. After 8:30pm, you can expect the innovative **Osteria dell'Ingegno** to be packed with local gourmands. Done up in bright, Cubist-style artwork, wicker chairs, and painted tabletops, the restaurant "of the ingenious" features a carefully selected menu of seasonal flavors, including such dishes as gnocchi in black truffle sauce and risotto with asparagus and saffron. **RipArte Café,** the art gallery–cum-bistro at the Ripa Suites Hotel [see Accommodations], has as many creative works in the kitchen as on the wall. Feast on *primi* such as ravioli stuffed with arugula and grouper, or belly up to the sushi bar—a concept that seems passé stateside, but is all the rage with image-conscious Romans. Alternatively, think canvas-covered chairs, stark white walls, and well-placed Asian accents, and you've got **Campo,** a modern restaurant more attuned to the New York or London scene than Rome's. The cuisine draws from the best of southern Italian cooking, with a focus on fish, but the menu is fashionably sparse. Before setting off on an all-nighter in the Centro, the young, see-and-be-seen crowd meets up at **Maccheroni** for pasta, Argentine-style steak, and occasional live music.

Chowin' down near the Colosseum... You don't have to wander far from the Colosseum to escape the overpriced, ubiquitous *menu turistico* and questionable street-vendor fare. **Il Tempio di Iside,** located on a side street off Via Labicana, serves all manner of *frutti di mare* at moderate prices. Just off the tourist beat, you can dine *al fresco* shaded by the trees of the Celian Park at **Taverna dei Quaranta.** Few tourists have happened upon this hideaway, and the basic Italian fare is fresh and cheap. Mama Lidia, who runs **Ristorante al Cardello** with her husband Angelo, will talk your ear off even if you don't speak Italian. Be warned, though, that lots of tourists (read: Americans) come here, sometimes making reservations weeks in advance. For that "I-can't-believe-I'm-in-Rome" experience (plus lotsa tourists, but the view is phenomenal), head up the stairs from Via dei Fori Imperiali to the **Hostaria**

del Nerone, which affords vistas of the Colosseum. Go at night, when the ruins are stunningly floodlit, and you just may be able to stomach fried brains, the house specialty.

Dishes your Jewish grandma would be proud of... After three generations of serving up traditional Roman specialties, **Da Giggetto** can't help but look a little rough around the edges. Still, this family-run restaurant in the shadow of the Portico d'Ottavia is one of the Ghetto's best for chowing on Jewish-style artichokes (*carciofi alla giudia*) and oxtail stew (*coda alla vaccinara*). Similarly, **Da Piperno** runs the gamut of Ghetto goodies, serving a knockout *fritto misto* (fried fish and vegetables) and a time-tested *trippa,* but it's often packed with as many tourists as locals. **Al 16 del Portico d'Ottavia** updates Jewish classics with house specials such as *pennete al 16* (sausage, eggplant, and tomatoes) and adds a gourmet touch to working-class *offal* dishes. While you can be assured that most restaurants in the Ghetto adhere to Jewish cooking practices, kosher kitchens are not the norm. Travelers who want to keep kosher can dine at **La Taverna del Ghetto,** which even has a kosher (but limited) wine list, or at **Zi Fenizia,** a kosher pizzeria. **Dar Filettaro di Santa Barbara,** known simply as **Filetti di Baccalà** after the sign above the door, is just out of the Ghetto proper close to Campo de' Fiori and has ample seating indoors or out for those hankering for a quick bite of salted codfish.

Vatican vittles... Stop by **Da Cesare,** a quiet Tuscan restaurant that contrasts nicely with the St. Peter's crowds. The *prezzo fisso* tasting menus include *primi* such as hearty minestrone and seafood risotto, generous servings of fish and beef for *secondi,* and dessert, and they're cheaper than going à la carte. **Lorodinapoli** serves Neapolitan specialties at relatively cheap prices in a reserved basement *trattoria.* Hot Roman days call for tropical flavor, including delicious Caribbean cuisine and rum punch served at outdoor tables at **Macondo.** Done up in the requisite red-and-white-checkered tablecloth look, **Arlù,** just two blocks from St. Peter's, is a surprisingly good value for its pan-Mediterranean cuisine, including Roman specialties and lots of seafood choices.

Taking a bite out of Trastevere... Trastevere justly deserves its props as Rome's best place to eat at neighborhood restaurants, though—incredibly—it's already becoming passé as more and more foreigners discover the area and move in. Nevertheless, you can still find great eats. Although **Pastarellaro di Severino** has been around since 1848 (and has a framed note on the wall from D'Annunzio to prove it), Roman standards like *bucatini all'amatriciana* and *coda alla vaccinara* (oxtail stew) still garner praise. And, considering its history, the prices aren't steep. **Roma Sparita,** which also serves traditional Roman and Jewish fare, is dirt-cheap given its location on the quiet (during the daytime, anyway) Piazza Santa Cecilia. **Asinocotto** may mean "cooked ass," but the creative cuisine here is far from unsavory. Dishes like artichokes stuffed with gorgonzola and gnocchi with clams and imaginative desserts have helped to restore the neighborhood's culinary status; service is just right, casual yet attentive. The place is also gay-owned—in case you couldn't tell by the rainbow flag proudly flying outside.

Eating on the tourist beat... The proprietress of **Dal Bolognese** can afford to be surly given the restaurant's prime spot on Piazza del Popolo. Enjoy specialties from the Emilia-Romagna region, including *tagliatelle al ragù*—which is incorrectly interpreted by Americans as *spaghetti bolognese*; purists would insist on the long, flat tagliatelle noodle instead of round, American-style spaghetti—outside on the edge of the square. For quicker service, or to mingle with Romans, choose a quiet indoor table. A perennial favorite, **Myosotis** sits on a quaint sidestreet between Piazza Navona and the Pantheon and serves dozens of *antipasti,* a lengthy and fairly inexpensive wine list, homemade breads and pastries, and service with a smile. **Armando al Pantheon** looks like a tourist dive, and prices have recently risen to compete with the cluster of tourist dives that surround it, but take heart—this small eatery is known to locals as a Mecca for ancient Roman cuisine, including such ingredients as guinea fowl and porcini mushrooms cooked in black beer. It also adheres to the usual daily schedule for local fare (gnocchi on Thursday, baccalà on Friday, and so forth). Campo de' Fiori's **La Carbonara,** where you can eat the pasta of the same name or fill up on *antipasti,* hasn't been completely destroyed by tourists, but its prices have risen in recent years to take advantage of them. **Hostaria Grappolo D'Oro,** also in the Campo area, is slowly but surely attracting more travelers than locals as it earns award after award for creative fresh pastas and desserts. Down the block, claustrophobes beware: **Da Pancrazio** is housed in cramped quarters adjacent to the ancient theater where Caesar was assassinated. Inventive dishes like ravioli stuffed with artichokes will make you forget that the crumbling walls are incredibly ancient; in any case, you're sure to make out better than old Julius did.

Up on the roof... If you'd rather forsake local flavor for a dazzling view and an astronomical bill, then rooftop dining is for you. For better or for worse, just about every hotel that's able to secure zoning approval has a rooftop restaurant or cafe. When the **Hotel Hassler Rooftop** opened in the 1950s, no one in town was dining on the roof; today, the hotel's über-elite clientele is still treated to heart-stopping views of central Rome from the sixth-floor windows, typical Italian cuisine, and black-tie service. No one can write a bad review about **La Pergola,** the Hotel Cavalieri Hilton's rooftop restaurant headed up by Chef Heinz Beck: The wide panoramas are spectacular, the Mediterranean fare is exceptional, and the wine list includes more than 1,300 labels. Still, the waiters will likely be the only Italians in the room, and the $80 you'll spend per person here adds up to more than a few "real" Roman meals (or a good shopping spree). **Les Etoiles,** perched atop the Hotel Atlante Star, has five-star meals and five-star prices, but the three telescopes set on St. Peter's are the real treat.

Eating out(side)... Just about every restaurant in Rome spills out onto a sidewalk or square in warm weather, but many have lackluster views of alleys, are spoiled by noise, or raise their prices substantially for outdoor tables. The best bet for a tranquil al fresco experience is in the neighborhood of Trastevere, which boasts dozens of outdoor options. **Sabatini** occupies a prime spot right on the Piazza di Santa Maria and is a haven for tourists. But it doesn't matter—locals feel comfortable splashing out for a meal here, too. On the weekend, **La Tana de' Noantri,** around the corner from Sabatini, has seating in a small medieval square behind the Santa Maria in Trastevere church. **Romolo nel Giardino di Raffaello e della Fornarina,** perhaps the most overhyped restaurant in all of Rome—it's located on the site where Raphael lived with his mistress—serves Roman classics like saltimbocca (veal cutlets covered with prosciutto, then breaded and fried; the name means "jump in the mouth") in a romantic inner courtyard. Most people don't go to **Caffè delle Arti,** the modern art gallery's stylish snack bar for the food, but rather for the view. During summer, you can sit on the terrace with a glass of wine or beer and a few appetizers and take in unspoiled views of the Villa Borghese. **San Teodoro** is a darling trat with memorable seafood dishes, but it's the restaurant's outdoor dining area near the Forum that really makes this a great spot for an evening meal. For something to eat on the antique beat, try **Osteria dell'Antiquario,** an upscale lunch option situated on a calm square on the Via dei Coronari. Finally, to dine among ancient ruins take a trip out to the Appia Antica [see Diversions] to **Hostaria Antica Roma.** You can enjoy recipes from the Imperial Age served in a former columbarium (an ancient storage place for funerary urns); the eerie atmosphere is unmatched.

In vino veritas... Cozy **Cul de Sac** is decorated with simple wooden booths, shelves of vino, and winking waiters. It completely lives up to its reputation as one of the coolest places in town. Get there early and you can dine on escargot, plates of prosciutto, or a creamy bowl of onion soup while you watch the queue extend down the street. **Angolo Divino,** a play on words meaning "wine corner" or "divine corner" is laid back despite its proximity to raucous Campo de' Fiori. Appetizers here are simple—think bruschetta or olives—and glasses of wine start at about $2. Celebs like Jack Nicholson and Claudia Schiffer have ducked into **Enoteca Antica di Via della Croce** for wine and privacy. This long, dark bar just a block or so from the Spanish Steps accommodates lazy lunches and its share of chic passers-by. Much of the food at **Vinamore** is pre-made, but somehow the staff manage to pull together tasty, mostly vegetarian hors d'oeuvres and entrees. Wine prices are a bit steeper here than at true *enoteche,* but you can stay as long as you like, reading a book or chatting with friends while you nurse your carafe. *Al fresco* dining at **La Buca di Bacco** only accommodates about two tables (indoors is a piano bar), but it's a fitting place to take a glass of wine and a plate of cheese for brunch or an afternoon snack. If good wine at outrageously low prices is all you're after, get ye to the **Vineria,** the city's most entertaining wine seller. The mess of tables outdoors and a long wooden bar indoors attract as many hip, young Romans as it does rowdy expats.

There's something fishy here... La Rosetta, near the Pantheon, has long been *the* place for seafood—if you could spare the expense. However, the recent addition of **Reef,** a trendy fish restaurant with a colorful decor inspired in equal parts by Philippe Starck and Salvador Dalì, has been bringing in the throngs by virtue of its creative Italian seafood entrées and good stabs at sushi and sashimi. Meanwhile, **Trattoria da Settimio all'Arancio** (near the Piazza di Spagna) and **Ripa 12** in Trastevere are two of the best-kept "seacrets" in the city. Locals pile into these two unassuming restaurants all week long for fresh fish, a friendly waitstaff, and extremely reasonable prices. Another local haunt is **Ristorante Il Pellicano,** which boasts a broad range of seafood dishes—most culled from traditional recipes of the Marche region—including several types of *brodetto,* a kind of fish stew.

Oh, please, not pasta again... Sick of paying 12 bucks for pasta and a mere dribble of red sauce? So take a break, already. The sushi craze is at full-throttle in Rome now, and the sleek Trastevere restaurant **ATM Sushi** is where to get it, even if it is overpriced—better hit the other kind of ATM before you visit. For a taste of Spain, **Tapa Loca** is excellent for paella (six varieties, including vegetarian) and sangria. To really spice things up, try **La Bodeguita del Malecon,** an authentic Cuban restaurant serving plates of roast pork, jerked beef, fried plantains, and black beans. Spankopita, tsatsiki, moussaka, and similar meals are done right at **Ouzerie,** a Greek social and cultural club that opens nightly for dinner and dancing. Pan-Asian fare, including recipes from the more exotic Indonesian, Malaysian, and Balinese cuisines, is well done at **Ketumbar,** a hip Testaccio restaurant featuring nightly DJs and ultra-cool scenesters. Finally, if you simply must eat steak or chicken wings in front of a big satellite TV—just like you'd do at home if you weren't on vacation—mosey over to **T-Bone Station,** near the Spanish Steps. It's an American-style steakhouse with filling side dishes.

When the moon hits your eye like a big pizza pie... You can get pizza *a taglio*—by the slice, that is, except that it's cut with kitchen scissors and sold by weight—all over the city, and if you're hurrying this is the quickest lunchtime option, not to mention probably just about only food you can get in the late afternoon when everyone else is closed. However, for a king-sized hunger you're better off going to a sit-down pizzeria, of which there are plenty. Romans flock to **PizzaRé,** a chain near Pizza del Popolo serving thick, Neopolitan-style pies. **Acchiappafantasmi,** which roughly translates as "ghost busters," is also a hit with everyone, especially kids, as the lively staff serve up pizzas decorated to look like spirits, with olives for eyes and other ingredients making spooky faces. Make a reservation for **Dar Poeta,** or else get there before 8pm. This wildly popular Trastevere dive has little in the way of decoration but makes a killer pizza. Sit near the back to get a good view of the *pizzaioli* (pizza baker) slinging dough. Meanwhile, **Supernatural** is the only strictly vegetarian pizzeria in Rome.

Mamma says eat your vegetables... **Margutta Vegetariano** was the first vegetarian restaurant in Rome and continues to be one of the most popular—largely due to its ultra-cool decor (Indian rugs, modern art) and health-conscious recipes like pasta with grilled veggies. They also squeeze fresh fruit and vegetable juices. **Govinda** serves ayurvedic, Indian-inspired dishes, including many varieties of curries, plus non-alcoholic beers and after-dinner liqueurs; just be warned that the bright-robed, beatific bald guys and gals in here are all Hare Krishna devotees and may press some philosophy on you. The area of San Lorenzo boasts a number of vegetarian options thanks to its large, eco-conscious student population. The two best are **Arcana,** an elegant, mostly vegan eatery, and **Arancia Blu,** technically a cultural association, which serves a broad palette of meat-free *primi* and *secondi* like pasta with *pecorino* (sheep's milk cheese) and truffles. The place also maintains an extensive wine list.

Food that's faster than a Formula One car... Three of Rome's best places for a fast meal are right off of the Campo de' Fiori. **Brek** has decent pasta, pizza by the slice, a wide selection of pastries, and ample seating for an afternoon breather. Less than a block away is **È Buono,** a *tavola calda* (hot-food bar) that's a big hit with the 20-somethings for its tantalizing choice of fresh salads, antipasti, daily soups, and *primi.* Early evening hunger pains call for deep-fried codfish, a specialty of **Dar Filettaro da Santa Barbara**, locally known as **Filetti di Baccalà**. A quick bite after sightseeing at the Trevi Fountain doesn't have to mean Dunkin' Donuts (sadly, now a fixture on the square). Walk up the same street to **Bruschetteria Nonna Papera,** a bright eat-and-go restaurant serving mostly *bruschetta* and salads. At least three daily choices of *primi,* sizable servings of *secondi,* and a buffet of *contorni* and sweets make the **Ristorante Self-Service del Palazzo delle Esposizioni** a favorite among Rome's business types. The large dining area makes the restaurant ideal for families and lone diners, too.

Noshing with the night owls... Sometimes you've just gotta eat late, whether it's a post-clubbing snack or to make up for a meal you missed earlier. Fortunately, you're in luck: A surprising number of kitchens in Rome stay open until at least 1 or 2am. **Steel,** a rather delicate, traditional trat despite its masculine moniker, stays open until an impressive 4:45am on weeknights, and until 5:45am on weekends. **La Tavernetta** serves up homemade raviolini (especially good when paired with porcini mushrooms), *spaghetti alla seppia* (squid ink), and more than 300 choices of wine until 2am. For a cheap, after-theater treat, think **Der Pallaro**—a simple, family-run restaurant. Party-types and night-owls head for **Bar San Calisto** in Trastevere for pizza or quick appetizers before moving on to the clubs. During the '60s and '70s, the spoons at this dive were often punched through with holes so that the hippie customers wouldn't steal them for heroin. Most of today's clientele are scooter-riding teens.

Getting just your desserts... Rome is awash with *dolci* (sweets) of all kinds. Gelato-making is a science at **Il Gelato di San Crispino,** a white-jacket kind of place where gelato is served only in cups—cones destroy the delicacy of the sweet stuff's flavor, don'tcha know? Concoctions here are made from everything, from Armagnac (a brandy blend) to standards like *stracciatella* (vanilla with chocolate chips), and are considered by some to be among the best in the world. **Blu Ice Gelateria,** a stroll away from Campo de' Fiori, lacks San Crispino's name recognition but still serves up some of the largest scoops of gelato you've ever seen. **Giolitti** is gelato for the old guard, offering flavors made from After Eight chocolate and Grand Marnier. **I Tre Scalini,** off of Piazza Navona, is known for its rich, chocolate *tartufo* (truffles) and decadent chocolate varieties. If flavored ice is your bag, look for a *grattachecca* vendor. This shaved-ice-and-syrup mixture is best at **Sora Mirella,** a family-run operation in Trastevere whose opening each March signals the start of summer. You can also get other sweet treats around town. When Romans need to buy a birthday cake, for instance, they make a beeline for **Vanni Café,** a *pasticceria* and caterer in the Centro Storico that's locally synonymous with rich cakes, tarts, and *crostate,* (a sort of dry cheesecake). Trastevere's **Pasticceria Valzani** is overseen by a quick-tempered older woman; ignore her manners, because her shop is tops for a Sacher Torte, biscotti, or *torrone* (a hard candy of almonds, honey, and nougat) that the store now manufactures under its own label). Come during Lenten festivals and you can pick up Easter treats like *frappe.* Also called *cenci* (lover's knots), these sweets are fried strips of dough flavored with sugar and brandy. Ignore the humongous wheel of cheese in the doorway at **Il Fornaio,** an extremely popular bakery near the Campo, and peruse the cases of sweets instead; Nutella-filled croissants and fruit tarts are made here daily, though they're often gone by noon. For Sicilian-style *dolci*, head to the Galleria Esedra (Repubblica), where you'll find **Dagnino** tucked among faceless discount shops and seedy bars. *Cannoli,* buns filled with marzipan, and little *bombes* (a rich yeast cake, often made with raisins or currants, and soaked in a rum syrup) are all here, served by pretty girls in frumpy aprons.

The Index

$$$$$	85,000L and up
$$$$	60,000–85,000L
$$$	40,000–60,000L
$$	20,000–40,000L
$	20,000L and less

Acchiappafantasmi. Pizza pies in spooky shapes.... *Tel 06/687 34 62. Via dei Cappellari 66, buses 35, 56, 60, 85, 116. Closed Tue and Oct–Mar. $–$$* **(see p. 56)**

Al 16 del Portico d'Ottavia. Traditional Roman cuisine with a gourmet touch. *Al fresco* dining available in summer at no extra charge.... *Tel 06/687 47 22. Via del Portico d'Ottavia 16, buses 23, 44, 56, 60, 65, 75, 170, 710, 774, 780. Closed Tue. $$* **(see p. 51)**

Alfredo alla Scrofa. The decor is wall-to-wall photos and memorabilia from movie stars, and the fettuccine is nothing you haven't eaten before, but you might as well taste the original.... *Tel 06/688 06 163. Via della Scrofa 104A, buses 64, 70, 75, 116. Closed Tue. $$$* **(see p. 49)**

Angolo Divino. An *enoteca* in Campo de' Fiori where you can hear yourself think. Order a glass of red or white and a plate of *bruschette* with olive, red pepper, or artichoke tapenade.... *Tel 06/686 44 13. Via dei Balestrari 12, buses 64, 492. Open daily. Closed Mon lunch. $$* **(see p. 54)**

Antico Caffe Greco. The legendary cafe has served everyone from Casanova to Valentino, but table service is pricey.... *Tel 06/678 25 54. Via Condotti 86, Metro Spagna. Open daily. $–$$* **(see p. 48)**

Arancia Blu. Vegetarian restaurant off the beaten path in San

Lorenzo. Actually a social club, so you'll need to fill out a (free) membership card before dining... *Tel 06/445 41 05. Via dei Latini 65, buses 11, 71, 492. Open daily for lunch and dinner. No credit cards. $$* **(see p. 56)**

Arcana. Organic and macrobiotic fare that actually tastes good. Friendly service and mostly smoke-free.... *Tel 06/445 52 46. Via degli Equi 39, buses 11, 71, 492. Closed Sun. No credit cards. $$* **(see p. 56)**

Arlù. Where good Catholics go for fish on Fridays. Otherwise, a mostly southern Italian trat just steps from St. Peter's... *Tel 06/686 89 36. Borgo Pio 135, Metro Ottaviano. Closed Wed. $$–$$$* **(see p. 51)**

Armando al Pantheon. Prices have increased over the years, but what could be better than ancient Roman cuisine just steps from the Pantheon?... *Tel 06/688 03 034. Salita de' Crescenzi 31, buses 64, 70, 75, 116. Open daily. $$–$$$* **(see p. 52)**

Asinocotto. Gay-owned and operated restaurant in Trastevere, overseen by star chef Giuliano Brenna. Mediterranean fusion cuisine includes gorgonzola-stuffed artichokes and tagliolini with sea bass and saffron. Also dabbles in Asian-inspired fare.... *Tel 06/589 89 85. Via dei Vascellari 48, buses 23, 97. Open daily, dinner only and Sun lunch. Closed Mon, Jan. $$$* **(see p. 52)**

ATM Sushi. Hip sushi bar within steps of the Regina Coeli prison where Mehmet Ali Agça, the man who tried to assassinate Pope John Paul II, is imprisoned... *Tel 06/683 07 053. Via della Penitenza 7, buses 23, 65, 280. Closed Mon and Aug. $$–$$$* **(see p. 55)**

Babington's Tea Rooms. A tourist haunt if there ever was one, but your only chance in town for the quintessential British snack. Proper tea and biscuits at improper prices.... *Tel 06/678 60 27. Piazza di Spagna 23, Metro Spagna. Open daily. $–$$* **(see p. 48)**

Bar San Calisto. Pizza and late-night snacks.... *No telephone. Piazza San Calisto, buses 23, 56, 60, 65, 75, 170, 280, trams 8, 30. Closed Sun. No credit cards. $–$$* **(see p. 57)**

Bar Sant'Eustachio. Bar none, the richest, sweetest, best coffee in the city.... *Tel 06/656 13 09. Piazza Sant'Eustachio 82, buses 64, 70, 75, 116. Open daily. $*
(see p. 48)

Blu Ice Gelateria. Roman gelato chain with 6 locations, the best of which is right off of Campo de' Fiori. Also has frozen yogurt and *granita.... Tel 06/687 61 14. Via dei Baullari 141, buses 64, 492. $* **(see p. 58)**

Brek. A quick stop for pastries, pasta, or pizza right across from the Area Sacra. The upstairs area is often filled with tourists pouring over their guidebooks.... *Tel 06/682 10 353. Largo Argentina 1, buses 64, 492. Open daily. $*
(see p. 57)

Bruschetteria Nonna Papera. *Bruschette,* crepes, and salads near Piazza Navona.... *Tel 06/678 35 10. Vicolo dei Modelli 60, buses 52, 53, 58, 60, 61, 62, 71, 95, 492. Closed Mon. $* **(see p. 57)**

Caffè delle Arti. Restaurant and bar attracting as many customers as the adjacent modern art museum. Ideal for a pleasant lunch and cocktails; the bar is good for a beer and snacks after a long museum tour, while the terrace hops during summer.... *Tel 06/326 51 236. Via Gramsci 73–75, Tram 30. Closed Mon. $–$$* **(see p. 54)**

Campo. Innovative Italian dining in a minimalist, Asian-inspired atmosphere of two stories. Restaurant has a non-smoking room; reservations are suggested.... *Tel 06/683 01 162, www.campo.it. Piazza della Cancelleria 64, buses 64, 492. $$$–$$$$* **(see p. 50)**

Checchino dal 1887. Rome's premier *offal* restaurant, yet paradoxically an elegant dining experience. Appropriately, it's right across from a former abbatoir.... *Tel 06/574 63 18. Via di Monte Testaccio 30, bus 92, Metro Piramide. Closed Sun and Mon. $$$$–$$$$$* **(see p. 49)**

Cul de Sac. This popular *enoteca* is at once intimate and lively, a favorite of just about everyone in the city. Remarkably good hors d'oeuvres, *primi* at reasonable prices, and plenty of wines by the glass, including an overwhelming variety of Italian labels.... *Tel 06/688 01 094. Piazza*

Pasquino 73, buses 46, 62, 64, 70, 81, 87, 186, 492. Open daily. Closed Mon lunch. No AE. $$ **(see p. 54)**

Da Cesare. Tuscan menus of 2 courses, dessert, and wine—a lunchtime bargain.... *Tel 06/686 19 12. Via Crescenzio 13, Metro Ottaviano. Closed Sun night. $$$$* **(see p. 51)**

Da Giggetto. Well-known trattoria in the Jewish quarter, looking out on the ruins of Teatro Marcello. Specialty dishes include tripe, fried brains with zucchini, *pajata* (veal intestines sautéed in olive oil), and *coda alla vaccinara* (oxtail sautéed in a celery and tomato broth). The artichokes *alla giudia* (flattened, battered, and fried) are some of the best in the neighborhood.... *Tel 06/686 11 05. Via Portico d'Ottavia 21/A-22, buses 23, 44, 56, 60, 65, 75, 170, 710, 774, 780. Closed Mon. $$* **(see p. 51)**

Dagnino. Sweet treats from Sicily, plus a daily *tavola calda.... Tel 06/481 86 60. Via Emanuele Orlando 75, Metro Repubblica. Open daily. $–$$* **(see p. 58)**

Dal Bolognese. Hearty fare from Bologna, Italy's culinary capital. Dine and people-watch indoors among artistic treasures and fine furnishings, or outdoors on the bustling Piazza del Popolo.... *Tel 06/361 14 26. Piazza del Popolo 1, Metro Flaminio. No AE. $$$–$$$$* **(see p. 52)**

Da Pancrazio. Underground setting and *nouvelle italiane* food duel it out in converted substructure of the Teatro di Pompeo (the site where Caesar was stabbed).... *Tel 06/686 12 46. Piazza del Biscione 92, buses 64, 492. Closed Wed. $$$* **(see p. 53)**

Da Piperno. One of the Ghetto's most expensive and congenial eateries, serving fried fish, tripe, and the like. Reserve well in advance.... *Tel 06/688 06 629. Via Monte de' Cenci 9, buses 23, 44, 56, 60, 65, 75, 170, 710, 774, 780. Closed Sun night, Mon, Aug, Easter, and Christmas. $$$$–$$$$$* **(see p. 51)**

Da Vezio. Have a latte with Lenin or a *granita* with Gramsci: This neighborhood bar is a Communist mecca from floor to ceiling.... *Tel 06/678 60 36. Via dei Delfini 23, buses*

23, 44, 56, 60, 65, 75, 170, 710, 774, 780. Closed Sun. No credit cards. $ **(see p. 48)**

Dar Filettaro di Santa Barbara. See Filetti di Baccalà, below. **(see pp. 51, 57)**

Dar Poeta. At least 15 different kinds of pizza, plus *bruschette.* Get a thick-crust pie for 2,000L by ordering it "più alta."... *Tel 06/588 05 16. Vicolo del Bologna 45, buses 23, 65. Closed Mon. Reservations recommended. $$* **(see p. 56)**

Der Pallaro. Traditional trat open 'til very late. Ideal for an after-theater meal.... *Tel 06/688 01 488. Largo del Pallaro 15, buses 64, 492. Closed Mon. No credit cards. $$–$$$* **(see p. 57)**

È Buono. *Tavola calda* (hot-food bar) popular with the young crowd. Many vegetarian selections.... *Tel 06/688 92 917, www.ebuono.com. Via di Torre Argentina 42, buses 64, 492. $* **(see p. 57)**

Enoteca Antica di Via della Croce. Sit on a stool at the long, wooden bar and you'll get quicker service. You might also get treated to a sample of cheese or antipasto. It's a local celeb hangout, too.... *Tel 06/679 08 96. Via della Croce 76b, Metro Spagna. Open daily. $–$$* **(see p. 54)**

Filetti di Baccalà. Deep-fried, salted codfish and a few other yummy takeout goodies. The outdoor tables in a tiny square off the Campo are just made for discreet people-watching.... *Tel 06/686 40 18. Largo Librai 88, buses 64, 492. Closed Sun and Aug. No credit cards. $* **(see pp. 51, 57)**

Giolitti. Rome's oldest combination *gelateria/pasticceria.* Try the Olympic Cup or the World Cup, decadent ice cream sundaes concocted to commemorate the 1960 Olympics and the 1990 World Cup, both held in Rome.... *Tel 06/679 42 06, www.giolitti.it. Via degli Uffici del Vicario 40, buses 56, 60, 85, 116, 492. $* **(see p. 58)**

Govinda. Vegetarian menu at low, low prices. Hare Krishna–run, thus does not serve alcoholic beverages....

Tel 06/688 91 540. Via Santa Maria del Pianto 15–16, buses 56, 60, 65, 170, 710, 718, 719. Closed Sat lunch. No credit cards. $–$$ **(see p. 56)**

'Gusto. A bookshop, restaurant, pizzeria, and *enoteca* (wine bar). Extensive menu and a mostly smoke-free environment.... *Tel 06/322 62 73. Piazza Augusto Imperatore 9, buses 90, 119, 913. Closed Mon. $$–$$$* **(see p. 49)**

Harry's Bar. Meeting place of old fogeys with money to burn, great for schmoozing over martinis. No relation to the famous cafe of the same name in Venice.... *Tel 06/484 643. Via V. Veneto 150, Metro Barberini, Spagna. Closed Sun. $$$$$* **(see p. 49)**

Hostaria Antica Roma. Fine dining near the catacombs. The rustic fare and ancient surroundings are worth the cab fare.... *Tel 06/513 28 88. Via Appia Antica 87. Closed Mon. $$$* **(see p. 54)**

Hostaria del Nerone. An honest eatery among a glut of tourist traps. Especially beguiling by night, when the Colosseum is flood-lit.... *Tel 06/474 52 07. Via delle Terme di Tito 96, Metro Colosseo. Closed Sun. No AE. $$* **(see p. 51)**

Hostaria Grappolo D'Oro. Despite its proximity to Campo de' Fiori, this award-winning restaurant is still a well-kept secret. Try simple dishes like pasta with tomato and ricotta or *risotto con funghi e tartufo*.... *Tel 06/686 41 18. Piazza della Cancelleria 80–81, buses 64, 492. Closed Sun and Aug. $$–$$$* **(see p. 53)**

Hotel Hassler Rooftop. Rome's first rooftop restaurant, situated atop the Spanish Steps. Undergoing extensive renovations during 2001.... *Tel 06/699 340. Piazza Trinità dei Monti 6, Metro Spagna. Open daily for dinner only. $$$$$* **(see p. 53)**

Il Fornaio. Probably the busiest bakery in town and always a madhouse at lunch, this small shop is filled to the brim with fresh-baked bread, focaccia, and pastries.... *Tel 06/688 03 947. Via dei Baullari 5–7, buses 64, 492. Closed Sun. $* **(see p. 58)**

Il Gelato di San Crispino. The high art of gelato, perfected to a science. Don't even think of ordering your scoop in a cone.... *Tel 06/679 39 24. Via della Panetteria 42, Metro Barberini. Closed Tue, Thur, and 2 weeks in Jan. No credit cards. $* **(see p. 58)**

Il Tempio di Iside. Modern gourmet restaurant untouched by the tourist hoards. Lots of fresh seafood.... *Tel 06/700 47 41. Via P. Verri 11, Metro Colosseo. Closed Sat lunch and Sun. $$$* **(see p. 50)**

I Tre Scalini. Where to get your gelato fix while you're hanging out in Piazza Navona.... *Tel 06/688 01 996. Piazza Navona 28–32, buses 46, 62, 64, 70, 81, 87, 186, 492. Closed Wed and Jan. No credit cards. $* **(see p. 58)**

Ketumbar. New Testaccio culinary hotspot, with an eye towards Asian fusion cuisine. Very popular with hip, young Romans.... *Tel 06/573 05 338. Via Galvani 24, bus 92. $$$* **(see p. 55)**

La Bodeguita del Malecon. Enjoy tasty tamales, friendly service, and live music (most nights).... *Tel 06/681 34 744. Largo del Teatro Valle, buses 64, 70, 75, 116. Open daily. $$–$$$* **(see p. 55)**

La Buca di Bacco. Small, down-to-earth bistro serving wine and antipasto accompanied by piano music. Sunday brunch includes omelets, pastas, and other light dishes; service is a bit erratic, though, even when the place is nearly empty.... *Tel 06/588 06 76. Via San Francesco a Ripa 165, buses 56, 60, 75, 170, 280, trams 8, 30. No AE. $–$$* **(see p. 55)**

La Campana. Quite possibly one of the oldest restaurants in the world. Serves all the standards, like *bucatini all'amatriciana.* Conservative setting and clientele.... *Tel 06/686 78 20. Vicolo della Campana 18, buses 70, 87, 119, 186. Closed Mon. $$$* **(see p. 49)**

La Carbonara. Tourists eat here. But the still-rustic food at lower-than-average prices gets it right on the bustling Campo de' Fiori.... *Tel 06/686 47 83. Campo de' Fiori 23, buses 64, 492. Closed Tue and Aug. $$–$$$* **(see p. 52)**

La Pergola di Cavalieri Hilton Hotel. One of the best meals you'll eat in Rome—and priced accordingly. Entrées of fish, beef, and rabbit, and exceptional desserts.... *Tel 06/350 92 211. Via A. Cadlolo 101. Open daily for dinner only. Reservations required. $$$$$* **(see p. 53)**

La Rosetta. Considered the best seafood restaurant in Rome for more than 30 years, thus the sky-high bills. Dishes such as rigatoni with rockfish and tuna carpaccio are standouts. Reservations required.... *Tel 06/686 10 02. Via della Rosetta 8, buses 64, 70, 75, 116. Closed Sun. $$$$$* **(see p. 55)**

La Tana de' Noantri. Above-average food served in a quiet Trastevere square. Daytime dining is best.... *Tel 06/580 64 04. Via della Paglia 1–3, buses 23, 56, 60, 65, 75, 170, 280, trams 8, 30. Open daily. $$–$$$* **(see p. 53)**

La Taverna del Ghetto. Kosher restaurant located in a 14th-century palazzo. The Roman/Jewish menu changes every 2 weeks; once a month, the kitchen experiments with Middle Eastern fare.... *Tel 06/688 09 771. Via del Portico d'Ottavia 8, buses 23, 44, 56, 60, 65, 75, 170, 710, 774, 780. Closed Fri night. $$–$$$* **(see p. 51)**

La Tavernetta. Homemade ravioli washed down with the proprietors' own red and white wines. Open every night until 2am, except Monday, when it closes at midnight.... *Tel 06/474 19 39. Via Sistina 147, Metro Spagna. Open daily. $$$–$$$$* **(see p. 57)**

La Tazza D'Oro. The powerful aroma of coffee from this big bar lures tourists and locals away from the Pantheon... *Tel 06/678 92 92. Via degli Orfani 84, buses 64, 70, 75, 116. Open daily. $* **(see p. 48)**

Les Etoiles. Impossibly fancy dishes made of such ingredients as truffles, snails, and quails' eggs eaten against the ornate backdrop of St. Peter's dome.... *Tel 06/687 32 33. Via Vitelleschi 34, buses 23, 49, 492, 990, J4. Open daily for dinner only. Reservations required. $$$$$* **(see p. 53)**

Lorodinapoli. Neopolitan cuisine near the Vatican.... *Tel 06/322 64 07. Via Fabio Massimo 101, Metro Ottaviano. Closed Sat lunch and Sun. $$$–$$$$* **(see p. 51)**

Maccheroni. Easy name to remember, food hard to forget. The wood-paneled walls and random pop art give this trendy trat an easy-going ambiance, while dishes like chicken cacciatore with grilled vegetables are sufficiently proper.... *Tel 06/683 07 895. Via delle Coppelle 44, buses 64, 70, 75, 116. Closed Sun. $$–$$$* **(see p. 50)**

Macondo. Classic Caribbean and Latin American dishes, including beans and rice, curried goat, and fried plantains.... *Tel 06/321 26 01. Via Marianna Dionigi 37, buses 49, 990. Closed Sun. $$–$$$* **(see p. 51)**

Margutta Vegetariano. Rome's premier vegetarian restaurant, now with 3 locations (also Le Cornacchie on Piazza Rondanini and Al Leoncino on Via del Leoncino); the daily prix-fixe buffet is a bargain. Also open for brunch.... *Tel 06/326 50 577. Via Margutta 118, Metro Spagna. Open daily. $$–$$$* **(see p. 56)**

Myosotis. Quick service, reasonable prices, and an outstanding menu. Ideal for lunch or dinner in the Centro Storico.... *Tel 06/686 55 54. Vicolo della Vaccarella 3–5, buses 70, 81, 87, 90, 186, 492. Closed Mon, Aug. $$$* **(see p. 52)**

Osteria dell'Antiquario. Intimate dining set in a converted antiques shop off of Via dei Coronari. Outdoor seating is in a pretty square.... *Tel 06/687 96 94. Piazzetta di San Simeone 26–27 (Via dei Coronari), buses 41, 280. Closed Sun. $$$* **(see p. 54)**

Osteria dell'Ingegno. Creative, pan-Mediterranean fare with hints of Latin and Asian inspiration. Tortilla soup, sea bass with artichokes and lemon grass, and gnocchi with black truffles are a few of the dishes that have appeared on the menu. Lunch is a bargain.... *Tel 06/678 06 62. Piazza di Pietra 45, buses 64, 70, 75, 116. Closed Sun. $$$* **(see p. 50)**

Ouzerie. A Greek social club-cum–restaurant in Trastevere that'll woo you until the obligatory after-dinner shot of *ouzo*. Traditional Greek music and dancing liven up Fridays and Saturdays. Reservations recommended.... *Tel 06/581 63 78. Via dei Salumi 2, buses 23, 56, 60, 65, 75, 170, 280, trams 8, 30. Closed Sun. No credit cards. $-$$* **(see p. 55)**

Pastarellaro di Severino. *Ossobuco*, tripe, and *coda alla vaccinara* are the specialties here. Good for an intimate, casual dinner for two.... *Tel 06/581 087. Piazza San Crisogono 33–35, trams 8, 30. Closed Wed. $$$-$$$$* **(see p. 52)**

Pasticceria Valzani. Trastevere bakery claiming to have the "best sacher torte in the world." Also makes its own brands of torrone, bignes, and other sweet treats.... *Tel 06/580 37 92. Via del Moro 37B, buses 23, 65. Closed Mon, Tue, and June–Sept 15. Open daily during the 30 days before Christmas and Easter. $* **(see p. 58)**

PizzaRé. Thick-crust, Naples-style pizza. Very popular for quick business lunches.... *Tel 06/321 14 68. Via di Ripetta 14, Metro Flaminio. Open daily except Sun lunch. $$* **(see p. 56)**

Reef. Bar of broken green glass and blown-up technicolor photos of fish give this hip new seafood restaurant a chic urban feel not found in many parts of Rome. Italian specialties, plus occasional dabbles in sushi.... *Tel 06/683 01 430. Piazza Augusto Imperatore 47, buses 90, 119, 913, Metro Flaminio. Closed Mon. No AE. $$* **(see p. 55)**

Ripa 12. Top choice for seafood lovers in Trastevere. Try traditional items like spaghetti with clam sauce, marinated tuna, or bass carpaccio.... *Tel 06/580 90 93. Via San Francesco a Ripa 12, buses 56, 60, 75, 170, 280, trams 8, 30. Closed Sun and Aug. $$$* **(see p. 55)**

RipArte Café. Trastevere hotspot with minimalist Italian fare and sushi; regularly hosts art installations and DJs.... *Tel 06/586 18 16. Via degli Orti di Trastevere 1, buses 56, 60, 75, 170, 280, trams 8, 30. Closed Sun night and Mon. $$–$$$* **(see p. 50)**

Ristorante al Cardello. Intimate and decidedly familial eatery on a quiet street near the Forum.... *Tel 06/474 52 59. Via del Cardello 1, near Forum. Closed Sun. No AE. Reservations recommended. $$* **(see p. 50)**

Ristorante Il Pellicano. Traditional, mostly fish dishes inspired by the Marche region and the owners' own whims. Pellicano's unique version of *olive ascolane* (fried, stuffed olives) are filled with shrimp.... *Tel 06/683 34 90. Via dei Gigli d'Oro 8, buses 46, 62, 64, 70, 81, 87, 186, 492. Closed Mon. $$$$* **(see p. 55)**

Ristorante Self-Service del Palazzo delle Esposizione. Climb the stairs to the left of the giant museum on Via Milano, then take the elevator to the top floor. Three *primi* and at least as many *secondi* daily, including a buffet of side dishes and desserts... *Tel 06/482 80 01. Via Milano 9, buses 64, 65, 70, 71, 75, 117, 170, Metro Repubblica. Open daily 12:30–3, closed Tue. $-$$$* **(see p. 57)**

Roma Sparita. Casual indoor and outdoor dining that should cost more, given the location. Roman cuisine and pizza, plus homemade desserts.... *Tel 06/580 07 57. Piazza Santa Cecilia 24, buses 23, 97. Closed Sun night and Mon. $$* **(see p. 52)**

Romolo nel Giardino di Rafaello e della Fornarina. Restaurant known more for its location than for its cuisine: Dining area is in the inner courtyard of Raphael's lover's house. Traditional Roman food and lots of tourists.... *Tel 06/581 82 84. Via Porta Settimiana 8, buses 23, 65. Closed Mon and Aug. $$$–$$$$* **(see p. 54)**

Sabatini. Go for the view (of Santa Maria in Trastevere square) and stay for the food, which includes *spaghetti alle vongole* and *rigatoni with pajata.* Undergoing renovations during 2001.... *Tel 06/581 20 26. Piazza Santa Maria in Trastevere 13, buses 23, 56, 60, 65, 75, 170, 280, trams 8, 30. Closed Wed. $$$$$* **(see pp. 49, 53)**

San Teodoro. Like you've died and gone to the Forum. A tiny traditional trat surrounded by the ruins of the Forum and the Palatine.... *Tel 06/678 09 33. Via dei Fienili 49–51, buses 15, 90. Open daily. $$$* **(see p. 54)**

Sora Lella. Hearty, home cooking on Tiber Island. Reservations suggested.... *Tel 06/686 16 01. Via Ponte Quattro Capi 16 (Isola Tiberina), buses 23, 44, 56, 60, 65, 75, 170, 710, 774, 780. Closed Sun and Aug. $$$$* **(see p. 49)**

Sora Mirella. The city's favorite *grattacheccheria,* better known to Americans as an Italian ice stand.... *No telephone. Lungotevere alla Anguillara at Ponte Sisto, buses 23, 97. Open daily March–Sept. No credit cards. $* **(see p. 58)**

Steel. Two floors of dining and drinking near the Pantheon. The lunchtime fixed-price menu is a bargain.... *Tel 06/682 10 099. Via delle Copelle 41, buses 64, 70, 75, 116. Open daily. $$–$$$* **(see p. 57)**

Supernatural. All you need is love—and a vegetarian pizzeria.... *Tel 06/326 50 577. Via del Leoncino 38, buses 35, 56, 60, 85, 116. Open daily. No AE. $$* **(see p. 56)**

Tapa Loca A lively paella restaurant by night becomes a relaxed tapas bar by day. Reservations suggested for dinner.... *Tel 06/683 22 66. Via di Tor Millina 4A–5, buses 46, 62, 64, 70, 81, 87, 186, 492. Open daily. No AE. $$* **(see p. 55)**

Taverna dei Quaranta. Inexpensive outdoor dining near Villa Celimontana. Provides a needed respite from the tourist hoards near the Colosseum.... *Tel 06/700 05 50. Via Claudia 24, buses 15, 118, 673. Open daily. $$* **(see p. 50)**

T-Bone Station. Exactly what it sounds like, plus burgers, ribs, and hot wings.... *Tel 06/678 76 50. Via Francesco Crispi 29, Metro Barberini. Open daily. $$$* **(see p. 56)**

Trattoria da Settimio all'Arancio. Friendly local restaurant just off the Via del Corso. Fresh fish every Tuesday and Friday.... *Tel 06/687 61 19. Via dell'Arancio 50, buses 35, 56, 60, 85, 116. Closed Sun. $$$* **(see p. 55)**

Vanni Café. Sugary cakes, pastries, espresso, and gelato. Catering also available.... *Tel 06/679 18 35. Via Frattina 94, Metro Spagna. $–$$* **(see. p. 58)**

Vinamore. *Enoteca* with an unusually select wine menu and surprisingly subdued atmosphere given its location next to Piazza Navona. Congenial service.... *Tel 06/683 00 159. Via di Monte Giordano 63, buses 46, 62, 64, 70, 81, 87, 186, 492. $$–$$$* **(see p. 54)**

Vineria. *Vino* at cheapo prices served by overly cheeky bartenders.... *Tel 06/688 03 268. Campo de' Fiori 15, buses 64, 492. Closed Sun. $* **(see. p. 55)**

Zi Fenizia. Even pizza lovers can be kosher here. More than 3 dozen varieties available by the slice.... *Tel 06/689 69 76. Via Santa Maria del Pianto 64–65, buses 23, 44, 56, 60, 65, 75, 170, 710, 774, 780. Closed Sat and Jewish holidays. No credit cards. $* **(see p. 51)**

Spanish Steps Dining

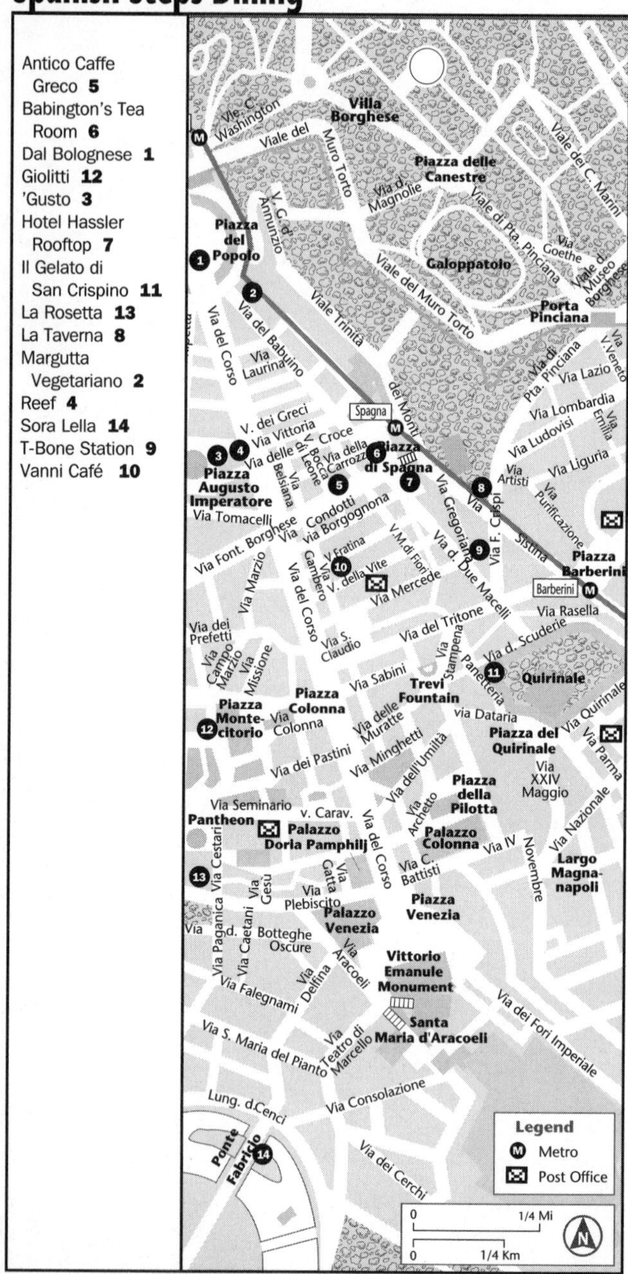

Via Veneto & Termini Dining

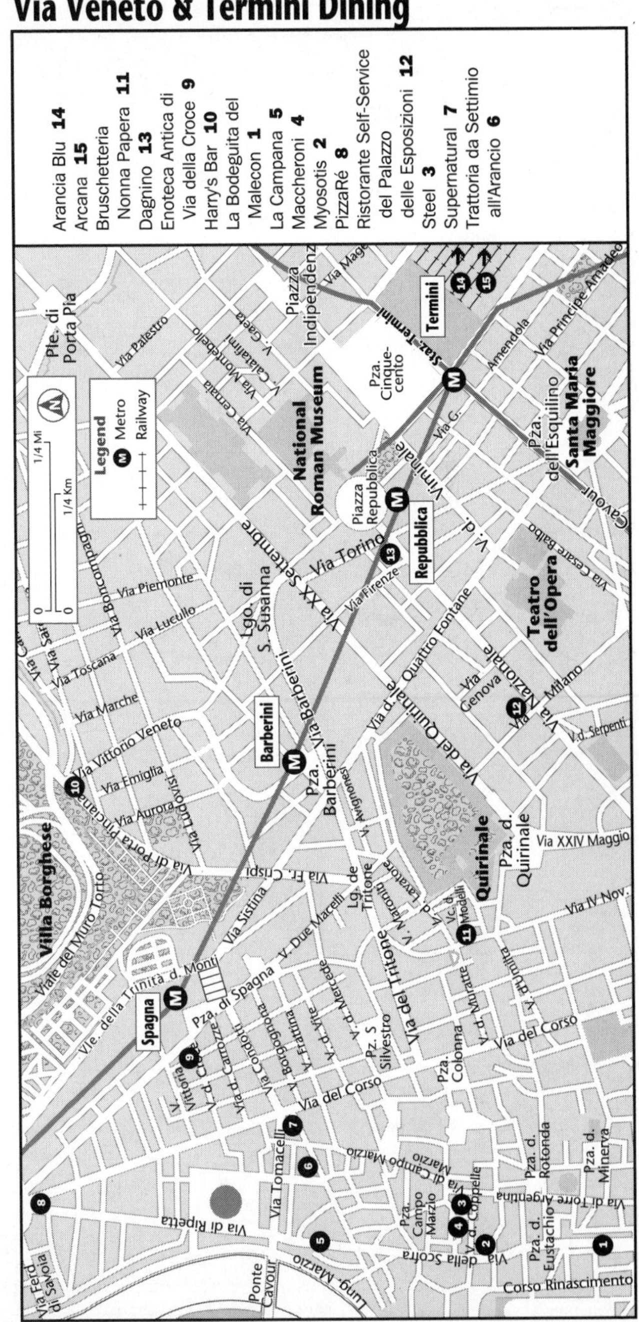

Campo de' Fiori & Piazza Navona Dining

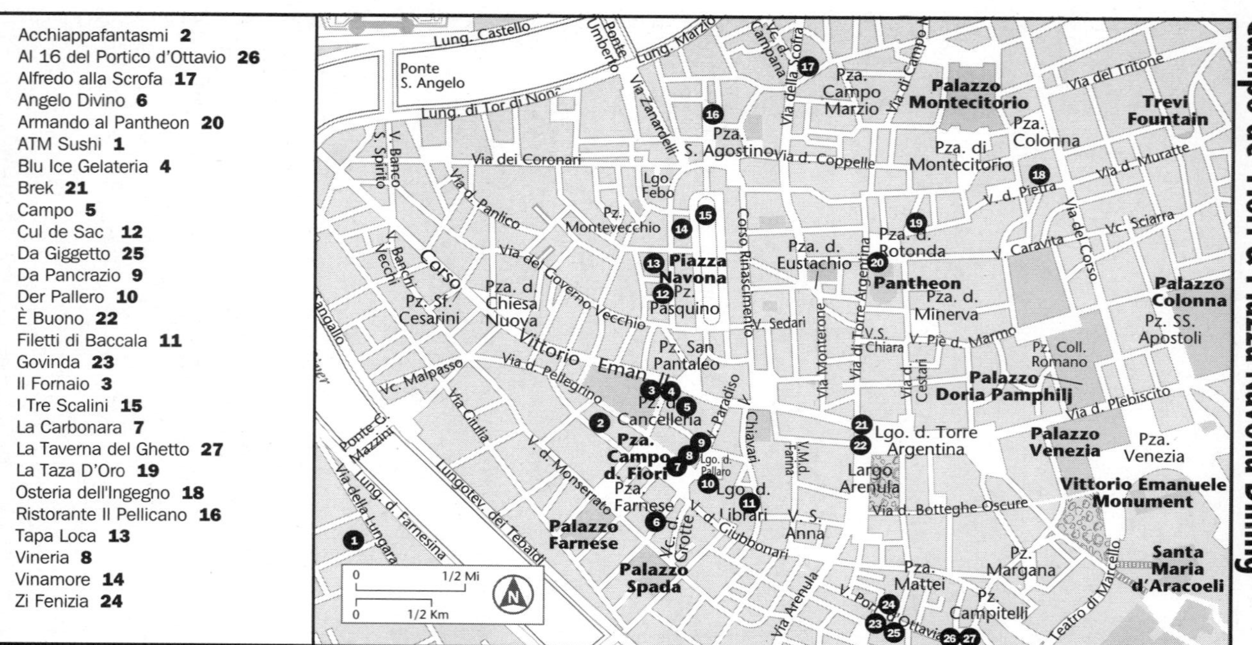

Vatican City Area Dining

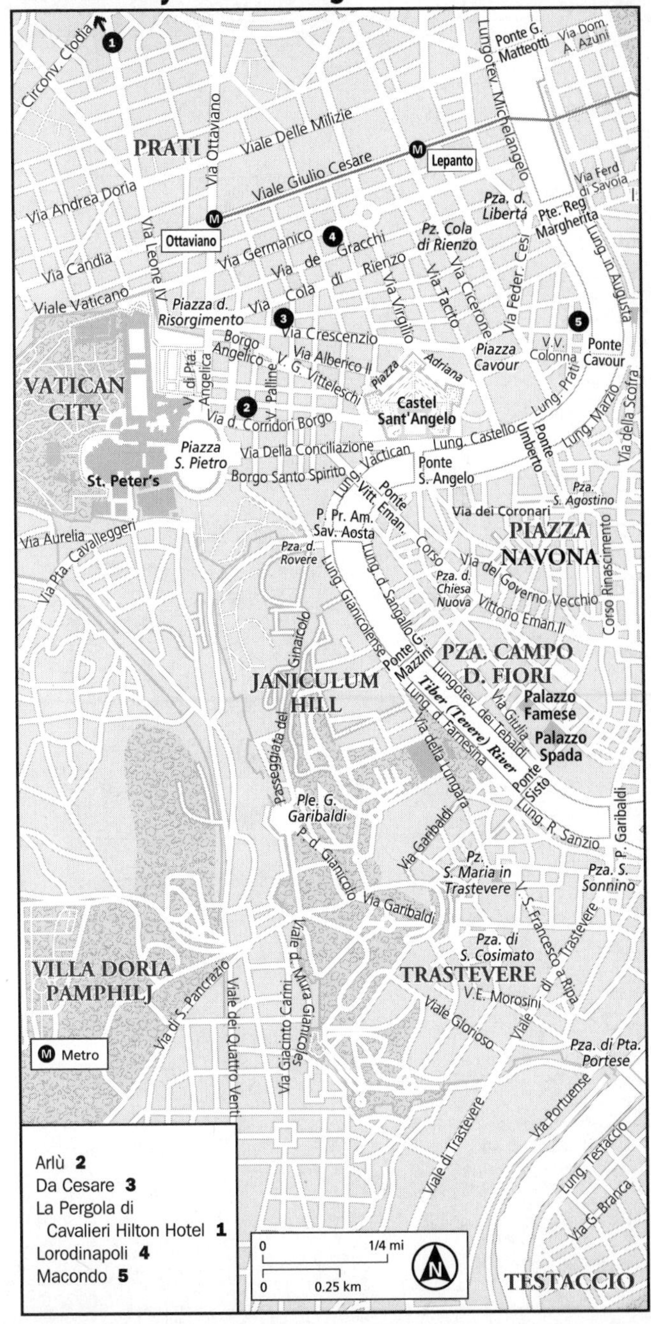

Rome Dining

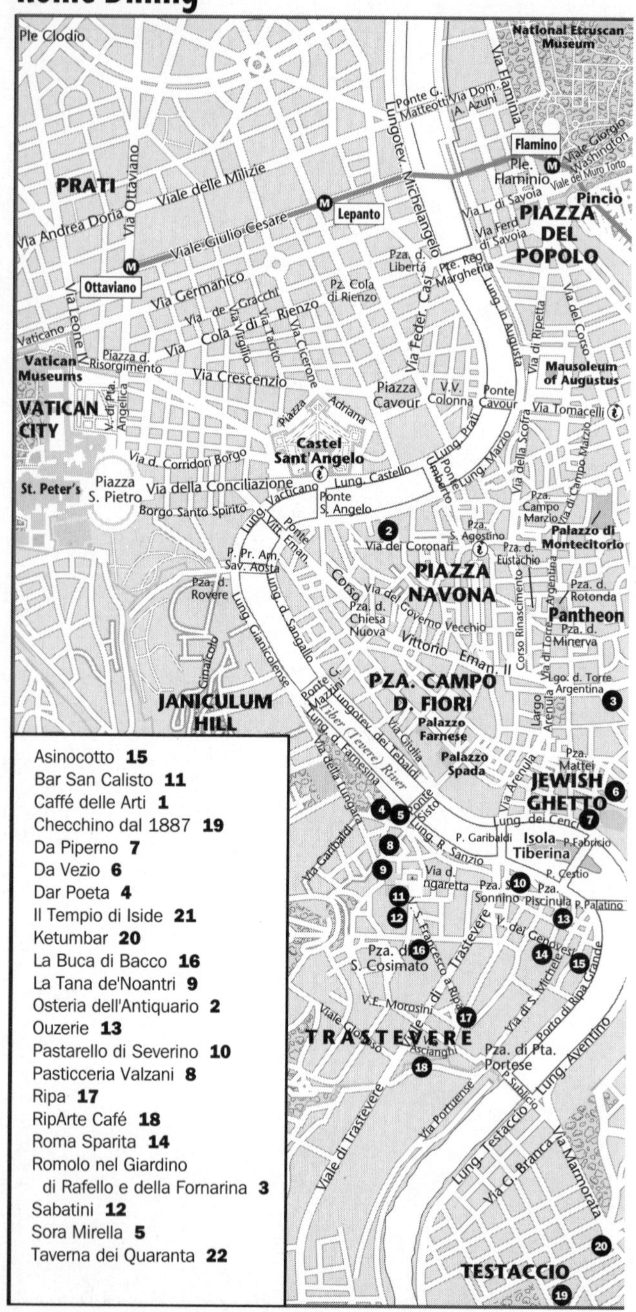

Ple Clodio
National Etruscan Museum
Via Flaminia
Ponte G. Matteotti
Via Dom. A. Azuni
Lungotev. Michelangelo
Flamino
Ple. Flaminio
Viale Giorgio Washington
Viale del Muro Torto
Pincio
PIAZZA DEL POPOLO
PRATI
Viale delle Milizie
Via Andrea Doria
Via Ottaviano
Viale Giulio Cesare
Lepanto
Ottaviano
Via Germanico
Via Cola di Rienzo
Pz. Cola di Rienzo
Pza. d. Libertá
Via Leone IV
Piazza d. Risorgimento
Via Crescenzio
Vatican Museums
VATICAN CITY
Mausoleum of Augustus
Via del Corso
Via di Ripetta
Piazza Cavour
Ponte Cavour
Via Tomacelli
Castel Sant'Angelo
Via della Conciliazione
Borgo Santo Spirito
St. Peter's
Piazza S. Pietro
Ponte S. Angelo
Via dei Coronari
Palazzo di Montecitorio
PIAZZA NAVONA
Pza. d. Rotonda
Pantheon
Pza. d. Minerva
Corso Vittorio Eman. II
Corso Rinascimento
Lgo. d. Torre Argentina
JANICULUM HILL
PZA. CAMPO D. FIORI
Palazzo Farnese
Palazzo Spada
Via Giulia
Tiber (Tevere) River
JEWISH GHETTO
Isola Tiberina
Ponte Sisto
TRASTEVERE
Viale di Trastevere
Pza. di Pta. Portese
Via Marmorata
TESTACCIO
Asinocotto 15
Bar San Calisto 11
Caffé delle Arti 1
Checchino dal 1887 19
Da Piperno 7
Da Vezio 6
Dar Poeta 4
Il Tempio di Iside 21
Ketumbar 20
La Buca di Bacco 16
La Tana de'Noantri 9
Osteria dell'Antiquario 2
Ouzerie 13
Pastarello di Severino 10
Pasticceria Valzani 8
Ripa 17
RipArte Café 18
Roma Sparita 14
Romolo nel Giardino di Rafello e della Fornarina 3
Sabatini 12
Sora Mirella 5
Taverna dei Quaranta 22

National Gallery of Modern Art
Galleria Borghese
VILLA BORGHESE
Piazza di Siena
SPANISH STEPS
Spagna
VIA VENETO
Barberini
PZA. BARBERINI
Keats-Shelley Memorial
National Gallery of Ancient Art
National Roman Museum
Piazza Indipendenza
Castro Pretorio
TERMINI
Piazza Repubblica
Repubblica
Stazione Termini
Termini
Palazzo del Quirinale
Trevi Fountain
Pza. d. Quirinale
Teatro dell'Opera
Santa Maria Maggiore
Palazzo Doria Pamphilj
Palazzo Colonna
Palazzo Venezia
Vittorio Emanuele Monument
Via Cavour
Vittorio Emanuele
Piazza Vittorio Eman. II
CAMPIDOGLIO
Capitoline Museums
San Pietro in Vincoli
Golden House of Nero
Colosseo
Colosseum
Roman Forum
ANCIENT ROME
Manzoni
PALATINE HILL
San Giovanni in Laterano
AVENTINE HILL
Circus Maximus
Circo Massimo
Piazza Albania
Baths of Caracalla
Pza. di Pla. Metronia
Piramide
Via Veneto
Via XX Settembre
Via Nazionale
Via del Corso
Via Cavour
Via Labicana
Via di S. Giovanni in Laterano
Viale Aventino
Via Merulana
Via Giovanni Giolitti
Via Marsala
Corso D'Italia
Via Po
Via Pinciana
Via Tritone
0 1/4 Mi
0 1/4 Km
N
Legend
Information
Metro
Railway

diver

3

sions

Sadly, travelers often avoid Rome simply because they're too lazy to make the trip down from Milan or Florence.

No matter that this is the Eternal City, chock full of the monuments and history that most people have read about since they were in grade school. Truth is, a lot of people decide to skip Rome because they've heard that the city is dirty and rampant with crime, and that residents are less genteel than their countrymen to the north.

These rumors are not entirely false. Pollution from cars, buses, and the ever-present *motorini* (motorized scooters) is stifling, especially in the dead of summer. Pickpockets and petty thieves patrol tourist areas, just as they would in big cities like New York, Paris, or Berlin. And many Romans do come off as impatient and cocky when compared to Venetians or Florentines. But give 'em a break: Like Washington, D.C., Rome is neither south nor north, eliciting a mild hatred from *both* regions, especially when it comes to governmental or religious matters; of course, this long-term dissing might have something to do with their surliness. That said, there's plenty to see and do here once you get past the attitude. Just be sure to plan carefully. Springtime is lovely, summer is stuffy and crowded, and winter can be a little dull. The Italians' long holiday weekends can be a good time if you know, in advance, when they'll be happening; however, public transport is either better or worse than usual during these times, depending on the region and holiday in question. The city is much more manageable in August, when Romans head for the beach or the hills to get away from the pressures of the big city—but it's also deathly hot, and besides, you'd be remiss to visit Rome when it's empty. Here, the people are just as much part of the landscape as the Colosseum or St. Peter's.

Getting Your Bearings

All roads lead to Rome—and then, they lead to confusion. Unlike Paris, Rome is not a planned city but rather a winding mass of cobbled streets and narrow alleys, grimy boulevards and traffic circles. The river Tiber snakes through the city to the west, separating the Centro Storico (Historic Center) from the neighborhood of Trastevere (literally, "across the Tiber"), the Vatican City, and the tonier Prati (Borgo) district. Rome's graffiti-tagged Metropolitana subway (Metro for short), which serves most areas (though not Trastevere or the Centro Storico), is easy to use and will get you close to almost all the major sites. Line A runs from just north of the Vatican (Battistini) to the southern suburbs (Anagnina); stops along the way include Piazza di Spagna (Spagna), Via Veneto (Barberini), and Termini Station. Line B also passes through Termini and covers the area between Rome's northern suburbs (Rebibbia) and the Fascist-designed EUR neighborhood. The stop for the Colosseum is on Line B. If you're pressed for time, avoid riding the Metro in the early evening, when—it seems—every kid and his mother is heading to the Spanish Steps. Buses are fairly reliable, though the main lines—numbers 64, 75, 492, and others—are usually standing room only. Keep good track of your wallet while riding public transportation and, if you're a woman, beware of *la mano morta;* the "dead (actually, wandering) hand" often comes to rest on unsuspecting derrières when rush hour forces people to pack in like cannoli. (For more information about public transport, see Hotlines and Basics.) The **Centro Storico,** which occupies the area within the bend of the Tiber, is the heart of Rome and contains scads of temples and churches—including the **Pantheon**—the wide pedestrian squares of Campo de' Fiori and Piazza Navona, and tons of hip shops, trendy wine bars, insider restaurants, and cafes. The main artery of the Centro is the Corso Vittorio Emanuele II, a traffic-clogged nightmare running roughly from Largo Argentina across the Tiber to the Vatican. Often missed among tourists is the small Ghetto area, where you'll find more traditional eateries, along with quiet *piazze* and medieval backstreets. From the Ghetto, cross Rome's oldest bridge—Ponte Fabricio, built in 62 B.C.—past Isola Tiberina (Tiber Island), to **Trastevere,** an ever-gentrifying artist enclave. Many say that this is the true heart of Rome, the place where "real Romans" live; but, by day, you can hardly tell, given the many foreign students slumming about. On the other hand, Trastevere comes alive at night when its many tiny restaurants and cafes spill out onto the streets. Hardly any tourists visit the **Janiculum,** and there's not really much to see here in this residential area, save for the **Botanical Gardens** [see Getting Outside] and some impressive panoramas of the city. Just north of here is the **Vatican City.** You can pick up the Metropolitana at Ottaviano station (Line A) and ride back over the Tiber to Rome's main shopping drag. Getting off at Flaminio station will bring you to Piazza del Popolo, apex of the **Tridente.** These three streets radiate out from the piazza. **Via di Ripetta,** once the old Tiber port, has some excellent upscale restaurants; the "Corso" **(Via del Corso)** is jammed with shopaholics and beggars at all hours of the day; and **Via del Babuino** gets its fair share of pedestrian traffic as it cuts a straight path down to **Piazza di Spagna.**

There's little reason to visit the tree-lined **Via Veneto** unless you enjoy overpriced cups of cappuccino. The famed street is overrun with hoards of American and German tourists trying to find the "sweet life," which never quite existed the way Fellini depicted it. The **Quirinale** and **Esquiline** areas form "uptown" Rome, a conglomeration of government buildings, tacky tourist shops, and smog-stained hotels and apartment houses. For travelers arriving by train at **Termini Station,** this first view of Rome is understandably disappointing. Although the spacious Piazza di San Giovanni is often the gathering point for raucous labor protests, the **Lateran** neighborhood resembles more a lazy, suburban area, what with its wider sidewalks, relatively quiet streets, and considerable dearth of good restaurants and shops. A short walk down **Via di San Giovanni** in Laterano brings you to the basilica of San Clemente and the **Colosseum** (see "Must-sees for first-time visitors from Springfield" below). Mussolini's wide boulevard **Via dei Fori Imperiali** was built to cut a direct path from the Forum and Colosseum to the dictator's headquarters in Piazza Venezia, symbolically linking him to the emperors of ancient Rome. More and more often, the city has been closing this street to traffic on the weekends, making it a pedestrian thoroughfare. Continued municipal concern for this traffic-choked, tourist-clogged avenue may make the closure a permanent reality in the not-so-distant future.

Discounts and Passes

Museum tickets can get a bit pricey in Rome, as most of the major sites charge an admission of 8,000 to 10,000 lira (approximately $4 to $5). Almost all state-owned sites offer discounts for children, students, and seniors, potentially cutting the cost of an outing; remember to inquire before purchasing tickets. A number of sites also offer joint tickets for other related attractions. For example, for about 20,000 lira you can get a three-day pass to the Colosseum, the Palatine, and the Museo Nazionale Romano. If you're really lucky, you'll visit Rome during the *Settimana dei Beni Culturali* (cultural heritage week), when admission to all the publicly owned museums is free; this annual event is usually scheduled for early spring, but check ahead. You should also be aware that in order to visit some Roman sites, you've gotta make reservations or get special government permission in advance—and the wheels of official Rome grind very slowly, so that means starting the process way in advance. You can purchase tickets and make reservations for certain visits to attractions like Nero's Golden House at the Centro Servizi per l'Archeologia (tel 06/481 55 76, Via O. Amendola 2 near Metro Termini; the office opens daily except Sunday from 9am to 1pm and 2 to 5pm). Other archaeological sites, such as the Area Sacra, require that you get permission from Ripartizione X (tel 06/6710 3819, fax 06/689 21 15) months in advance. See individual listings in the Index below for details.

The Lowdown

Must-sees for first-time visitors from Springfield... With gold, marble, and Michelangelo's *Pietà,* **St. Peter's Basilica** has everything you'd expect from the largest church in Christendom. The "newest" (but also shortest-running) attraction at St. Peter's is the massive bronze Holy Door, which was opened during the year 2000 for the Jubilee (a celebration that occurs once every 25 years), then resealed at the end of the year. If you missed it, too bad for you; at least a nearby plaque commemorates the occasion. A majority of the galleries in the **Vatican Museums** underwent restoration in the years preceding the Jubilee. Rooms that had previously been under wraps, such as the Raphael Rooms, are now open to visitors, and statues like the ancient *Laocoön* have been dusted off and polished up. Of course, most visitors pay little attention to these treasures, instead heading straight for the **Sistine Chapel.** The most famous little chapel in the world—even more astounding now after 20 years of cleaning—never disappoints. Unfortunately, you'll have to endure standing-room-only crowds if you really want to give the frescoes of Michelangelo and other Renaissance artists a good once-over. It's not likely that you'll bump into buff Russell Crowe while visiting the **Colosseum.** Instead, overweight and overly friendly gladiator wannabes may offer you a whimsical photo-op (for a few thousand lira) while you wait in line. First-time tourists go to the Colosseum because it will be the one attraction that the relatives back home will ask about; returning visitors drop by to snap a few photos of the landmark's unforgettable facade. The **Roman Forum,** site of the Temple of Julius Caesar, the House of the Vestal Virgins, and numerous other remnants from ancient history, is also worth multiple visits. Crowds are a problem here, too—heck, so is mud after a good rain—but entrance is free. Legend has it that if you toss a coin into the **Trevi Fountain,** you're guaranteed to return to the Eternal City. (Of course, if you toss *all* your coins in you may not be able to afford to leave. One of Rome's more romantic tourist traps, the fountain is at its most spellbinding at, oh, around 4am when there's nary a tourist or vendor in sight. The rest of the time, the steps in front are swamped with coin-tossing tourists, scam artists, and roving Casanovas. Gargantuan granite columns, an unsupported dome, and decorative marble flooring easily make the **Pantheon** one of Rome's most impressive architectural spectacles. The "temple of all the gods,"completed about 50 years after the Colosseum's debut, houses the Tomb of Raphael and the tombs of the kings of modern Italy. Everyone's favorite spots to people-watch—the **Spanish Steps** and **Piazza Navona**—are great places to take a load off. During sun-drenched days, both are flooded with lounging tourists and locals from dawn to dusk. The piazza takes on a carnival-like atmosphere during the Christmas season, when dozens of vendors sell ornaments, stocking stuffers, chocolates, and roasted chestnuts.

Only in Rome... For Catholics and other curious tourists, a trip to Rome means an audience with the pope. Usually held in the Papal Audience Chamber or in **St. Peter's Square**, the gathering is slightly more intimate than a high school graduation ceremony. You should apply several weeks in advance if you want to attend, but if time is on your side try to apply several *months* in advance. Contact the **Prefettura della Casa Pontifica** (tel 06/698 83 017, fax 06/698 85 863, mailing address Città del Vaticano 00120) several weeks before you want to visit. (In a pinch you might also be able to gain same-day admission by applying at the Portone di Bronzo—the big bronze door—located in the right colonnade of St. Peter's Square, but don't just assume they'll have room for you.) The cult of coffee is greater in Rome than anywhere else, and its oldest place of worship is **Antico Caffè Greco** [see Dining]. Operating since 1760, the grand cafe has served the likes of Goethe, Wagner, and Casanova. (Top that, Sardi's.) The espresso here is standard, but the atmosphere is the thing. An attraction that drives kids and Japanese tourists wild is the **Bocca della Verità** (the "mouth of truth"), located at the entrance of **Santa Maria in Cosmedin.** Stick your hand into the mouth of the ancient sewer cover à la Audrey Hepburn in

Roman Holiday. Legend says that if you've been untruthful, the mouth should clamp down and cut your hand off.

Remains of the day... If you've seen *Gladiator,* you've seen the **Colosseum.** Well, sort of. The crowds to get into the amphitheater are about the same as they were back then, but the entertainment is lacking. However, year 2000 saw the construction of a wooden platform over one part of the excavations. And, for a few months during the summer, plays were staged here for the first time in more than 1,500 years. City fathers are debating whether to make this shindig a regular event or not. If you really want to get a good view of the **Roman Forum** or the **Circus Maximus,** go up to the **Palatine,** the hill on which wealthy Romans like Augustus built their palaces. Not as many tourists visit the ruins on the Palatine, which include the Huts of Romulus and the Palace of Septimus Severus, so you won't have to contend with tour groups galore. What's more, groves of fragrant orange trees and trickling fountains (part of the Farnese Gardens) will make you feel like you've escaped the city altogether. Parts of the **Appian Way** (in Italian, the Appia Antica), the superhighway that stretched from Rome all the way to Brindisi on the southern Adriatic coast, are still open to traffic, though public transportation to this famous road is unreliable. The **Archeobus** (tel 06/469 54 695; see Hotlines and Other Basics), on the other hand, costs about seven bucks and takes you to all the sites on the Appian Way, including the **Catacombs of San Sebastiano** and the **Tomb of Cecilia Metella.** Up until recently, one of the most significant monuments of ancient Rome, the **Ara Pacis** (Altar of Peace), sat inconspicuously on Via Ripetta. Built to celebrate Augustus' victories in Spain and Gaul, this first-century B.C. monument of Carrara marble is intricately detailed with reliefs of the emperor's family, including a frieze that depicts the entire clan by rank. Thankfully, city fathers decided a grand building was needed to house the altar; construction on a pavilion and exhibition space for *Ara Pacis*–related relics is expected to last through early 2002. Most of the other notable ruins in Rome, including the **Area Sacra,** the **Theater of Marcellus,** and the **Imperial Forum,** including **Trajan's Markets**—across the Via dei Fori Imperiali from the Roman Forum—are open only by written permission from the Ripartizione X (see "Discounts and Passes" above). Call or fax the office a few weeks prior to your visit to save yourself frustration.

Rub-a-dub-dub... More than just a place to wash off the grime of the day, those enormous bathing complexes that the emperors built for themselves and their subjects were integral to social interaction. In fact, some of the notorious orgies that took place during Rome's glory days often got started in the enormous baths. The **Baths of Diocletian,** Rome's most extensive network of baths, could hold up to 3,000 bathers simultaneously. Today, the best preserved sections of the complex house Michelangelo's **Santa Maria degli Angeli e dei Martiri** church and the **Museo Nazionale Romano,** which has a vast store of relics from Etruscan and Roman times. More impressive, probably because they sit on a quiet patch of land in the valley of the Aventine hill, are the **Baths of Caracalla.** Up until several years ago, operas and other performances were staged in the cavernous ruins of the *Calidarium, Tepidarium, and Frigidarium*; then archaeologists realized that the booming sound systems were damaging the foundations of the baths. After walking what seems like miles inside these sites, you, too, may want to engage in a bit of hedonistic pleasure at a modern-day spa. Enjoy a massage or an aromatherapy treatment at the **Hotel de Russie** [see Accommodations], which houses the chicest spa in town.

Daily columns... Reminders that Rome was once the *Caput Mundi* (Capital of the World) stand all over the city, jutting up from squares like huge phalluses intent on proving their virility (and Rome's might). The fact that just about all these obelisks were pilfered from Egypt during Imperial times is lost on most people; today, Rome's obelisks and columns are simply points of reference. The **Obelisk of Piazza San Giovanni in Laterano** (the largest) and the **Obelisk of Piazza del Popolo** once decorated the *spina* (long, raised mound) of the **Circus Maximus**. The **Obelisk of Montecitorio** served as the "hand" on a sundial during the reign of Augustus, while the **Obelisk of Santa Maria Sopra Minerva** is beloved for the Bernini elephant sculpture that supports it. Mussolini brought back the **Obelisk of Axum** as a war trophy from Africa. Likewise, the soaring **Column of Trajan** and the **Column**

of Marcus Aurelius (which was mostly a knock-off of the former) recall Roman military victories.

Architecture Romans love to hate... No Roman will admit that he actually likes **Il Vittoriano,** the monstrosity that squats at the south end of Piazza Venezia. Often referred to as the "wedding cake," the "typewriter," or even "the dentures" (yuck), the grandiose monument to Rome's first king is a garish heap of white Brescian marble and Teutonic equestrian statues completely out of proportion and character with the rest of Rome's ochre-toned buildings. Nevertheless, when the Vittoriano opened in spring 2001, many Romans were oh-so-eager to climb its many flights of stairs to enjoy the panoramic views. Equally despised is the **Palazzo di Giustizia** (the Palace of Justice), the oversized building on the Vatican side of the Tiber. Romans have many reasons to hate the "ugly, old palace" (palazzacio, in Italian). For one, the neo-Baroque structure, built between 1888 and 1910, is too ornate for its nearby surroundings, especially compared to its medieval neighbor **Castel Sant' Angelo** (see "Who's afraid of the Dark Ages?" below). Second, the *palazzacio,* a government building, stands as yet another reminder of Roman red tape. Finally, topping the list, is the fact that this massive structure began to sink under its own weight by the 1970s. How could Romans respect a building that can't hold its own for at least a thousand years? (The Palazzo di Giustizia has since been restored.)

Christianity's Top Ten... All good Catholics wouldn't think of going to Rome without making a stop at **St. Peter's Basilica.** The really pious ones will go out of their way to see the other three basilicas that make up the "Big Four" pilgrimage churches: **San Giovanni in Laterano, Santa Maria Maggiore,** and **San Paolo Fuori le Mura.** San Giovanni in Laterano (St. John Lateran), the church of the Bishop of Rome (the pope, to you and me), is clear on the other side of town from St. Peter's, but ranks a very close second as the most important cathedral in the city. Every pope from the fourth through the 14th centuries lived in the adjoining Lateran Palace. And, until 1870, papal coronation ceremonies were held here. The basilica has undergone renovations over the years, due to extensive damage by an earthquake in 896 A.D. and two fires (in 1308 and 1360); inside, a fresco of Boniface VII is attributed to Giotto. The main facade, featuring giant statues of Christ and the apostles, was designed by Alessandro Galilei between 1730 and 1740. A fifth-century church with a baroque facade, Santa Maria Maggiore isn't located in the best neighborhood. Discount stores and souvenir shops occupy most of the real estate across from the church piazza, and seedy Termini Station is only a few blocks away. But pilgrims ignore the peripheral riff-raff and flock to this basilica to view recently-restored fifth-century mosaics, a Medieval enthroned Christ, and a spectacularly coffered ceiling, apparently decorated with gold that Columbus brought back from the Americas. Saint Paul being one of the two patron saints of Rome (Saint Peter is the other), it's only natural that one of the pilgrimage churches bears his name. San Paolo Fuori le Mura, located on the outskirts of town, is a reconstruction of a fifth-century church that was mostly destroyed by fire in 1823. Like Santa Maria Maggiore, San Paolo contains some restored fifth-century mosaics. The multiple layers, including Medieval apse mosaics and a 19th-century facade, add to the church's simple, solemn character. *Tondi* (round paintings) of all of the popes, in chronological order, decorate the upper walls of the basilica, and there are spaces left for only a few more. (Some say that once the spaces run out, the apocalypse is nigh.) Two other pilgrimage sites near San Giovanni are also worth noting. The **Scala Santa,** or "Holy Stairs," are said to be the steps that Christ ascended in Pontius Pilate's house during his trial. No feet are allowed to touch the Scala Santa, and true pilgrims are expected to get on their knees in order to climb the 28 marble steps (long since fitted with wooden planks). Also in the building that houses the Scala Santa is **Sancta Sanctorum,** the pope's private chapel. **Santa Croce in Gerusalemme** isn't one of the "Big Four," but pilgrims-in-the-know stop off here to view what are believed to be actual pieces of Christ's cross, a nail, two thorns from Christ's crown, and St. Thomas's doubting finger.

Champagne art on a beer budget... You could be down to your last lire and still enjoy some of best paintings and sculpture created by the heavyweights of Italian art. Rome's historic center alone boasts works by Fra Filippo Lippi, Michelangelo, Bramante, Raphael, Caravaggio, and Bernini, to name just a few. If you're a fan of *trompe l'oeil* design, walk east to **Sant'Ignazio di Loyola.** Bowing to the request of Dominican neighbors, who were worried that a domed church would block the sunlight, Andrea Pozzo got creative and designed a ceiling that appears to curve upwards into a dome. The effects are astonishing if you stand on the disc embedded in the floor. Another Jesuit church not far from here is the **Gesù.** Over-the-top Baroque sculpture by Pozzo and lesser-known Jesuit artists dominate the church, and, like Sant'Ignazio, the nave and dome feature illusionistic decoration. **Chiesa Nuova,** on the Corso Vittorio Emanuele II, is unspectacular but for three altar paintings by the Flemish artist Peter Paul Rubens. From the outside, **Santa Maria del Popolo**—just to the left of the piazza entrance of the Porta del Popolo—doesn't look like much, but inside lies a treasure trove. Raphael's ornate Chigi Chapel is tucked away in the back, while two of Caravaggio's finest works—*Crucifixion of St. Peter* and *Conversion of St. Paul*—and Carracci's are in the Cerasi chapel. Three more Caravaggios can be found in **San Luigi dei Francesi,** near Piazza Navona. Raphael's *Sybil* frescoes, featured in **Santa Maria della Pace** (also near Piazza Navona) were restored in 2000.

It's kosher with us... Passing by Catholic church after church, you would hardly know that Rome is home to the largest Jewish community in Italy. Yet about 16,000 Jews still live in Rome, mostly in the original Ghetto area that was established by papal bulls in the 16th century. For a small entrance fee, you can visit the gorgeous, 20th-century **Synagogue** and a smallish museum that houses priceless parokhets (decorative curtains that hang within holy arks), old photos, and other valuable items. Some traditional Roman dishes originated in the Ghetto, including *carciofi alla giudia* (deep-fried artichokes) and *filetti di baccalà* (deep-fried codfish), and there are quite a few restaurants in the neighborhood that do these dishes serious justice [see Dining]. Out of Manischewitz? **Kasher**—the city's only kosher *enoteca* (wine store) is just around the corner [see Shopping].

Museums you could lose yourself in... The biggest complaint overheard in the halls of the **Vatican Museums** usually sounds something like this: "We want to see the

Michelangelos. Who cares about the rest of this stuff?" It's true that you'll start seeing signs for the Sistine Chapel immediately upon entrance into the museums, even though it's the very last room on the tour. But if it weren't for this clever herding system, most travelers would miss the embarrassment of riches that make up the vast Vatican collections: Egyptian mummies, Etruscan vases, and frescoes by a veritable who's-who of Renaissance artists are just the tip of the iceberg. A map and an audio-tour (available from the reception desk in multiple languages, including English) are the best ways to approach the galleries, allowing you to zip around the obtrusive tour groups and drown out their din. At last, there's the Sistine Chapel. After 20 years of restoration—and several doses of criticism—the "new and improved" Sistine Chapel is absolutely stunning. Find a good standing position among all the other gawkers, and take time to admire Michelangelo's altarpiece *Last Judgment* and ceiling with scenes from the Old Testament, including *The Creation of Adam* and *Original Sin*. There are also wall frescoes by Perugino (*Christ Handing Over the Keys to St. Peter*), Botticelli, Ghirlandaio, and others. If you bring a small pair of binoculars, you can get even closer to the details. For instance, with some optical assistance, you can make out the grimaces of the condemned in the *Last Judgment,* the delicate clothing on the Delphic Sybil, and the fig leaves on Adam and Eve as they flee from Eden. Bottom line with these museums? Go early, and expect to spend at least three hours wandering around amongst the vast treasures. **Capitoline Museums,** home of the famous *She Wolf* statue, reopened in 2000 after more than two years of renovations. The Palazzo Nuovo and the Palazzo dei Conservatori are now linked by an underground passage that showcases an ancient Tabularium—an archive storage area in the ancient temple—over which the museums were built. The walkway is swell, but most visitors want to see the other new attraction: the rooftop cafe. Café Capitolino has one of the freshest snack bars around—and great views to boot. Proportions, rather than name, usually draw tourists in off of Via Nazionale to the **Palazzo delle Esposizioni,** or PalaExpo for short. Up to three major exhibitions, on topics ranging from ancient artifacts to photography, are held simultaneously, and installations change about once every three months. The ultra-modern gift shop and self-serve cafeteria are reason enough to drop in. Further afield in the northern environs of the **Villa Borghese** (see "A brush with the modern world" below), the **Villa Giulia** is home to Italy's foremost museum of Etruscan and Faliscan artifacts. Within the museum is a vast store of relics from early towns such as Veio and Cerveteri, including a sixth-century B.C. husband and wife sarcophagus, myriad vases, and intricate mosaics. Built originally as a "country" house for Pope Julius III, the Villa Giulia is especially delightful in the summer, when it plays host to outdoor classical concerts by the Accademia Nazionale di Santa Cecilia [see Entertainment].

Michelangelo was here... Michelangelo Buonarotti is associated more with the city of Florence, despite having designed St. Peter's, the *Pietà,* and the amazing frescoes in the **Sistine Chapel.** However, there are a few other masterpieces from the Renaissance artist are scattered about Rome. A usual stop-off after a tour of the Colosseum is at the church **San Pietro in Vincoli,** which houses the tremendous, stern statue of *Moses.* The 7-foot tall sculpture underwent extensive renovation during 2001, with the entire project being broadcast over the Internet. To see a record of the restoration efforts, check out www.progettomose.com (the site's narration is in Italian only, however). Less spectacular is *Risen Christ,* which stands to the left of the altar in **Santa Maria Sopra Minerva.** Knowing that the piece was actually finished by a student of Michelangelo, or that the genitals of the statue were later covered with a ridiculous-looking golden loincloth, perhaps takes away from the beauty of the work. Nonetheless, this was designed by the Great One and deserves a look. Michelangelo also took on a few architectural projects during his stay in Rome. Buonarotti laid down the plans for the wide stairs of the cordonata (a passageway meant for both humans and horses) leading up to the **Campidoglio,** as well as the black-and-white, geometrically patterned marble piazza at the top designed as a way to beautify the muddy Capitoline hill. Although Michelangelo saw only the cordonata through to completion, the piazza design remained largely true to the original. The same did not hold true for **Santa Maria degli Angeli e dei Martiri,** Michelangelo's attempt to transform the Baths of Diocletian into a place of worship.

There's an exhibition in the church's sacristy that details the original plan.

A Bernini bonanza... You can hardly walk down the street or wander through a church without coming across a painting or sculpture by Baroque artist extraordinaire Gian Lorenzo Bernini. Rome's golden boy left his imprint on almost every quadrant of the city. In **Piazza Barberini,** named for Bernini's biggest patrons, you can check out the Fontana del Tritone, which depicts the sea god Triton spurting water through a conch shell; just across the Via Veneto, the Fontana delle Api (Fountain of the Bees) features the ubiquitous Barberini symbol of bees, which is found all over Rome. **Piazza Navona** also lays claim to two Bernini fountains: the **Fontana dei Quattro Fiumi** (his most famous) and the Fontana del Moro. One of Bernini's favorite subjects—religious ecstasy—is portrayed on two remarkable sculptures in Rome, and you can view them virtually undisturbed. In **Santa Maria della Vittoria** rests the *Ecstasy of St. Teresa,* a sculpture that combines equal parts sensuality, peacefulness, and morbidity. Similarly, the *Ecstasy of Beata Ludovica Albertoni* in **San Francesco a Ripa** shows the saint clutching her breast in a state of rapture. It's amazing the artist got away with such blatantly sexual sculptures. Bernini's best stuff arguably rests in the **Museo Borghese.** *Apollo and Daphne* and *Pluto and Persephone* are testaments to what is possible with a hunk of marble and a chisel.

Home is where the art is... Quite a few aristocratic families still live in some of Rome's *palazzi*, or at least keep their art collections in them. The 18th-century **Galleria Colonna** opens only on Saturday mornings, offering culture vultures who didn't stay up too late the night before a chance to see *The Bean Eater,* probably Caracci's most famous work. The most extensive private art collection in Rome is owned by the Doria Pamphili family, the same folks who lent their name to the ill-fated ship, the *Andrea Doria.* **Galleria Doria Pamphili** has works by Titian, Caravaggio, Correggio, Velázquez, and Dutch and Flemish masters. Raphael's *Triumph of Galatea,* in the **Villa Farnesina** (now operated by the National Academy of Lincei), is gorgeous. But, the price of admission seems hardly worth it—only three rooms are open to the public.

A brush with the modern world... In their rush to see ancient Rome, many tourists completely miss the wide range of museums and galleries, big and small, that make up the contemporary art scene. First and foremost is the **Galleria Nazionale d'Arte Moderna e Contemporanea,** the high palace of modern art at the top of the **Villa Borghese**. For those who aren't well-versed in 19th- and 20th- century art, there are few standouts here, save for a van Gogh, a Klimt, and a relaxing little cafe that looks out onto the park. The majority of the collection features works by Modigliani, de Chirico, and other Italian artists you may have never heard of. The city's modern art gallery, the **Galleria Comunale d'Arte Moderna e Contemporanea** is smaller and features much of the same. Meanwhile, a more ambitious municipal modern art space—**Galleria Comunale d'Arte Moderna e Contemporanea ex-Birreria Peroni**—recycles the old Peroni brewery to make room for about 4,000 works of contemporary Italian art. The huge industrial complex, which opened in 1999, will also be host to larger traveling exhibitions. The **Chiostro del Bramante,** a cloister revamped as a cultural complex, opened in 1997 with a large Andy Warhol retrospective. Since then, the gallery has hosted exhibits by such bigwigs as Roy Lichtenstein and Keith Haring. Larger spaces that often host contemporary art shows are the **Complesso del Vittoriano, PalaExpo (Palazzo delle Esposizioni),** and the **Museo del Corso.** (Here's a hot insider's tip: The latter even has a cyber cafe.) If you're wandering around Trastevere, also be on the lookout for impromptu gallery exhibits of no-name artists. You may just discover the next big thing.

Museums only Italians (and you, now) know about... If your plans to hang out at the Trevi Fountain get rained out, walk over to the **Museo Nazionale della Paste Alimentari** (National Pasta Museum) to gobble up some propaganda about the traditional dish. The 30-minute audio tour, which is complimentary with admission, will likely bore you to tears. At least you'll learn all you ever wanted to know about pasta production and the importance of the phrase *al dente.* The **Museo Napoleonico** displays all sorts of personal effects, from original letters to uniforms, from Napoleon and his clan, some of whom lived in the palazzo where the museum is housed. One of Rome's smallest and most fascinating museums recalls the dark days between 1943 and 1944 when the Nazis occupied the city. The **Museo Storico della Liberazione di Roma** is located in a nondescript apartment building just off of Piazza San Giovanni in Laterano—the very building where the Germans imprisoned and tortured approximately 100 Roman partisans.

Marble madness... It all started in the early 1500s when a shopkeeper named **Pasquino** was so fed up with papal rule that he decided to air his beefs about the system and the events of the day by posting anonymous, satirical comments on an old statue outside his store. The phenomenon grew, and soon Pasquino (the adopted name of the statue) began "talking" to other statues around town via anonymous notes, often written in Latin or Roman dialect. Sadly, Pasquino isn't as outspoken as he used to be—a lot of the posted messages today read (in Italian, of course) "For a good time, call...." It's been said that approximately half of the population of ancient Rome was made up of statues. Fragments of these are not just in museums, but lying around on the street. The **Piè di Marmo** is a random hunk of marble you may stumble across while strolling around the Centro Storico. This big, marble foot was probably part of a large statue dedicated to an Egyptian god.

A river runs through it... The **Isola Tiberina** (Tiber Island) will get you as close as you'll want to get to the dirty Tiber. Connected on one side by the **Ponte Fabricio,** Rome's oldest bridge still in use, and the equally aged **Ponte Cestio,** the island is the site of one of Rome's hospitals, a church, and a medieval tower. Isola Tiberina is low-key and not especially interesting—but it *is* a great spot to soak up some rays. Take the stairs down to the travertine walkway for views across the river to Trastevere (which means, incidentally, "across the Tiber"). While you're down there, you can also get a closer look at the **Ponte Rotto,** one of Rome's earliest bridges. Otherwise, there's really not much else here—but at least you can cross Rome's river off your to-do list for the rest of the trip.

Paydirt for bookworms... It's no coincidence that the big names of the Romantic Movement spent some time in Rome, and you can easily make up a short itinerary designed to hit Rome's most interesting and important literary landmarks. The **Keats-Shelley Memorial House,** right at the bottom of the Spanish Steps, is usually the first stop for lit-lovers. The small home has a few relics from the pair and some original manuscripts. True literary pilgrims should skip the house and head to the lovely **Protestant Cemetery,** where the two are buried. Goethe wrote much of his travelogue *Italian Journey* in his apartment on Via del Corso. The **Casa di Goethe** features permanent and temporary exhibits on the life and times of the German author. Skipping ahead to the 20th century, you can visit the house in which disillusioned Sicilian playwright Luigi Pirandello lived while in Rome. The **Casa di Pirandello** has a display of original furnishings and documents.

Who's afraid of the Dark Ages?... Rome is the last place people consider when thinking about the Middle Ages, as monuments from this period are either long-gone or overshadowed by ones from antiquity or the Renaissance. An exception is **Castel Sant'Angelo,** a Medieval fortress built atop the Mausoleum of Hadrian to safeguard the papal strongbox. In troubled times, the pope could scurry across the Vatican Corridor (a fortified walkway from the pope's quarters to the castle, not open to the public) to escape invading armies. The most notable art from this period can be found in **Santa Maria in Trastevere,** which features dazzling mosaics, and in the cloisters of **San Giovanni in Laterano. Santa Maria Sopra Minerva,** built in the 13th century, is the best example of Gothic architecture in Rome. Dedicated in 2000, the museum of **Crypta Balbi** is actually an excavation of several layers of Roman history, including a medieval street. Rather sober but extensive collections of artifacts from the Middle Ages are on display in **Palazzo Venezia** and the **Museo dell'Alto Medioevo** (Medieval Museum).

On top of the world... You had better believe that a city of seven hills—and a few foothills—has some excellent vistas. The best thing about getting up on high is getting a look at a Rome mostly undisturbed by traffic and people. The most popular viewing spot is the **Pincio Gardens,** just above the Piazza del Popolo and a short stroll from the top of the Spanish Steps. This is where you'll see the clutter of towers and domes—including St. Peter's—that is so often photographed for picture books.

Then, there's the lookout from the perch just outside of **Santa Maria in Aracoeli,** one of Rome's quietest churches because most people who climb the 124 marble steps to get to it rarely go inside. (Maybe they're too tired?) If you do go inside, take note of the Santo Bambino, a statue said to have been carved from a tree that stood in the garden of Gethsemane. Admission to the **Capitoline Museums** will get you an even better view from the rooftop cafe. Before you bolt down the steps from **Piazza del Quirinale**—with its mustard-colored residence of the president of the Republic of Italy—toward the Trevi Fountain, pause a moment to take in the view of St. Peter's a mile or so in the distance. In comparison to the other panoramic points, the piazza is usually fairly empty, but occasionally swarming with nattily attired *carabinieri* (police) and unsmiling guards keeping watch over the presidential palace. Romans and tourists-in-the-know head to the **Aventine** hill for their viewing pleasure. Here, from the headquarters of **The Order of the Knights of Malta,** is a panorama of St. Peter's perfectly framed by a keyhole. Go by night for fewer interruptions by, er, knights. You can get a closer view of St. Peter's and the pope's fortified walkway from the terrace of **Castel Sant'Angelo.** If you want to get closer still, why not climb the dome itself? Just 575 lung-stretching steps (no, there's no elevator) separate you from a God's-eye-view of Rome from the dome of **St. Peter's Basilica**—a hike you won't mind because, as they say, "you must suffer before you get to Heaven." Looking out, you'll see the Colosseum and the Capitol to the east, as well as numerous spires and domes from various churches. The panorama is impressive; the only disappointment is the absence of the basilica's signature dome (on which you stand) amidst it all.

What lies beneath... An entire other city of roads, homes, and places of worship is buried under modern-day Rome. No one knows for certain the extent of what's beneath the surface. (Some Romans even go so far as to hide the fact that they can access antiquity from their basement, lest the government claim the subterranean discoveries for the state.) In 1999, construction began on an underground parking garage near the Vatican that was to accommodate millions of Holy Year pilgrims arriving by car and by tour bus. Work stopped for about a month when workers discovered ancient relics and a room of frescoes believed to be part of the Agrippina Palace—home of Agrippina, who was only the granddaughter of Augustus, mother of Caligula, and grandmother of Nero—but, sadly, construction soon resumed. The pope inaugurated "God's Garage" just in time for the Jubilee. The underground cities that comprise the **Catacombs of San Sebastiano** and the **Catacombs of Domitilla** are obvious and old news, though worth checking out if you're into old tombs. A new-found appreciation for what lies beneath has been spurred on largely by the excavations of **Nero's Golden House (Domus Aurea)** and the multilayered **Crypta Balbi.** The infamous he-fiddled-while-it-happened fire in 64 A.D. enabled Nero to build his enormous palace on the Oppian Hill (now overlooking the Colosseum). Today, no fewer than 145 rooms of the Golden House have been unearthed. Numerous "grotesque" paintings are still visible on the walls, as is some graffiti left by Renaissance artists who were inspired by the artwork in the grottoes. The Crypta Balbi, opened in 2000 as part of the National Roman Museum, contains remnants of the Roman, Medieval, and Renaissance Ages, one above the other. For the record, Rome's original multilayered site is the basilica of **San Clemente,** where stands a 12th-century church, on top of a fourth-century church—on top of a first-century B.C. temple dedicated to the cult of Mithras. You can explore all of these sites on your own or, better yet, call on one of the tour companies now specializing in the growing fascination with subterranean Rome. **Genti e Paesi** (tel 06/85 30 17 55, fax 06/85 30 17 57, e-mail genti&paesi@uni.net) at Via Adda 111 and **Palladio** (tel 06/686 78 97, fax 06/687 66 70) can also take you on guided tours of some of Rome's lesser-known archaeological finds, such as the **Excubitorium** (26 feet below modern street level) and the Mithraeum under **Circus Maximus.**

Grave sites of the rich and famous... Rome may not have Jim Morrison's final resting place (that's in Paris), but it's got some heavyweight grave stones of its own. The **Tomb of Cecilia Metella** featured prominently in many early sketches of the Roman *campagna,* but there's really not much to it. A real gem, and probably the most tranquil spot in all of Rome, is the **Protestant Cemetery,** where non-Catholics, like Keats and Shelley, and Communists, like Antonio Gramsci, rest in peace amidst docile cats and meticulously landscaped environs. Right next door, looking as absurd today as it must have when it was built, is the **Pyramid of Caius Cestius**, tomb of a first-century B.C. Roman magistrate (not open to the public). Dozens of Popes are entombed in the Necropolis under **St. Peter's Basilica.** If you're looking for the burial spots of some of Italy's great artists, go to the **Pantheon** to see Raphael's tomb; **Santa Maria Sopra Minerva** for Fra Angelico's grave; and **Santa Maria Maggiore** to see the modest gravestone for Gianlorenzo Bernini.

On the not-so-lighter side... Rome has seen her share of war, torture, and death over the years, so it's not too surprising that you can plan a fairly gory itinerary. If you can fit in only one gruesome attraction, by all means visit the **Crypt of the Capuchin Monks** beneath the church of **Santa Maria della Concezione.** Here you will find the skeletal remains of some 4,000 capuchin monks affixed to walls, arranged into chandeliers and combined to form some of the most beautiful (and bizarre) crypt decorations you'll ever see. Staring back at you are petite monk skulls, stacked in perfect formation, as well as several mummified monks still in their cassocks. A plaque at the end of the crypt reminds you of the grim reality that you, too, "will be what we are now." Less morbid but still pretty freaky is the tiny **Museum of Purgatory,** which features bibles, pieces of cloth, and other items "touched" by souls waiting to enter heaven (significant scorch marks are the proof). While it's not for certain that St. Peter was indeed incarcerated here, many prisoners of Caesar's Rome were tortured and executed in dark, dank **Mamertine Prison.**

Roaming around Trastevere... Residents of Trastevere claim to be the "true Romans," as a community has lived in this area across the Tiber since the city's inception in 753 B.C. Definitely quirky, this is the neighborhood to visit if you want to dine under clotheslines of laundry, listen to aging hippies strum their guitars, stumble over drunken punk rockers and their mangy mutts, or visit funky, one-off art galleries. The **Museum of Folklore,**

now part of the **Museo di Roma in Trastevere,** has some amateurish waxwork recreations of taverns and street scenes that are supposed to depict typical Roman life in the 18th and 19th centuries. The rarely visited Museo di Roma shifted gears, and at the end of 1999 reopened with a focus on less rustic (read "sexier") themes. Some of the temporary exhibits have been "Rome on Film" and "100 Year of Soccer...and Counting." According to Trastevere's old-timers, the charm of the community has faded over the past few years as expats have taken over rent-controlled lofts and tourists have invaded once-secret nooks and sidestreets. Tourists usually come to the neighborhood to visit the three main churches—**Santa Maria in Trastevere, San Francesco a Ripa,** and **Santa Cecilia in Trastevere** (whose sculpture is based on the position of Santa Cecilia's body when she was disinterred from her tomb)—stick around to dine *al fresco* on the traffic-free square, then start making their ways back to their comfy hotels in the Centro before it gets too dark. This suits the residents just fine—Trastevere's best-kept secrets are its restaurants, the finest (and also the rowdiest) of which open only in the evening, when most of the tourists are long-gone.

Where tourists are still an endangered species... The neighborhoods of **Testaccio** and **San Lorenzo** are in direct competition with Trastevere as the current hot hangout of hip young things. Testaccio has a strictly working-class feel by day, but by night the area is club central, teeming with college kids, gay boys, ravers, and handfuls of transvestites and prostitutes. San Lorenzo has long been home base for Rome's Communists and anarchists, not coincidentally due to its proximity to the campus of Rome's La Sapienza University. Visually speaking, the area is ugly, with few fancy public spaces and charmless architecture; but its tattoo parlors, cheap pizza joints, pubs, and college-town personality adds to San Lorenzo's down-to-earth appeal. A complete U-turn from San Lorenzo is **EUR** (Esposizione Universale di Roma, pronounced ay-yur), Mussolini's fantasyland, replete with imposing Fascist architecture. This southern suburb, now paradoxically home to snotty rich kids, was planned as an exhibition area for the dictator's "Work Olympics," which were then cancelled due to WWII. The few tourists who take the trip out here come to visit the **Museo dell'Alto Medioevo,** crammed full of medieval treasures, or the **Museo della Civiltà Romana,**

which features scaled-down versions of some of Imperial Rome's most adored monuments. Also cutting a sharp image in EUR is the **Palazzo della Civiltà del Lavoro,** known locally as the "square Colosseum." Largely an office building, the square Colosseum is one of the most unmistakable landmarks you'll see on your way from Fiumicino Airport.

Kid stuff... Children with even an ounce of imagination ooh and aah when confronted with such landmarks as the Colosseum, but that doesn't mean they're gonna want to waste their pent-up energy looking at ruins, and they certainly don't want to schlep through museums. Wide-open spaces, like those found at **Villa Borghese,** are sure to run them down. Here, you can rent bikes, rent in-line skates, or kick around the soccer ball. Also tucked away on this swath of park land is the zoo, today known as the **Bioparco**—which is slowly revamping the cramped quarters where it keeps its animals—and the **Museo Civico di Zoologia** (Museum of Zoology), which features a 50-foot long whale skeleton as well as exhibits on local flora and fauna. Wildly popular with younger tikes is the the not-open-to-the-public but visible from the exterior "Monster House," otherwise known as the **Palazetto Zuccari** on Via Gregoriana—its entrance looks like a monster's gaping mouth, and its windows look like eyes—and the ancient sewer cover is the **Bocca della Verità.** It ain't Six Flags, but Roman kids make do with **LUNEUR** (a.k.a., Luna Park), a hokey little amusement park in the suburbs. Even better news is on the horizon: By the end of 2001, children will have their own museum at the all-new **Museo dei Bambini** (Children's Museum), which rides on the whole trend of interactive museums so popular in the United States. More and more museums in Rome are offering docent-led tours and activities for kids. Check the weekly guide *Roma C'è* for more information on kid stuff.

Where to spot the next Michelangelo... Rather than snap away at the scenery with your camera, why not awaken your inner Michelangelo? A favorite challenge for burgeoning artists is trying to draw the "twin" churches **Santa Maria dei Miracoli** and **Santa Maria in Montesanto** in **Piazza del Popolo.** Or, take a seat at the **Colle Oppio,** the hilltop park overlooking the Colosseum.

Many American art students sit for hours in **Piazza Santa Maria in Trastevere,** sketching the square's fountain and namesake church. If you're drawn to the Roman *campagna,* à la Goethe, spend a day on the **Appian Way,** sketching aqueduct ruins and those unforgettable umbrella pines.

The Index

Appian Way. Rome's first paved road, built in 312 B.C. Original pathway to the campagna, also featuring a vast network of tombs and catacombs.... *For information, contact Parco Regionale Dell'Appia Antica at Via Appia Antica 42. Tel 06/512 63 14, fax 06/518 83 879, www.parcoappiaantica.org.* **(see pp. 85, 101)**

Ara Pacis. Built by Augustus, this "Altar of Peace" is one of the most important monuments from ancient times. Undergoing extensive renovations in 2001.... *Tel 06/671 10 35. Via di Ripetta, buses 70, 81, 115, 186. Open Tue–Sat 9am–5pm, Sun 9am–1pm. Admission charged.* **(see p. 85)**

Area Sacra. Cat-filled plot where Caesar was apparently assassinated on the Ides of March. Three more temple ruins here as well.... *No telephone. Largo di Torre Argentina, buses 44, 46, 56, 60, 62, 64, 70, 81, 492. Open by appt only, apply for permit from Ufficio Monumenti Antichi e Scavi (see page 83 above for details).* **(see p. 85)**

Baths of Caracalla. Rome's most picturesque baths.... *Tel 06/575 86 26. Viale delle Terme di Caracalla 52, buses 160, 628, 760. Open Tue–Sat 9am–sunset, Sun–Mon 9am–1pm. Closed Jan 1, May 1, and Dec 25. Admission charged.* **(see p. 86)**

Baths of Diocletian. Baths reconverted into a church, Santa Maria degli Angeli e dei Martiri. Also house a large collection

from the Museo Nazionale Romano.... *Tel 06/488 05 30. Terme di Diocleziano, Piazza della Repubblica, buses 57, 64, 65, 75, 170, 492, 910, Metro Repubblica and Termini.*
(see p. 86)

Bioparco. More depressing than the eco-friendlier zoos in the U.S., but Rome's zoo is slowly cleaning up its act.... *Tel 06/360 82 11. Via del Giardino Zoologico 1, tram 30. Open daily 9:30am–6pm. Admission charged.* **(see p. 100)**

Bocca della Verità. Ancient sewer cover turned tourist attraction and lie detector... *Tel 06/678 14 19. Piazza della Bocca della Verità 18, buses 23, 81, 160, 204. Open daily 9am–1pm and 2:30–6pm, until 5 pm in winter.* **(see pp. 84, 100)**

Campidoglio. Michelangelo-designed black-and-white cobblestone piazza with wide cordonata; a copy of the equestrian statue of Marcus Aurelius stands in the middle of the square.... *No telephone. Piazza del Campidoglio, buses 44, 46, 64, 70, 81, 110 and other routes to Piazza Venezia.*
(see p. 91)

Capitoline Museums. The Palazzo Nuovo and the Palazzo dei Conservatori contain a vast collection of classical busts, statues, and Renaissance paintings. Home of equestrian statue of Marcus Aurelius, giant marble pointing finger of Constantine, and the She Wolf statue.... *Tel 06/671 02 071. Piazza del Campidoglio, buses 44, 46, 64, 70, 81, 110 and other routes to Piazza Venezia. Open Tue–Sun 9am–7pm, public holidays 9am–1:45pm. Closed Jan 1, May 1, and Dec 25. Admission charged, free last Sun of month.*
(see pp. 90, 96)

Casa di Goethe. Former apartment of the German author displays sketches and paintings from his times, as well as some personal effects.... *Tel 06/326 50 412. Via del Corso, 18–20, buses 81, 115, 117, 204. Open Wed–Mon 11am–6pm. Admission charged.* **(see p. 95)**

Casa di Pirandello. Residential home of the Italian playwright turned Fascist sympathizer.... *Tel 06/442 91 853. Via Bosio 13/15, bus 36. Open by appointment only.* **(see p.95)**

Castel Sant'Angelo. Medieval fortress built atop Hadrian's mausoleum.... *Tel 06/687 50 36. Lungotevere Castello,* *buses 23, 34, 64, 70, 186, 280, Metro Lepanto. Open Tue–Sun 9am–6pm (last admission one hour before closing). Closed public holidays and 2nd and 4th Tue of month. Admission charged.* **(see pp. 87, 95, 96)**

Catacombs of Domitilla. Rome's largest network of catacombs, containing one of the earliest depictions of Christ as the Good Shepherd.... *Tel 06/511 03 42. Via delle Sette Chiese 282, buses 218, 660. Open Wed–Mon 8:30am–noon and 2:30–5:30pm, until 5pm Oct–March . Closed Jan. Admission charged.* **(see p. 97)**

Catacombs of San Sebastiano. The remains of Saints Peter and Paul may have been moved here for a short time during the persecution of Christians by Romans.... *Tel 06/788 70 35. Via Appia Antica 136, buses 218, 660. Open Mon–Sat 9am–noon and 2:30–5:30pm, until 6:30 May–Sep . Closed Nov. Admission charged.* **(see pp. 85, 97)**

Chiesa Nuova. "New Church," with altarpieces by Rubens and the tomb of Counter Reformation leader St. Philip Neri.... *Tel 06/687 52 89. Piazza della Chiesa Nuova, buses 46, 62, 64. Open daily 7:30am–noon and 4:30–7pm.* **(see p. 89)**

Chiostro del Bramante. Cultural complex hosting regular exhibitions of 20th-century art.... *Tel 06/688 09 035. Vicolo del Arco della Pace 5, buses 70, 81, 87, 116, 186, 492. Open Tue–Sun 10am–7pm, Fri–Sat until midnight. Admission charged.* **(see p. 93)**

Circus Maximus. Scene of ancient chariot races and modern-day picnics.... *No telephone. Via del Circo Massimo, buses 81, 10, 175, 628, tram 30, Metro Circo Massimo.* **(see pp. 85, 86, 97)**

The Colosseum. Former fighting ground of gladiators and the symbolic heart of Rome.... *Tel 06/700 42 61. Piazza del Colosseo, buses 27, 81, 85, 87, Metro Colosseo. Open Mon–Sat 9am–one hour before sunset, Sun 9am–2pm. Closed Jan 1, May 1, and Dec 25. Admission charged.* **(see pp. 82, 83, 85)**

Column of Marcus Aurelius. Marcus Aurelius's self-congratulatory tribute to his military prowess.... *No telephone. Piazza Colonna, buses 56, 60, 85, 116, 492.* **(see pp. 86)**

Column of Trajan. Giant column commemorating Trajan's victories in Dacia (Romania).... *No telephone. Via dei Fori Imperiali, buses 27, 81, 85, 87, 186, Metro Colosseo.* **(see pp. 85, 86)**

Complesso del Vittoriano. Part of the Vittoriano complex, housing exclusive temporary exhibits, often of modern art.... *Tel 06/678 06 64. Via San Pietro in Carcere, buses 85, 87, 170, Metro Colosseo. Open Tue–Sun 9am–8pm, Fri–Sat until 11pm. Admission charged.* **(see p. 93)**

Crypta Balbi. An underground look at ancient and medieval Rome.... *Tel 06/39 74 99 07. Via delle Botteghe Oscure 31, buses 44, 46, 56, 60, 62, 64, 65, 70, 75, 81, 492, and many other routes to Largo Argentina. Open Tue–Sun 9am–7:45pm. Admission charged.* **(see pp. 95, 97)**

Crypt of the Capuchin Monks. Above-ground monastic cemetery featuring numerous skulls. Hands-down the creepiest sight in Rome.... *Tel 06/488 27 48. Via Veneto 27, buses 52, 53, 56, 58, 58b, 490, 495, Metro Barberini. Open daily 7am–noon, 3:45–7:30pm; Crypt open Fri–Wed 9am–noon, 3–6pm. Donation expected.* **(see p. 98)**

Excubitorium. Former guard house and fire station during the time of Augustus. Frescoes and ancient graffiti on the walls of the building are still visible.... *No telephone. Via della VII Coorte 9, buses 23, 60, 75, 280, tram 8. Open Sat and Sun 10am–1pm. Donations expected.* **(see p. 97)**

Fontana dei Quattro Fiumi. Bernini's signature fountain in Piazza Navona, representing the 4 largest rivers known at the time: the Danube, the Ganges, the Nile, and the Plata. Its obelisk, swiped and carried from Egypt, once stood on the Appian Way.... *No telephone. Piazza Navona, buses 46, 62, 64, 70, 81, 87, 186, 492.* **(see p. 92)**

The Forum. Rome's biggest marble graveyard. Early-morning visits are the most satisfying.... *Tel 06/699 01 10. Via dei Fori Imperiali (entrances at Largo Romolo e Remo and by the Arch of Titus), buses 11, 27, 81, 85, 87, 186, Metro Colosseo. Open March–Oct Mon–Sat 9am–dusk, Sun 9am–1pm, Nov–Feb Mon–Sat 9am–3pm, Sun 9am–1pm. Closed Jan 1, May 1, and Dec 25. Admission free.* **(see pp. 83, 85)**

Galleria Colonna. Home of Caracci's *The Bean Eater.... Tel 06/679 43 62. Via della Pilotta 17, buses 64, 65, 70, 75, 170. Open Sat only 9am–1pm (last admission at noon). Closed Aug and public holidays. Admission charged.*
(see p. 92)

Galleria Comunale d'Arte Moderna e Contemporanea. Rome's municipal museum for modern art. Focuses on small exhibitions of individual artists.... *Tel 06/47 42 84 89 09. Via F. Crispi 24, buses 52, 53, 58, 61, 62, 63, 95, 492, Metro Barberini. Open Tue–Sat 10am–1:30pm, 2:30–6:30pm, Sun 9:30am–1:30pm. Admission charged.* **(see p. 93)**

Galleria Comunale d'Arte Moderna e Contemporanea ex-Birreria Peroni. City's newest and best space for contemporary art. Housed in the former Peroni brewery.... *Tel 06/884 49 30. Via Reggio Emilia 84, buses 36, 60, 62, 63, 317, 490, 495. Open Tue–Sun 9am–7pm. Admission charged.*
(see p. 93)

Galleria Doria Pamphili. Perhaps the finest of Rome's private art collections. Caravaggio, Titian, and Raphael, among others, represented.... *Tel 06/679 73 23. Piazza del Collegio Romana 2, buses 44, 46, 94, 710, 718, 719, and other buses to Piazza Venezia. Open daily except Thursday 10am–5pm. Admission charged.* **(see p. 92)**

Galleria Nazionale d'Arte Moderna e Contemporanea. Huge museum on Villa Borghese grounds featuring Italy's largest collection of modern art by Italian artists.... *Tel 06/322 41 52. Viale delle Belle Arti 131, tram 19, 30. Open Tue–Sat 9am–7pm, Sun 9am–1pm. Admission charged.* **(see p. 93)**

Gesù. Rome's first Jesuit church; fantastic nave and dome, each frescoed by Baroque artist Il Baciccia.... *Tel 06/678 63 41. Piazza del Gesù, buses 44, 46, 56, 60, 62, 64, 65, 70, 81, and other routes to Piazza Venezia or Largo di Torre Argentina. Open daily 7am–12:30pm and 4–7:15pm.* **(see p. 89)**

Il Vittoriano. Rome's largest—and most detested—monument, reviled as "the typewriter".... *Tel 06/36 00 43 99. Piazza Venezia, buses 44, 46, 94, 710, 718, 719, and other buses to Piazza Venezia. Open Tue–Sun 10am–4pm.* **(see p. 87)**

Imperial Forum. Across Via dei Fori Imperiali from the main

Forum, this one was built to deal with a Roman population boom—and the egos of the emperors.... *No telephone. Via dei Fori Imperiali, buses 11, 27, 81, 85, 87, 186, Metro Colosseo. Open only with permission from Ripartizione X (see page 83 above for details).* **(see p. 85)**

Isola Tiberina. Building on an ancient Roman myth, early city architects constructed a travertine platform around the island so that it would resemble a ship. Today, the stern is suitable for sunning. Isola Tiberina has its own hospital and small church.... *No telephone. Isola Tiberina, buses 23, 44, 56, 60, 65, 75, 170, 710, 774, 780.* **(see p. 94)**

Keats-Shelley Memorial House. Shrine to English Romantic poets who lived in Italy. Advance reservations suggested.... *Tel 06/678 42 35. Piazza di Spagna 26, buses 117, Metro Spagna. Open Mon–Fri 9am–1pm and 3–6pm, Oct–March 2:30–5:30pm. Closed public holidays and 10 days in Aug. Admission charged.* **(see p. 95)**

LUNEUR (Luna Park). Second-rate amusement park in Rome's EUR suburbs.... *Tel 06/591 44 01, www.luneur.it. Via delle Tre Fontane (EUR), buses 706, 707, 714, 717, 765, 771, Metro Magliana, Palasport, or EUR Fermi. Open mid-June through mid-Sept Mon–Thur 4pm–1am, Fri–Sat 4pm–2am, Sun 10am–1am, mid-Sept through mid-June Mon–Thur 3pm–9pm, Fri–Sat 3pm–2am, Sun 10am–11pm (closed Tue). Admission charged.* **(see p. 100)**

Mamertine Prison. Torture and execution chamber of choice for Rome's enemies during Imperial times. Legend portends that St. Peter was imprisoned here.... *Tel 06/679 29 02. Clivo Argentino 1, buses 81, 85, 87, 186. Open Apr–Sept daily 9am–noon and 2:30–6pm, Oct–March daily 9am–noon and 2–5pm. Donation expected.* **(see p. 98)**

Museo Nazionali Romani. Mind-boggling collection of Etruscan and early Roman artifacts, including stone inscriptions, vase fragments, everyday tools, marble busts, and mosaics. So vast, it's housed in 3 separate buildings: Palazzo Massimo (tel 06/481 55 76, Largo di Via Peretti 1); Palazzo Altemps (tel 06/390 871, Piazza San Apollinare 44); and main one at the Baths of Diocletian.... *Tel 06/399 67 700. Piazza dei Cinquecento 78, Metro Termini. Open Tue–Sun 9am–7pm. 3-museum admission pass 30,000L,* *individual museums 8000–12,000L per museum.* **(see p. 86)**

Museo Borghese. Borghese family villa, featuring Bernini's sculptures of Apollo and Daphne, Pluto and Persephone, and David. Patrons must reserve tickets for visits on weekends.... *Tel 06/84 24 16 07. Villa Borghese, Piazzale Scipione Borghese 5, buses 52, 53, 116, 910 to Via Pinciana, 3, 4, 57 to Via Po, trams 19, 30b to Viale delle Belle Arti. Open Tue–Sat 9am–5pm, Sun 9am–1pm (longer hours in the summer). Closed public holidays. Admission charged.* **(see p. 92)**

Museo Civico di Zoologia. Natural history museum with exhibits of indigenous flora and fauna and a 50-foot whale skeleton.... *Tel 06/321 65 86. Via Aldrovandi 18, tram 30. Open Tue–Sun 9am–5pm. Admission charged. Children under 18 free.* **(see p. 100)**

Museo dei Bambini. Hands-on children's museum scheduled to open at the end of 2001.... *Tel 06/361 37 76, www.mdbr.it (in Italian). Via Flaminia 80, buses 490, 495, Metro Flaminio. Call for hours and admission fees.* **(see p. 100)**

Museo del Corso. Museum where old works of art meet modern-day technology; see original paintings firsthand, then learn more about them through virtual imaging.... *Tel 06/678 62 09, www.museodelcorso.it (in Italian). Via del Corso 320, buses 35, 56, 60, 85, 116. Open Tue–Sun 11am–8pm. Admission charged.* **(see p. 93)**

Museo dell'Alto Medioevo. Works of art and relics from medieval Rome.... *Tel 06/54 22 81 99. Viale Lincoln 3, Metro Marconi. Open Tue–Sat 9am–2pm, Sun 9am–1pm. Admission charged.* **(see pp. 95, 99)**

Museo della Civiltà Romana. Highlights include small-scale and full-scale models of ancient Roman buildings and monuments.... *Tel 06/592 60 41. Piazza Giovanni Agnelli 10, Metro EUR Palasport. Open Tue–Sat 9am–7pm, Sun 9am–1pm. Admission charged.* **(see p. 99)**

Museo di Roma in Trastevere. Originally the Museum of Folklore, but retooled in 2000 to include space for one-off exhibits on contemporary Roman culture, multimedia installations, and a research area with database.... *Tel 06/581 65 63.*

Piazza Sant'Egidio 1, buses 23, 56, 60, 65, 280, tram 8. Open Tue–Sun 10am–8pm. **(see p. 99)**

Museo Napoleonico. Portraits, original letters, and memorabilia from the Bonaparte clan.... *Tel 06/688 06 286. Piazza di Ponte Umberto 1, buses 70, 81, 87, 280, 492. Open Tue–Sat 9am–7pm, Sun 9am–1:30pm. Closed Jan 1, May 1, and Dec 25. Admission charged.* **(see p. 93)**

Museo Nazionale della Paste Alimentari. Well-organized tour of the pasta-making process. Photos of celebrity pasta eaters are worth a look.... *Tel 06/69 91 119. Piazza Scanderberg, buses 52, 53, 58, 60, 61, 62, 71, 95, 492. Open Tue–Sat 9am–7pm, Sun 9am–2pm. Admission charged.* **(see p. 93)**

Museo Storico della Liberazione di Roma. Little-known museum housing original cell-blocks and memorabilia left by Roman partisans imprisoned during Nazi occupation of Italy.... *Tel 06/700 38 66. Via Tasso 145, buses 16, 85, 87, 117, trams 13, 30, Metro Manzoni. Open Tue, Thur, and Fri 4–7pm, Sat–Sun 9:30am–12:30pm. Donations expected.* **(see p. 94)**

Museum of Purgatory. Two display cases worth of money, clothing, and bibles "burned" by the fingers of souls in purgatory.... *Tel 06/680 65 17. Sacro Cuore Church, Lungotevere 12, buses 34, 49, 87, 926, 990, Metro Lepanto. Open daily 7–11am and 4:30–7pm. Admission free.* **(see p. 98)**

Nero's Golden House (Domus Aurea). Remnants of early "grotesque" frescoes are still visible in the crazy emperor's abode.... *Tel 06/699 01 10. Via Labicana 136, buses 85, 87, 117, 186, tram 30, Metro Colosseo. Open daily 9am–5pm. Admission charged. Reserve tickets with the Centro Servizi per l'Archeologia (see page 82 above for details).* **(see p. 97)**

Obelisk of Axum. Rome's "newest" obelisk, looted by Mussolini after victory in Ethiopia.... *No telephone. Viale delle Terme di Caracalla, buses 27, 81, 118, 628, tram 30, Metro Circo Massimo.* **(see p. 86)**

Obelisk of Montecitorio. Once part of Rome's first sundial.... *No telephone. Piazza di Montecitorio, buses 56, 60, 85, 116, 492.* **(see p. 86)**

Obelisk of Piazza del Popolo. Obelisk once stood in the Circus Maximus.... *No telephone. Piazza del Popolo, buses 81, 95, 115, 117, 204, Metro Flaminio.* **(see p. 86)**

Obelisk of Piazza San Giovanni in Laterano. Rome's largest obelisk.... *No telephone. Piazza San Giovanni in Laterano, buses 16, 85, 87, 117, Metro San Giovanni.* **(see p. 86)**

Obelisk of Santa Maria Sopra Minerva. Bernini designed the adorable elephant on whose back the obelisk sits.... *No telephone. Piazza della Minverva, buses 56, 64, 70, 81, 116.* **(see p. 86)**

Order of the Knights of Malta. Exceptional view of St. Peter's through the bronze keyhole.... *No telephone. Piazza dei Cavalieri di Malta, buses 23, 95, 175, 715, Metro Circo Massimo.* **(see p. 96)**

Palatine. Hill contains the ruins of ancient palaces and the Huts of Romulus. The Palatine Museum houses more ancient artifacts.... *Tel 06/699 01 10. Entrance on Via di San Gregorio or via the Forum, buses 27, 81, 85, 87, 186, Metro Colosseo. Open Mon–Sat 9am–dusk, Sun 9am–2pm, Oct–March, Mon–Sat 9am–3pm, Sun 9am–2pm. Admission charged.* **(see p. 85)**

Palazetto Zuccari (Monster House). Former home of architect Federico Zuccari and designed to look like a large stone beast; now home to a fine arts society.... *No telephone. Via Gregoriana 30, Metro Spagna. Not open to the public.* **(see p. 100)**

Palazzo della Civiltà del Lavoro. The Fascist version of the Colosseum (the "square Colosseum" or the "Colosseo quadrato") and the centerpiece of the EUR neighborhood.... *No telephone. Viale della Civiltà del Lavoro, Metro EUR Palasport. Not open to the public.* **(see p. 100)**

Palazzo delle Esposizioni. Large museum featuring classic and modern exhibitions. The museum's self-serve cafeteria is one of the best in Rome.... *Tel 06/474 59 03, Via Nazionale 194, buses 64, 65, 70, 71, 75, 117, 170. Open Wed–Mon 10am–9pm (last admission at 8:30pm). Closed Jan 1, May 1, and Dec 25. Admission charged.* **(see pp. 90, 93)**

Palazzo Venezia. Palace built in 1455; later Mussolini's headquarters (he gave rousing speeches from its balcony). Museum holds rotating exhibits of Renaissance art, sculpture, and tapestries.... *Tel 06/798 865. Via del Plebiscito 118, buses 44, 46, 56, 57, 60, 64, 65, 70, 75, 90, 170, 492. Open Tue–Sat 9am–2pm, Sun 9am–1pm. Admission charged.* **(see p. 95)**

Pantheon. The oldest and best preserved of all of Rome's ancient temples. Tombs of King Umberto I, Vittorio Emanuele II, and Raphael are here, among others.... *Tel 06/613 00 230. Piazza della Rotonda, buses 64, 70, 75, 116. Open Mon–Sat 9am–6:30pm, Sun and public holidays 9am–1pm. Closed Jan 1, May 1, and Dec 25. Admission free.* **(see pp. 84, 98)**

Pasquino. Rome's "talking" statue.... *No telephone. Piazza di Pasquino, buses 46, 62, 64, 70, 81, 87, 492.* **(see p. 94)**

Piazza Barberini. Medium-sized piazza at the foot of the Via Veneto; features Bernini's Fontana del Tritone. Across the way, slightly catty-corner, is the artist's Fontana delle Api, with potable water.... *No telephone. Piazza Barberini, buses 52, 53, 56, 58, 58b, 490, 495, Metro Barberini.* **(see p. 92)**

Piazza del Popolo. Nexus point of Via Ripetta, Via del Corso, and Via del Babuino and home to a 3,000-year-old obelisk, the square was once the site of public executions; today, it's traffic-free and used for demonstrations and holiday gatherings.... *No telephone. Piazza del Popolo, buses 81, 95, 115, 117, 204, Metro Flaminio.* **(see p. 100)**

Piazza del Quirinale. Wide piazza notable for Italian president's residence; also features a small fountain and an obelisk flanked by Castor, Pollux, and horses—thus the nickname Monte Cavallo (Horse Hill).... *No telephone. Piazza del Quirinale, buses 52, 53, 56, 60, 61, 62, 71, 95, 117, 492.* **(see p. 96)**

Piazza Navona. Once the site of an ancient stadium, now a favorite place for people-watching.... *No telephone. Piazza Navona, buses 46, 62, 64, 70, 81, 87, 186, 492.* **(see p. 84, 92)**

Piazza Santa Maria in Trastevere. Square at the heart of

Trastevere, flanked by a medieval church and numerous restaurants and cafes. Central fountain was designed by Carlo Fontana.... *No telephone. Piazza Santa Maria in Trastevere, buses 44, 56, 60, 75, tram 8.* **(see p. 101)**

Piè di Marmo. A big, marble foot that once belonged to a bigger statue.... *No telephone. Via di Santo Stefano del Cacco, Bus 56, 64, 70, 81, 116.* **(see p. 94)**

Pincio Gardens. Great views of the city.... *No telephone. Il Pincio, buses 95, 117, 204, Metro Flaminio.* **(see p. 95)**

Ponte Cestio. Built in the 1st century B.C., this bridge was restored in 370 A.D. Names of Byzantine emperors are inscribed upon it.... *No telephone. Ponte Cestio, buses 23, 44, 56, 60, 65, 75, 170, 710, 774, 780.* **(see p. 94)**

Ponte Fabricio. Rome's oldest bridge, built in 62 B.C., and still used today as a footbridge. During the Middle Ages, two powerful families (the Pierleoni and the Caetani) controlled its use by erecting a toll tower, still standing today.... *No telephone. Ponte Fabricio, buses 23, 44, 56, 60, 65, 75, 170, 710, 774, 780.* **(see p. 94)**

Ponte Rotto. The "broken bridge." Best viewed from Isola Tiberina.... *No telephone. Below Ponte Palatino, buses 23, 44, 56, 60, 65, 75, 170, 710, 774, 780.* **(see p. 94)**

Protestant Cemetery. Final resting place of Keats, Shelley, Gramsci, and other non-Catholics.... *Tel 06/574 19 00. Via Caio Cestio 6, buses 23, 27, 95, 716, trams 13, 30b, Metro Piramide. Open Tue–Sun 9am–6pm, until 5pm Oct–March. Last admission 30 min before closing. Donation expected.* **(see pp. 95, 98)**

Pyramid of Caius Cestius. Tomb of a wealthy Roman who died in 12 B.C.... *No telephone. Piazzale Ostiense, buses 123, 27, 95, 716, trams 13, 30b, Metro Piramide. Not open to the public.* **(see p. 98)**

San Clemente. A Medieval church built upon an ancient Mithraeum. Just steps from the Colosseum.... *Tel 06/70 45 10 18. Via di San Giovanni in Laterano, buses 16, 81, 85, 87, 810, Metro Colosseo. Open Mon–Sat 9am–12:30pm and 3:30–6:30pm, until 6pm Oct–March, Sun*

10am–12:30pm, 3:30–6:30pm and Admission charged for excavations. **(see p. 97)**

San Francesco a Ripa. Modest church in old Trastevere, a hospice when St. Francis of Assisi visited Rome in 1219; still contains his crucifix and stone pillow, as well as Bernini's *Ecstasy of Beata Ludovica Albertoni.... Tel 06/581 90 20. Piazza San Francesco d'Assisi 88, buses 23, 44, 100, 175. Open daily 7:30am–noon and 4–7pm.* **(see pp. 92, 99)**

San Giovanni in Laterano. Dominated by oversized statues. Before the papacy moved to France in 1309, this and the adjoining Lateran Palace were the main church and residence of the pope.... *Tel 06/77 20 79 91. Piazza di San Giovanni in Laterano 4, buses 4, 16, 85, 87, trams 13, 30b, Metro San Giovanni. Open daily 7am–7pm, until 6pm Oct–March. Admission charged for Cloister.* **(see pp. 87, 95)**

San Luigi dei Francesi. French expats claim this church as their own, as a number of renowned Frenchmen were buried here. Most remarkable for its 3 Caravaggio masterpieces, located in the 5th chapel on the left.... *Tel 06/688 271. Via Santa Giovanna d'Arco, Bus 70, 81, 87, 116, 492. Open daily 8am–12:30pm and 3:30–7pm, closed Thur in evenings. Admission free.* **(see p. 89)**

San Paolo Fuori le Mura. Pilgrimage church standing on the site of a 4th-century basilica destroyed by fire.... *Tel 06/541 03 41. Via Ostiense 186, buses 23, 170, 673, Metro San Paolo. Open daily 7:30am–6:40pm (last admission 15 min before closing). Admission free.* **(see p. 87)**

San Pietro in Vincoli. "St. Peter in Chains" features the shackles that supposedly held St. Peter captive in Mamertine Prison, but Michelangelo's giant Moses is the reason most people go out of their way to find this church.... *Tel 06/488 28 65. Piazza di San Pietro in Vincoli 4A, buses 27, 115, 117, 204. Open daily 7am–12:30pm and 3:30–7pm, until 6pm Oct–March. Admission free.* **(see p. 91)**

Santa Cecilia in Trastevere. Cavallini frescoes and a morbid sculpture of Santa Cecilia are the highlights of this pretty church.... *Tel 06/581 90 20. Piazza Santa Cecilia, buses 23, 44, 100, 175, tram 8. Open daily 7:30am–noon and 4–7pm.* **(see p. 99)**

Santa Croce in Gerusalemme. Three pieces of the cross, a nail, and 2 thorns are kept in a display case in a chapel to the left of the altar. Also be on the lookout for a finger, said to be the very one doubting St. Thomas stuck into Christ's wound.... *Tel 06/701 47 69. Piazza di Santa Croce in Gerusalemme 12, buses 9, Tram 13, 30b. Open daily 6am–12:30pm and 3:30–7pm.* **(see p. 88)**

Santa Maria degli Angeli e dei Martiri. Most of Michelangelo's original plans for this church were ignored, but there are displays of his blueprints in the sacristy and Domenichino's Martyrdom of St. Sebastian, too.... *Tel 06/488 08 12. Piazza della Repubblica, buses 57, 65, 75, 170, 492, 910, Metro Repubblica, Termini. Open daily 8am–12:30pm and 4–7pm, until 6:30pm in winter.* **(see pp. 86, 91)**

Santa Maria dei Miracoli e Santa Maria in Montesanto. Twin churches on the Piazza del Popolo.... *Miracoli tel 06/361 02 50; Montesanto tel 06/361 05 94. Piazza del Popolo, buses 81, 115, 117, 204, Metro Flaminio. Miracoli open Mon–Sat 6am–1pm and 4:30–7:45pm, Sun 4:30–7:45pm. Montesanto open daily 4–7pm. Closed Aug.* **(see p. 100)**

Santa Maria del Popolo. Two of Carvaggio's most important works reside in this church's Cerasi Chapel, and the Raphael-designed Chigi Chapel houses sculpture by both Lorenzetto and Bernini.... *Tel 06/361 08 36. Piazza del Popolo 12, buses 81, 95, 115, 117, 204, Metro Flaminio. Open Mon–Sat 7am–noon and 4–7pm, Sun 8am–2pm and 4:30–7:30pm.* **(see p. 89)**

Santa Maria della Concezione. Grisly yet peaceful Capuchin crypt, with thousands of friars' bones sculpted into sunbursts and lattice patterns.... *Tel 06/488 27 48. Via Veneto 27, buses 52, 53, 56, 58, 58b, 490, 495, Metro Barberini. Open daily 7am–noon and 3:45–7:30pm, Crypt open Fri–Wed 9am–noon and 3–6pm. Donation expected.* **(see p. 98)**

Santa Maria della Pace. Location of Raphael's Sybil frescoes.... *Tel 06/686 11 56. Vicolo del Arco della Pace 5, buses 70, 81, 87, 116, 186, 492. Open Tue–Sat 10am–noon and 4–6pm, Sun 9–11am.* **(see p. 89)**

Santa Maria della Vittoria. Home to Bernini's *Ecstasy of St. Teresa.... Tel 06/482 61 90. Via XX Settembre 17, buses 16,*

36, 37, 60. Open daily 6:30–noon and 4:30-6pm.
(see p. 92)

Santa Maria in Aracoeli. Church at the top of the long staircase featuring the Santo Bambino, a statue said to have been carved from a tree that stood in the garden of Gethsemane. Both church and icon were restored in 2000.... *Tel 06/679 81 55. Piazza d'Aracoeli, buses 64, 65, 70, 75, or 170 from Termini, 56, 60, or 492 from Piazza Barberini and buses 44, 46, 57, 90, and 90b. Open daily 7am–noon and 4–5:30pm, until 6:30pm June–Sept .* **(see p. 96)**

Santa Maria in Cosmedin. The most important Greek church in Rome. Site of the Bocca della Verità and Byzantine mosaics.... *Tel 06/678 14 19. Piazza della Bocca della Verità 18, buses 23, 81, 160, 204. Open daily 9am–1pm and 2:30–6pm, until 5pm in winter .* **(see p. 84)**

Santa Maria Maggiore. On the pilgrimage route, Santa Maria Maggiore contains a series of 5th-century biblical mosaics on its triumphal arch.... *Tel 06/48 31 95. Piazza di Santa Maria Maggiore, buses 16, 27, 70, 71, Metro Termini or Cavour. Open daily 7am–7pm (last admission 15 min before closing).*
(see pp. 87, 98)

Santa Maria Sopra Minerva. Tombs of Fra Angelico and St. Catherine of Siena are the highlights of Rome's only Gothic-style church.... *Tel 06/679 39 26. Piazza della Minerva 42, buses 56, 64, 70, 81, 116. Open daily 7am–noon and 4–7pm, Cloister open Mon–Sat 8:30am–1pm and 4–7pm.*
(see pp. 91, 95, 98)

Santa Maria in Trastevere. Medieval church whose facade and apse glisten with golden, 12th-century mosaics. Life of the Virgi mosaics above the altar were designed by Cavallini.... *Tel 06/581 94 43. Piazza Santa Maria in Trastevere, buses 44, 56, 60, 75, tram 8.* **(see p. 95, 99)**

Sant'Ignazio di Loyola. Sister church of the Gesù; Jesuit church's dome is one of the finest examples of trompe l'oeil in the city.... *Tel 06/679 44 06. Piazza di Sant'Ignazio, Bus 56, 60, 81, 85, 492. Open daily 7:30am–12:30pm and 4–7:15pm.* **(see p. 89)**

Scala Santa and Sancta Sanctorum. Penance of climbing the

Scala Santa (on your knees) is often carried out on Good Friday.... *Tel 06/70 49 44 89. Piazza di San Giovanni in Laterano 14, buses 4, 16, 85, 87, trams 13, 30b, Metro San Giovanni. Open daily 6:30am–11:50pm and 3:30–6:45pm.* **(see p. 88)**

Sistine Chapel. Small chapel built for Pope Sixtus IV and frescoed by heavyweights of the Italian Renaissance. Also the site of papal elections.... *Tel 06/698 83 333. Città del Vaticano, Metro Ottaviano. Open Mon–Sat 8:45am–1:45pm, until 4:45pm Mar–June and Sep–Oct, free on last Sun of month. Admission charged.* **(see pp. 83, 91)**

The Spanish Steps. Teenagers, families, and weary tourists all use the Spanish Steps to take a breather from their busy Roman days here in the Piazza di Spagna. Stairs were added in the 17th century at the behest of the owners of the Trinità dei Monti church.... *No telephone. Piazza di Spagna, buses 117, Metro Spagna. Admission free.* **(see p. 84)**

St. Peter's Basilica. The largest church in Chistendom ('nuff said).... *Tel 06/698 84 466 or 06/698 84 866. Piazza San Pietro, buses 64, 23, 81, 492, 991, tram 19, Metro Ottaviano. Open daily 7am–7pm, until 6pm Oct–March, Treasury open 9am–6:30pm, until 5:30pm Oct–March, Vatican Grottoes open 7am–6pm, until 5pm Oct–March, Dome open 8am–6pm, until 5 pm Oct–March. Admission charged to Treasury and Dome.* **(see pp. 83, 87, 96, 98)**

Synagogue. Admission includes a tour of the on-site museum containing important relics from Rome's large and longstanding Jewish community.... *Tel 06/68 40 06 61. Lungotevere dei Cenci, buses 23, 44, 56, 60, 65, 75, 170, 710, 774, 780. Open Mon–Thur 9am–5pm, Fri 9am–2pm, Sun 9:30am–12:30pm. Closed Sat and public holidays. Admission charged.* **(see p. 89)**

Theater of Marcellus. Ancient theater reborn as Renaissance palace. Forms the outer edge of the Ghetto area.... *Tel 06/481 48 00. Via del Teatro di Marcello, buses 23, 81, 95, 160, 204, 717, 744, 780. Closed to the public except during summer concerts [see Nightlife].* **(see p. 85)**

Tomb of Cecilia Metella. The famed round "drum" featured in romantic depictions of the Roman campagna.... *Tel 06/780*

24 65. Via Appia Antica, bus 660. Open Tue–Sat 9am–1pm hour before sunset, Sun–Mon 9am–1pm. Closed public holidays. Admission charged. **(see pp. 85, 97)**

Trajan's Markets. Ruins of an ancient shopping center, located across from the Forum.... *Tel 06/679 00 48. Via IV Novembre, buses 64, 65, 70, 75, 170. Open Tue–Sat 9am–7pm, Sun 9am–1pm (last admission one hour before closing). Admission charged.* **(see p. 85)**

Trevi Fountain (Fontana di Trevi). Rome's most famous and theatrical fountain. Pickpocket central.... *No telephone. Fontana di Trevi, buses 52, 53, 58, 60, 61, 62, 71, 95, 492.* **(see p. 83)**

Vatican Museums. Former papal palaces containing some of the most priceless works of art in the world. Raphael Rooms, Map Room, collections of Egyptian and Etruscan art, and Sistine Chapel are not to be missed.... *Tel 06/698 83 333. Città del Vaticano, Metro Ottaviano. Open Mon–Sat 8:45am–1:45pm, until 4:45pm Mar–June and Sep–Oct, free on last Sun of month. Admission charged.* **(see pp. 83, 89)**

Villa Borghese. Rome's main (and huge) urban park, with grounds including a zoo, natural history museum, and contemporary art museum. On the weekends, you can rent a bike or in-line skate to cruise around on.... *See individual attractions for Bioparco, Museo Nazionale dell'Arte Moderna e Contemporanea, and Villa Giulia.* **(see pp. 91, 93, 100)**

Villa Farnesina. Former Farnese family villa, now home to Raphael's famous Triumph of Galatea fresco.... *Tel 06/688 01 767 or 06/669 80 230. Via della Lungara 230, buses 23, 65, 280 to Lungotevere Farnesina. Open Mon–Sat 9am–1pm; Gabinetto open Tue–Sat 9am–1pm. Admission charged.* **(see p. 92)**

Villa Giulia. Home of the National Etruscan Museum. Of note are 6th-century ceramics and the Nypheum, a sunken courtyard decorated with period mosaics.... *Tel 06/322 65 71. Piazzale di Villa Giulia 9, buses 52, 95, 490, 495, trams 19, 30. Open Tue–Sat 9am–7pm, Sun 9am–1pm. Admission charged.* **(see p. 91)**

Spanish Steps Diversions

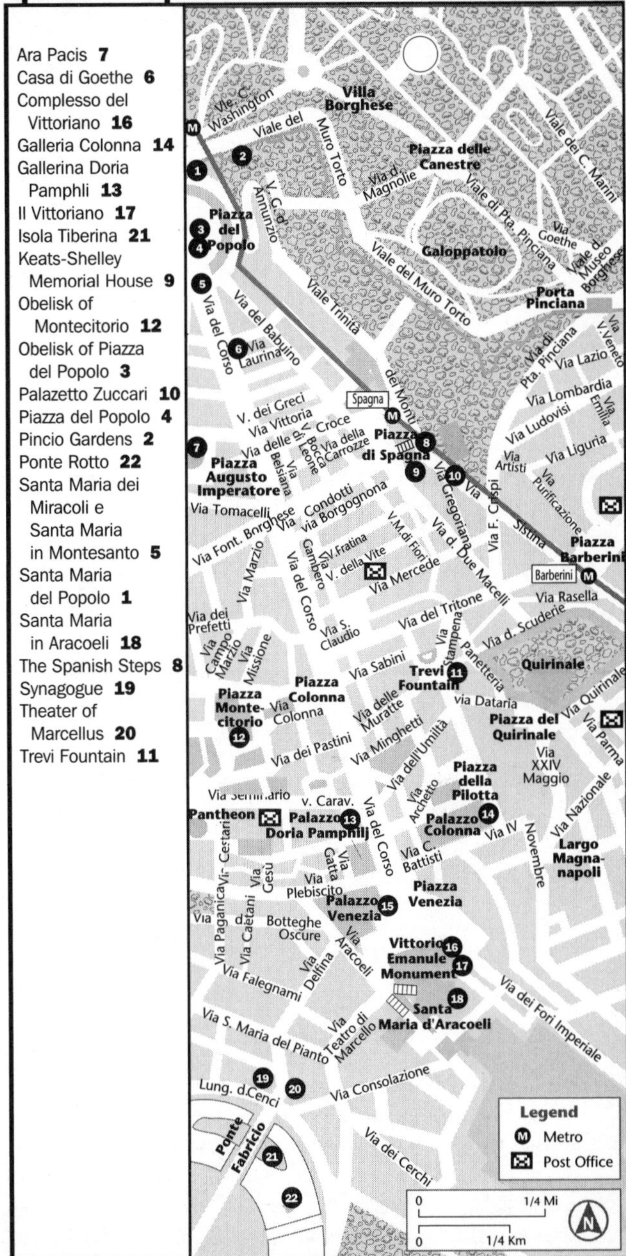

Via Veneto & Termini Diversions

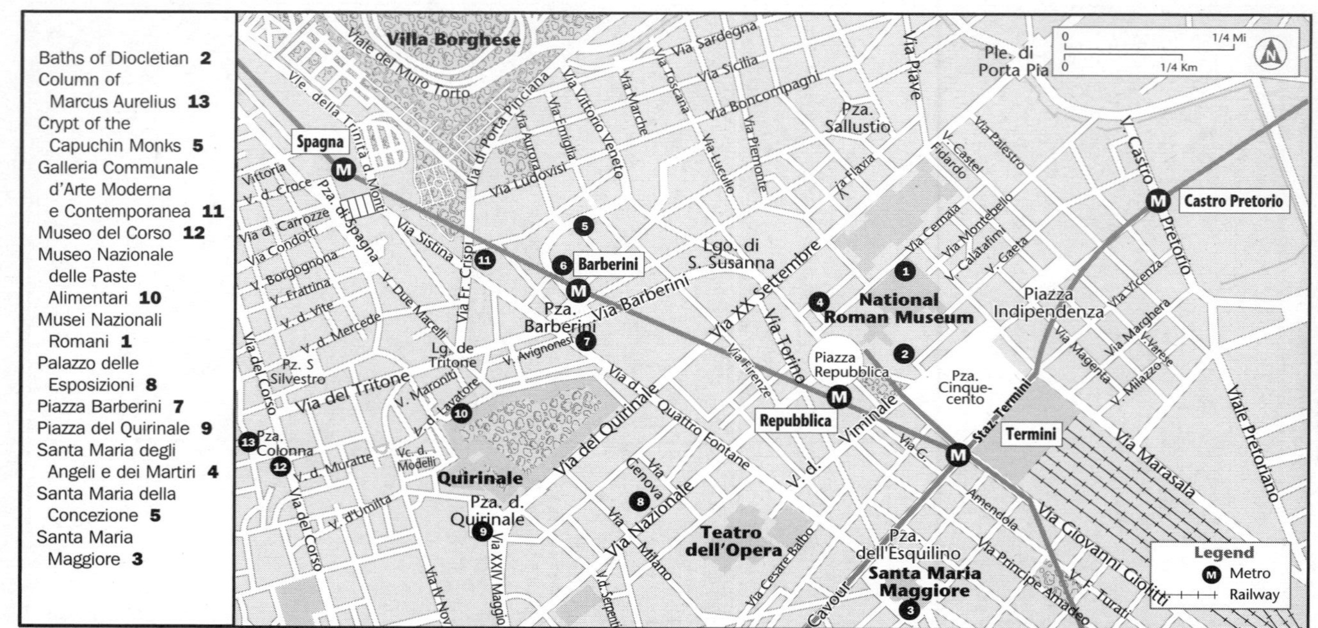

Campo de' Fiori & Piazza Navona Diversions

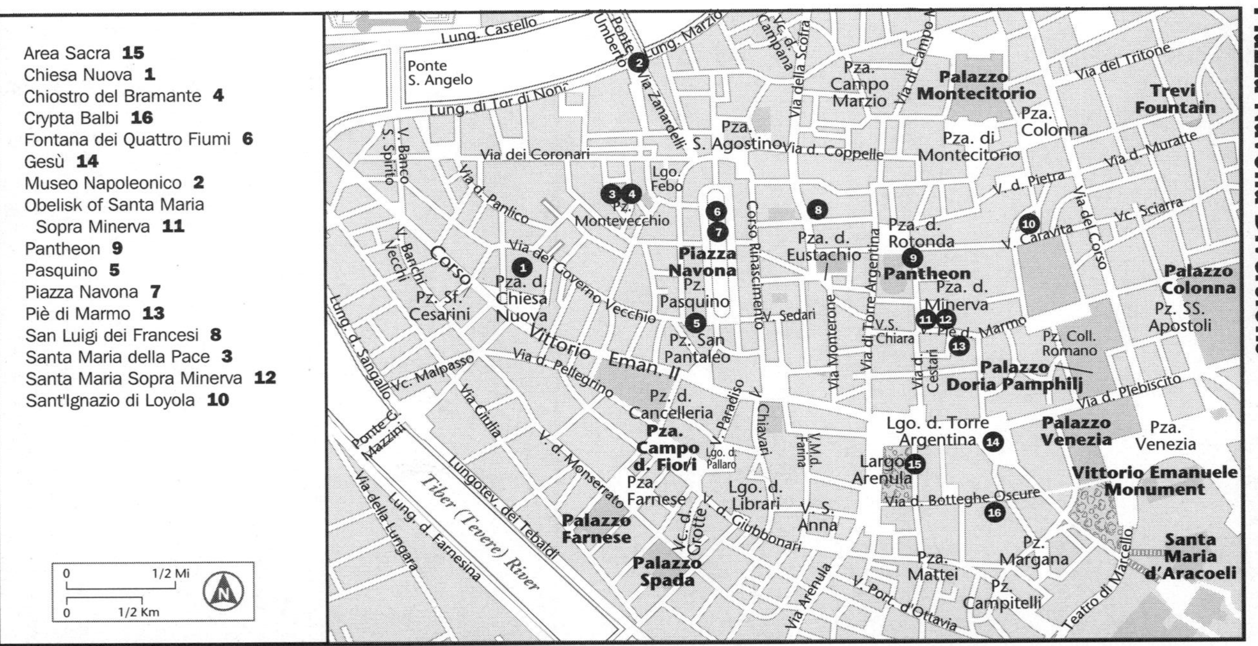

Vatican City Area Diversions

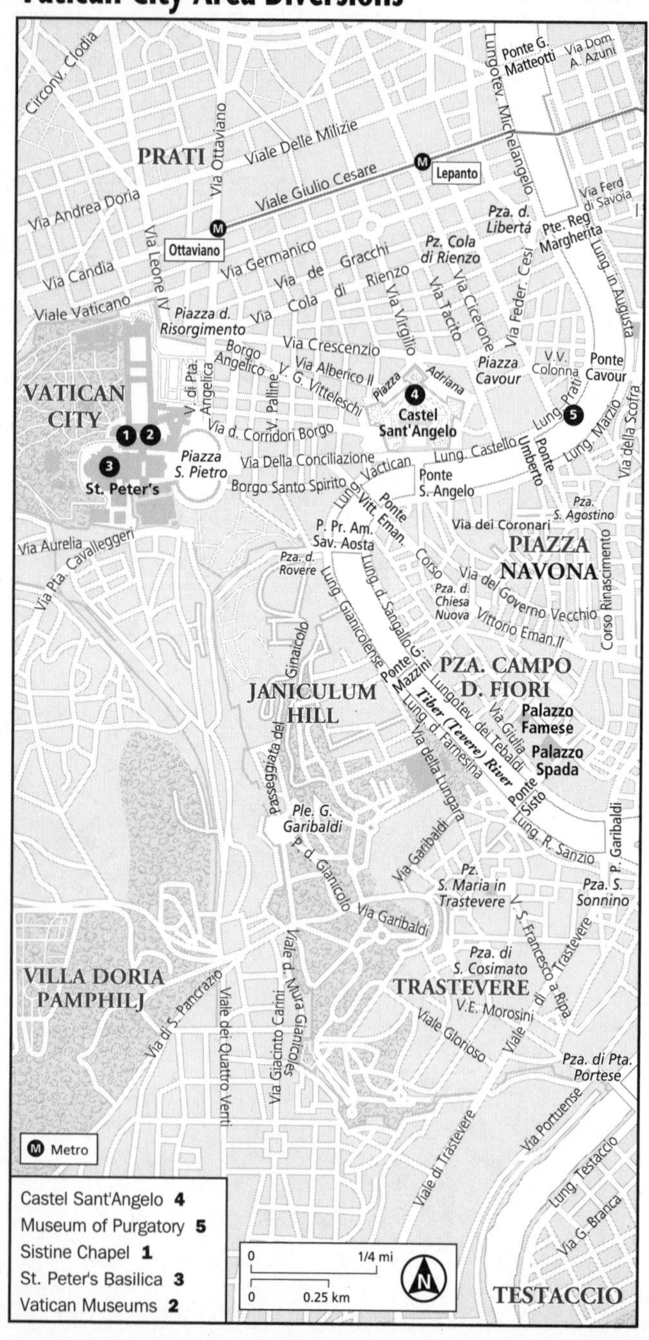

Ancient Rome Diversions

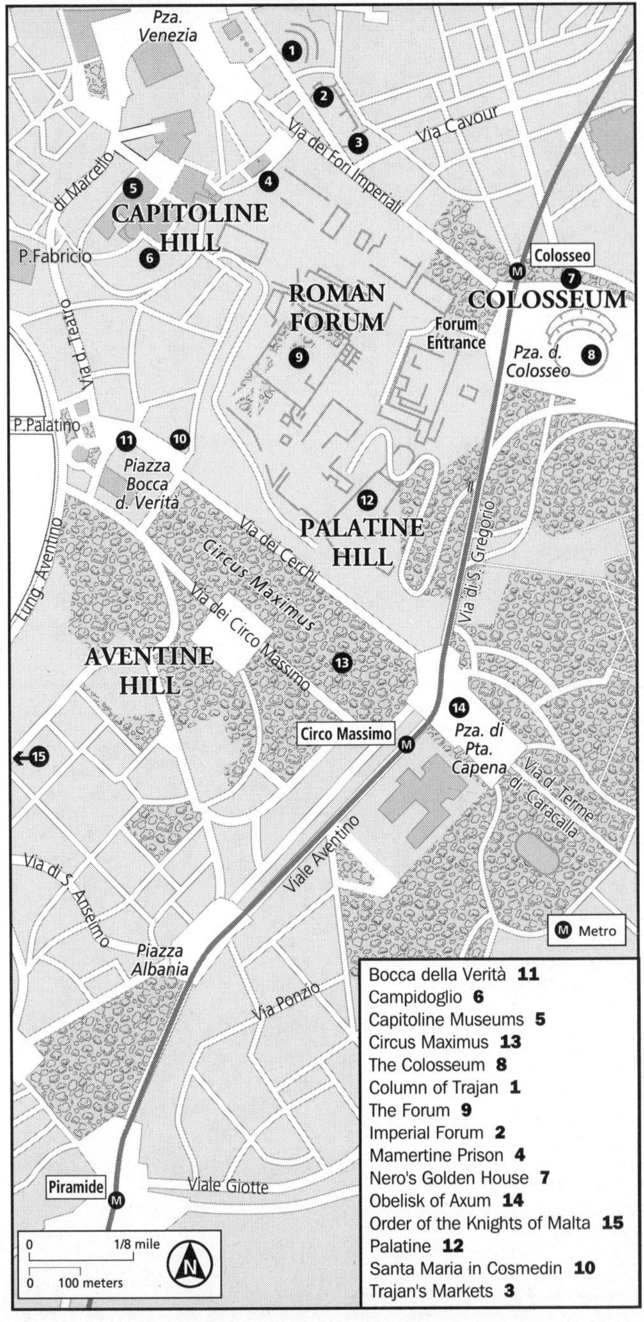

Bocca della Verità **11**
Campidoglio **6**
Capitoline Museums **5**
Circus Maximus **13**
The Colosseum **8**
Column of Trajan **1**
The Forum **9**
Imperial Forum **2**
Mamertine Prison **4**
Nero's Golden House **7**
Obelisk of Axum **14**
Order of the Knights of Malta **15**
Palatine **12**
Santa Maria in Cosmedin **10**
Trajan's Markets **3**

Rome Diversions

National Gallery of Modern Art
Galleria Borghese
Piazza di Siena
VILLA BORGHESE
SPANISH STEPS
VIA VENETO
Spagna
Barberini
PZA. BARBERINI
Keats-Shelley Memorial
National Gallery of Ancient Art
National Roman Museum
TERMINI
Stazione Termini
Castro Pretorio
Piazza Indipendenza
Repubblica
Termini
Palazzo del Quirinale
Trevi Fountain
Teatro dell'Opera
Santa Maria Maggiore
Palazzo Doria Pamphilj
Palazzo Colonna
Palazzo Venezia
Vittorio Emanuele Monument
Via Cavour
Vittorio Emanuele
Piazza Vittorio Eman. II
CAMPIDOGLIO
Capitoline Museums
San Pietro in Vincoli
Golden House of Nero
Colosseo
Roman Forum
Colosseum
ANCIENT ROME
Manzoni
PALATINE HILL
San Giovanni in Laterano
AVENTINE HILL
Circo Massimo
Baths of Caracalla
Piramide
Legend
Information
Metro
Railway
0 1/4 Mi
0 1/4 Km

getting

4
outside

Depending on the time of day, Rome's parks are crowded with spoiled brats, dog-walkers, flashers, and horny teens. Unlike Parisians, who tend to manicure their gardens into oblivion, Romans are very practical when it comes to their green spaces. Hardly any of Rome's parks have "Do Not Walk on the Grass" signs—and if they do, Romans ignore them. For the most part, wherever there's a patch of grass, most likely you're allowed to sit, walk your dog, play soccer, or have a picnic. Just watch out for the *cacca.* Romans rarely scoop their pets' poop. Perhaps the reason parks in Rome are so user-friendly is that they provide the only respite from summer's unbearable heat, air pollution, and noise. True, few Romans stick around to see the city at its stickiest—most pack up and scoot off to the beach or the mountains during August. But for those who are left behind, these parks are a cool escape—and often the scene of film festivals, plays, and sporting expositions [see Entertainment].

The Lowdown

It's not easy being green... Rome may feel like an asphalt jungle, but it somehow also horns in around 130 square feet of parks and gardens per capita—impressive, although sometimes you have to hunt to find the greenery. **Circus Maximus** (Metro: Circo Massimo), that storied venue for ancient Rome's chariot races, now looks like an oversized football field, which makes it a favorite for jogging and impromptu soccer matches on its flat end. Locals also lounge on its grassy knoll or take Fido out for his daily walk. Once the retreat for the noble Mattei family in the 16th century, **Villa Celimontana** (buses 81, 810, tram 30) on the Celian Hill near the Colosseum is now a public park where you'll encounter neighborhood nannies with pesky kids in tow as well as lovers stretched out on a blanket during their lunch breaks. A few lazy cats, a merry-go-round, and giant shade trees are the highlights here, as well as a paved and relatively unused jogging trail. A smaller park is the **Colle Oppio** (Metro: Colosseo), more memorable for its crumbling, oversized, graffiti-tagged, concrete fountains than its grass, but still very convenient as a breather after visiting the Colosseum or the Domus Aurea. A small cafe with surly service opens near the eastern entrance in the afternoons from March through October. Sooner or later, you're going to visit **Villa Borghese** (Metro: Spagna), Rome's best-known and biggest recreational area. With a circumference of about 4 miles, including the areas between the Pincio Gardens and the Via Veneto, the park has an artificial lake, jogging and rollerblading areas, a depressing zoo, a contemporary art museum, and acres of grass shaded by umbrella pines. On weekends, the park is teeming with fashionable joggers, screaming kids, and young lovers. By night, the park becomes Make-Out Central, and (unfortunately) a favored hangout of voyeurs and perverts; avoid it after dark. Connected to Villa Borghese by Via Salaria, **Villa Ada** (buses 3, 4, 57, 319) is the former residence of the royal Savoy family and the public park of choice for affluent *Pariolini.* (Parioli is that slightly snooty northern Rome neighborhood just above the Villa Borghese.) The vegetation here is thick, with lots of huge pines, cypresses, and palm trees, and the wildlife is abundant, making it the perfect headquarters for the Italian bureau of the World Wildlife Fund. The park is completely off the beaten track from the center, but attractions like a merry-go-round and a passable playground are enough to keep the wee ones occupied for a while. Wedged between Trastevere and the Vatican is the hill known as the **Janiculum** (bus 870), with little in the way of tourist attractions but lots of green space. At the foot of the hill sits the **Botanical Gardens** (buses 23, 65, 280; admission charged), a nicely landscaped collection of trees, flowers, and tropical grasses maintained by local university students and overseen by a curmudgeon. This is one of the quieter places accessible by foot via the alleyways of Trastevere. (If you're there around noon, don't worry—Rome is not being bombed; each day, at 12 on the nose, the cannon on the hill by the Garibaldi monument is fired. You'll jump a mile if you're caught unaware.) Farther afield from the Janiculum is **Villa Doria Pamphili** (bus 75), an impossibly gorgeous formal garden with geometrical flower beds, grottoes, walking trails, and rolling meadows. Also called **Belrespiro** (roughly speaking, "good air"), this garden was once the estate of Camillo Pamphili (Pope Innocent X's nephew), and is now Rome's largest park, spanning roughly 455 acres.

Stopping to smell the roses... Rome's many gardens are well-maintained, mostly by the city these days rather than the wealthy families who started the tradition. Though not very large, the **Farnese Gardens** (buses 11, 27, 81, 85, 87) at the top of the Palatine [see Diversions] are the sort you would expect in a Mediterranean setting: Groves of orange trees, manicured bushes, pretty flowers, and some well-placed fountains are worth the climb (and the admission fee) up the hill. The **Roseto** (buses 23, 95, 175, 715) on the **Aventine** hill is a real treat in May, when rows of red, yellow, pink, and white roses pop open in blossom. Because the blooming season is so short, this rose garden is usually packed with admirers during that one month, and there's really no good way to avoid the crowds at that time. But what the heck, you only live once, right? The **Botanical Gardens** (see above) offer a series of different ecosystems to explore, including a bamboo forest, rose garden, and greenhouse of carnivorous plants. There's also a small **Garden of the Blind** here, which contains flower and tree varieties that appeal to the other senses and placards with info printed in Braille. For an outdoor art show, trek up to the northernmost reaches of the city to **Villa Glori** (buses 53, 217, 910) where you'll find the **Parco di Scultura Comtemporanea** (no telephone, small fee charged) or Contemporary Sculpture Park. Eleven avant garde works with names like *Grass Man* make up Rome's first permanent installation of outdoor art.

On your own two feet... Just don't feel right without that 10-mile run before breakfast? Well, you're not in California anymore, bub; Romans tend to get their daily exercise by walking, bicycling, gesticulating, and arguing rather than actually breaking a sweat. Track stars who just can't kick the habit, though, can get in a kind of workout at **Circus Maximus,** where one lap equals about two and a half times around a standard American track. However, meandering tourists and dog-walkers tend to get in the way of a productive jog. You might feel a little less out of place in your shorts and tank top running along **Via delle Terme di Caracalla** (Metro: Circo Massimo); just across the way from the Circus, this jogging area attracts a crowd of die-hard runners. **Villa Borghese** has a bunch of wooded trails that wind around statues, neo-classical temples, and man-made ponds, making for a pleasant jog on weekday mornings. Go on Saturday or Sunday, though, and you'll have to contend with the rear ends of rollerbladers, cyclists, and a see-and-be-scene of weekend warriors in Prada workout gear. **Villa Doria Pamphili** has plenty of room for walkers and runners, as well as exercise stations along the way. Marathoners might want to consider coming to Rome in late March, when the **Maratona di Roma** (tel 06/406 50 64, www.maratonadiroma.com) is held. What's cooler than a traffic-free jog past the Colosseum, the Forum, and St. Peter's? You do have to qualify to run in this big boy, but take heart—there's also a 3.1-mile fun run called the *Stracittadina* on the same day, and it's open to amateurs. That means you.

Pedal pushers... Italians love their bicycles (you *have* seen the classic Italian flick *The Bicycle Thief,* haven't you? No? Rent it at once!), though the crush of Rome's auto traffic can make cycling around the city hairy at times; hence, most Italians go with snappy motorized scooters instead and expertly (if dangerously) weave in and out of the city traffic. You can rent both bikes and scooters at **Villa Borghese** from **I Bike Rome** (tel 06/322 52 40). **Collati** (tel 06/688 01 084, Via del Pellegrino 82, buses 64, 492), a small shop just a few steps away from Campo de' Fiori, rents out bikes (and all-important helmets for your noggin) to tourists brave enough to navigate the cobblestones. **Francesco Tranchina** (tel 06/481 58 669, Via Cavour 80a, csdovt@tin.it) runs a professional rental shop not far from Termini station; old-school bikes (you know, the kind without gears), new-fangled Vespas, and souped-up motorcycles are all available for hire. A bike rental should run you somewhere between 5,000L (just $2.50) per hour and 20,000L (about $10) a day, while most scooter rentals start at 50,000L a day—depending on the make and model—and go up from there. You'll also need to leave a credit card or large cash deposit when renting a scooter from most agencies. Finally, by all means bite the bullet and pay a little extra for the personal accident insurance when you rent a motorcycle—the streets of Rome are like something out of *Thunderdome.*

Horsing around on land or water... Horses have come a long way since the days when Romans would shove hot tar into their bums and then watch them gallop down Via del Corso like bats out of hell. Today, the **Gallopatoio** (tel 06/322 67 97) in **Villa Borghese** is a much kinder, gentler, horseback riding club—and the only one in the city proper. It's not cheap, though: Lessons cost upwards of 200,000L (that's about $100) per 1-hour session. If your idea of horsing around involves water polo instead of actual horses, you can also swim your way around Rome.

Hotel pools are your best when you need to cool off in a hurry. The **Cavalieri Hilton,** the Sol Melia Aurelia Antica, and the Delta Colosseo [see Accommodations] all offer free pool privileges to hotel guests. Fees for non-guests range between 70,000 and 90,000L per day for adults and 30,000 to 50,000L per day for kids under 12 (that's about $35 to $45 daily for adults, and $15 to $25 daily for the tykes). EUR's Olympic-sized **Piscina delle Rose** (tel 06/592 67 17, Viale America 20, Metro EUR Palasport), with rates ranging from 15,000L per half-day to 20,000L per day, is much more reasonable. So is the **Oasi delle Pace** (tel 06/718 45 50, Via degli Eugeni 2), an outdoor facility located off of Via Appia Antica. If you're staying north of town, stop by the **Centro Sportivo Italiano** (tel 06/323 47 32, Lungotevere Flaminio 59, buses 490, 495), where a dip costs around 25,000L. All pools in Rome are open roughly from June through September.

Playing with the swing set... For those who are determined to get in a round of golf or a tennis match, Rome has a few options. If one of your dreams includes becoming the next Tiger Woods, your cheapest option in the city is the **Circolo Golf di Roma** (tel 06/780 34 07, Via Appia Nuova 716a), which requires greens' fees of 50,000L per person (and up to 100,000L per person on the weekend); it's open Tuesday through Sunday from 8am until dusk. As do most European links, this one requires that you bring a membership card from your home club. No membership? No dice. If you're on your way out of town, the 18-hole **Sheraton Golf Club** (tel 06/655 34 77, Villa Parco de' Medici 20), open daily except Tuesdays from 8am until dusk in the Parco de' Medici—it's near Fiumicino Airport—also requires a member ID from your home club. Fees here range from 80,000 to 100,000L per person for 18 holes. With more than 350 tennis clubs, a tennis match is a bit easier to arrange in Rome—though, more often than not, you'll have to play at a private club, where a small membership fee (and the whitest of tennis whites) are required. Look for clay and grass courts at **Circolo della Stampa** (Piazza Mancini, tel 06/323 24 52), owned by the Italian Journalists Association. Fees run approximately 24,000L per hour per court, including lights—which is unusual, as many clubs charge you extra to flip 'em on at night. Both **Tennis Belle Arti** (tel 06/360 06 02, Via Flaminia 158) in the heart of Villa Borghese and **Tennis**

Lazio (tel 06/332 48 42, Lungotevere Flaminio 55) charge similar fees for their clay courts. Tennis fans flock to Rome each May for the **Italian Open,** played on the clay courts at the **Foro Italico** (tel 06/368 58 218, Viale dei Gladiatori 31). This is a big-time event, with a multimillion dollar purse, drawing such international stars as Andre Agassi, Martina Hingis, and the Williams sisters; if you're nuts about tennis, try to make it.

Get out of town!... A number of Rome's neighboring towns make great low-key day trips. The hill town of **Tivoli,** for instance, attracts a lot of tourists. That's not only because it's so easy to get to—you simply take a COTRAL bus from the Metro station called Rebibbia, or else a train from Termini or Tiburtina stations to Avezzano—but also because it boasts some of the most gorgeous country estates in the area surrounding the city. **Villa d'Este** (tel 0774/31 20 70, Piazza Trento), a former Benedictine convent, has an Avenue of 100 Fountains—known here as Viale delle Cento Fontane—with terraced gardens, decorative grottoes, and fragrant flower beds. If the villa's fountains are turned on (half the time they're being repaired), the sound of water is overwhelming. **Hadrian's Villa** (tel 0774/53 02 03) was, in part, the emperor's twisted take on Egypt: It features a faux Nile river decorated with sunbathing marble crocodiles and encompassed by pillars in the shapes of women; an elaborate bathing complex; and a playground for his homosexual lover. The ancient port city of **Ostia Antica** (take the Metro to Magliana station, then catch a train to Ostia) is a pleasantly quiet way to spend a warm weekday. (Warning: Tourists come in droves on the weekends.) Larger than Pompeii, but without any of the messy volcanic history (it was slowly besieged by mud after the Tiber was dammed), Ostia has a lot of well-kept black-and-white mosaics, a large amphitheater (still used for plays in the summer; see Entertainment), and ruins of columns, houses, shops, and tombs. If it's summer and you want to do as the Romans do—in other words, head for the beach—try **Lido Centro** (one train stop beyond the Ostia Antica ruins) or **Fregene**. Fregene, reached by a COTRAL bus from Metro station Lepanto, is where the majority of Rome's nightclubs move in summer, and the beach takes on a similarly festive scene during the daytime hours.

shop

5

ping

Many travelers to Italy pooh-pooh shopping in Rome, thinking that Milan is the be-all and end-all. True, there are deals to be had in Milan, such as those found at the sample sales of Milan-based designers. But in Rome you'll find more diversity—and more bargains—than in pricey northern Italy. No woman worth her weight in Visa cards should have trouble finding something to buy here—and men shouldn't have a problem, either, given Italy's world-class reputation for men's fashion. Shoes, shirts, boots, handbags, and belts are usually the first objects of desire; then there's designer clothing and accessories from Prada, Valentino, Gucci, Fendi, Armani, and all the big Italian names to choose from. Among the designer wares, there are plenty of moderately priced boutiques, artisan clothiers and jewelers, plus a handful of markets selling vintage coats, skirts, ties, and scarves for next to nothing. While you don't have to be rich to shop well in Rome, it helps if you have the figure of a 17-year-old, because most clothes are cut for trim figures. You'll also find that many stores in the city get away with refusing to allow customers to try on blouses, worried that patrons will get makeup or—God forbid—deodorant on them. And, during the end-of-season sales, many won't even let you try on pants. Bottom line? If you know you're not a perfect size 8, hope for the best—these clothing stores do not accept returns. Of course, Rome's shopping scene is not all about clothing. There's a sprinkling of antiques stores specializing in everything from 17th-century furniture to 1940s-era decor. *Alimentari* (delicatessens) and *enoteche* (wine shops) have wines, pastas, liqueurs, and sweets worth bringing back home—most reasonably priced, the rest splurge-worthy. Or, why not bring back an item that screams *Rome*? Pick up a bottle opener engraved with the likeness of the pope from any of the local kitsch vendors or pay a visit to the ecclesiastical shops near the Pantheon for an ornate rosary and a pair of beet-red cardinal socks. Even better, if you're in Rome at Christmastime stroll over to Piazza Navona, where you can buy locally made holiday ornaments and treats.

Target Zones

Sure, high fashion and big money will get you a long way on the Via Veneto, but the street of the "sweet life" is no place for a shopping spree. Instead, think **Via Condotti,** the ultimate address for the hotshots of Italian and international design. Start at the end of the street just below the Spanish Steps, where the boutique names read like a fashion mag—Prada, Gucci, Valentino, Ferragamo, Bulgari. The pretentiousness is thicker than a 3-inch stacked heel. Parallel streets Via Frattina and Via Borgognona are filled with shops of equal stature and lack Condotti's hype—so they're a bit quieter. Moving on to more plebeian environs, you'll find **Via del Corso,** a narrow, almost unbearably congested street running smack down the middle of the Centro Storico. Hundreds of shops selling trendy fashions at fairly reasonable prices bring Romans and tourists here in droves. Meanwhile, **Trastevere,** with its random new and used boutiques, is where self-styled bohos go. If another's trash is your treasure, Rome also offers a number of markets full of secondhand wares, plus antiques shops galore. The famous **Porta Portese** is only enjoyable if you like giving up your otherwise quiet Sunday morning to stand shoulder-to-shoulder with meandering bargain-seekers. If you're up for the challenge, you can stand to find handmade linens, marble curios, interesting kitchen gadgets, and anything else you've got on your list here. But, in the summer—fuhgeddaboutit! The outdoor market, despite some interesting knick-knacks, is more like an overheated junkyard. The market at **Via Sannio** is a better bet for those who are potentially claustrophobic. It's mellow, sells both new and used items (including a wide array of leather jackets and soccer wear)—and you can do the whole thing in half an hour. Antiques shops, once found mostly only around the **Via dei Coronari,** have lately sprouted up all over the Centro Storico as well as on the **Via Babuino** (in the Trident area) and the **Via del Pellegrino** (near Campo de' Fiori).

Hours of Business

Stores in Rome open at 9:30 or 10am, close for up to three hours for lunch around noon or 12:30, then reopen from about 3:30 until 7:30pm (and usually until 8pm in the summer). Most department stores and some entrepreneurial boutiques keep "orario non-stop," meaning that they don't close for lunch. (This doesn't mean they stay open 24/7, however.) Sundays and Mondays are when most shop owners take a *riposo,* closing for part or all of the day. However, die-hard shoppers will be happy to learn that Sunday is no longer sacred in Rome; many boutiques, especially those on the Via del Corso, keep afternoon hours. An ungodly number of shops close for the entire month of August so that employees can escape to cooler climes, so if you're coming that month don't expect the full range of places listed below to be open.

Sales Tax

Look for shops that display the "Euro Tax Free" sticker. If you purchase goods worth more than 300,000 lira (about $150) in one of these stores, you are entitled to receive a VAT—or IVA, in Italian—refund of the 12- to 35-percent tax you paid when purchasing the item or items. (No word yet on how many Euros you will have to spend to get a tax refund once the common European currency comes into play. (It is scheduled to do so in January 2002.) Most likely, it will still run the equivalent of $100 to $150. The shop should give you a VAT refund form at the checkout so that you can show it—and your purchases—to customs officials upon departure from Italy. Note that items that have been bought used will not be considered eligible for this rebate. For more on taxes, see Hotlines and Other Basics.

The Lowdown

The bargain hunt is on... Being around so many ancient relics seems to make Romans crave something *nuovo,* as many would rather cut off their noses than wear last year's fashions. Good for them—and for you. Here's why: The city is ideal for procuring chic cast-offs, from Fendi trench coats to mod minis that are already somehow out of style. Secondhand bargains, designer and otherwise, lie in messy piles in the stalls of the **Porta Portese** and **Via Sannio** markets, most of them priced by the kilo. Looking for a Pucci scarf or a classic motorcycle jacket? You may just find it here if you look hard enough. Even Romans—who normally scoff at anything used—frequent the **Atelier Ritz,** an *alta moda* extravaganza held twice monthly on a quiet street at the northwest edge of Villa Borghese. Here, haughty women dispose of last season's trends, many of which have yet to come into fashion in the United States. Of course, you don't *have* to sort through mounds of junk to find affordable fashions. Moderately priced boutiques of varying quality occupy the majority of the storefronts along Via del Corso. If purple suede pants are the "it" item of the season, you can bet that these stores—and almost every other one on the block—will "translate" (read: knock off) the look. **United Colors of Benetton,** Italy's answer to the Gap, is much cheaper here than in the United States and sells a much larger selection of hip, casual wear for men and women. **Sisley,** a slightly more upscale brand that's sold in Benetton stores in the States, has several branches in the Centro. **Max & Co.,** a less expensive line from **MaxMara,** has trendy business and street apparel for shoppers with mid-range budgets. You can also sometimes find good—though disposable—knock-offs of the season's accessories at the dime stores **Oviesse** and **Upim.** Sure, you may look like a cheap poseur while you're still in Rome—but who cares? Friends back home will never know how much you paid. The best thing about traveling to Rome during off-peak times is the chance to shop the end-of-season sales. During February, while most Americans are still digging out from the umpteenth snowstorm, Rome enjoys springlike weather and some excellent bargain basement sales. Wool coats and leather jackets that went for $300 may be on sale for $90, and boots and sweaters are marked down drastically. July is the time to pick up the remnants of summer clothing—though it's not especially pleasant to window-shop in the sweltering, smoggy, and crowded conditions. Be wary of stores that advertise *vendite promozionali* (promotional sale), as this is usually just a way to entice sales-crazed shoppers to browse. *Liquidazioni*, however, are genuine going-out-of-business sales and may be worth checking out.

The fine art of Italian negotiation... For Romans, haggling is in the blood, so you'll be considered a sucker if you don't try to talk down prices at flea markets and antiques shops. Typical of many markets and second-hand outlets worldwide, prices for a lot of items here are marked up at least 50 percent above what the vendor actually expects to receive. Offer a price or ask for a *sconto* (discount), and you may just get a deal. If the vendor won't budge on something you know is worth much less, feel free to roll your eyes and affect the do-you-think-I'm-a-fool hand gesture: Bring fingers to thumb, palms pointing upward, then wag the hand back and forth (toward you, then away from you). This can be done with one hand, or—for full effect—with both. A little local color might go a long way. On the other hand, while haggling works, it can't be done everywhere. The prices in retail stores are usually fixed (*prezzo fisso*) and are often indicated as such with handmade signs in display windows or near registers. In these cases, getting a discount can be virtually impossible, though you may be able to score a two-for-one deal at a smaller, family-run boutique during the big, annual end-of-season sales when stores are eager to move old merchandise out and make way for the new lines. Be sure not to let a bargain become a bust; some items may be stretched out, broken, or dirty by the time the sell-off begins. It's also very important that you get a receipt (*scontrino*) from every store where you've bought, as you and the shop owner can each be held liable—and fined—if there's no record of your purchase. God only knows why the Italian government puts the onus on the customer for this one, but it does: Every merchant fears the dreaded fiscal police, who occasionally drop in—or waylay pedestrians—checking for receipts. Minding your *scontrino* will also help you ensure that a shop isn't charging you more than what's on the tag. Sad to say it, but those *prezzi fissi* are occasionally "readjusted" by salesmen at purchase time.

One-stop shopping... Romans are rabid shoppers, but even they get tired of meandering from store to store to comparison-shop. If they must shop in a department store, many prefer the tried and true **Rinascente.** Occupying a 5-floor palazzo on the Via del Corso, Rinascente is the place to go for pretty dresses, conservative suits, and quality accessories for men and women. What's more, the store is open every night of the week, including Sunday, until 10pm: unheard of in Italy. **Coin,** which operates three stores in the city, features Italian, French, and American name brands, good deals at the makeup counter, and an overwhelming selection of goodies in the accessories section. The branch in the Lateran neighborhood also has a top-floor cafe/restaurant with a view over San Giovanni in Laterano, good for brunch or evening cocktails. The shopping mall is still quite a new concept in Italy, but the **Centro Commerciale Cinecittà Due** has been reeling them in since 1988 with great success. Most of the 100 stores featured here are the same chains you'll see on the Via del Corso, but thankfully the price tags reflect suburban storefront rents instead of urban ones.

Dressing to the nines... Rome's lavish *alta moda* boutiques stretch along Via Condotti and the other small streets between the Spanish Steps and the Via del Corso, and they're as much a part of many travelers' itineraries as the Colosseum or St. Peter's. Hip Japanese tourists have been known to line up outside of **Prada** and **Gucci** well before opening hours, waiting to get their hands on the newest in overpriced club duds. **Valentino Uomo/Donna,** one of the few Italian designers to keep his headquarters in Rome, has a pretentious 2-floor boutique connected by a red-carpeted staircase more intimidating than any of the store's salesmen-slash-bodyguards. Another design family that keeps things local is **Fendi,** creator of the ubiquitous "double-F" logo and the much-heralded "baguette" bag from a few seasons back. Fendi caters to ladies who lunch—the ones who still wear fur and big, gaudy sunglasses (coincidentally, looking a whole lot like Fendi's current head designer, Karl Lagerfeld). Meanwhile, the third-generation of the Fendi family—Maria Teresa, Federica, and Maria Ilaria—has its own, smarter line, **Fendissime** (very Fendi). Other VIPs of the Italian design world, like **Dolce & Gabbana, Giorgio Armani, Missoni,** and **Versace,** keep a high-profile presence in the fashion district, while the big names in accessories—**Bottega Veneta** and **Furla**—are just off the Corso. If you'd rather shop for a lot of labels at the same time, check out **Gente.** Here you can find original couture pieces from all the best labels. Looking for designer clothes at cut-rate prices? If secondhand shopping doesn't give you the heebie-jeebies, visit the **Atelier Ritz,** a twice-monthly market where chic Romans unload everything from Valentino gowns to Prada slippers to Francesco Biasia handbags. Because these items are from previous seasons, Roman *fashionistas* no longer have a use for them. All the better for you—most things look like they've never been worn.

Every girl's crazy 'bout a sharp-dressed man... Trade in those sweatpants, already! Roman men primp and preen just as much as the women do, giving way to dozens of stores specializing in custom-made shirts and suits, haberdashery, and masculine accessories. With more than 50 years in the business, **Brioni** is one of the best-known names in men's *haute couture.* Pick up classic ties, sober suits, or even something in suede, safe in the knowledge that these guys designed Pierce Brosnan's dapper clothing for recent James Bond flicks. Now all you need is a snazzy BMW. If you can manage to spit out the name of **Ermenegildo Zegna**—another big-timer on the menswear scene—then you're well on your way to shopping for ready-to-wear suits and accessories. Zegna also stocks casual shirts and pants, in case you're in the market for a $200 polo shirt. When politicians need to dress the part, they stop by **Davide Cenci,** a popular place for custom-made men's shirts and suits just down the street from the Palazzo Montecitorio (Rome's parliament building). Meanwhile, younger guys go for the clean lines and sharp looks at **Testa.** Unable to spend time getting measured? You can save time and money at **David Saddler,** an off-the-rack clothier with a decent selection of work shirts, casual pants, and belts. Saddler has several locations throughout the city, all of which sell basically the same stuff—but the one on Via del Corso is open daily (even on Mondays) until at least 8pm. For name-brand bargains, you can go through the racks at **VestiAStock.** If you're lucky, you'll find a chic cast-off from Valentino or Armani—but double-check for flaws before you buy. For a nice tie or two, stop by **La Cravatta su Misura,** where the choices are limitless. Also check out **Etro.** Pricey, yes—but its bright signature ties in florals and paisleys are unmistakable.

Hot (no, not haute) couture... You've gotta move fast to keep up with the changing Italian fashion picture. But a few guidelines can help you try to compete. Most young Romans wouldn't be caught dead wearing their mothers' designer duds, preferring to pick up one-of-a-kind (or what they think are one-of-a-kind) items from lesser labels. Italian mega-trendsetter **Diesel** is the first and last name in cool for teenagers and 20-somethings, selling jeans and casual urban wear with a high-tech slant. Paint-splattered jeans and barely there tops are the big sellers at cutesy **Fiorucci**—if Britney Spears were Italian, she'd probably shop here—while **Onyx** gets away with selling T-shirts and flimsy accessories for teens with more flash than cash. **Energie** sells an assortment of sportswear and clothing from popular brands like Diesel and Kappa in a techno-blaring storefront on Via del Corso. For those who prefer more subtle stylings, **Ethic** is the place to go. Floral dresses, colorful capri pants, and classic skirts in funky patterns are the rage here. Young dandies shop at **Empresa,** which has a selection of suits as well as hip sweaters and footwear for men. Meanwhile, Trussardi's line for the younger fashion set is available at the all new **T'Store.**

Doing the Imelda Marcos thing... Women who encounter Rome's abundant, sexy selection of footwear for the first time may think they've died and gone to hell, because only Satan would provide such a mouth-watering choice of shoes and boots and so little time to choose from among them. **Salvatore Ferragamo** is known on both sides of the drink as the purveyor of glamorous, classic-style pumps, while **Bruno Magli** remains the king of easy loafers and dress shoes for men. Spanish chain **Camper** started the whole bowling-shoe-as-fashion-statement look, and its new store right on Piazza di Spagna sells colorful versions for both sexes. **Dominici** on Via del Corso and **Loco** in Campo de' Fiori both offer a range of sandals, mules, and boots in snakeskin, pony, or dyed leather. You'll pay a bit more for their unique looks, but it'll be well worth it when you stand out from the pack back home. On the other hand, if you want to look like everyone else, affordable knock-offs of all the latest styles are prevalent throughout the city. Stock up at **Romy Shop** or **Bata.** If you just can't find anything that fits, you may want to head to one of Rome's best-known shoe shops, **Carlotto Rio,** where the footwear is made to order. No doubt, Rio's custom-made shoes cost a bit more, but the craftsmanship is well worth it, if you've got time to spare.

Tuning in to the leather channel... Make no mistake: Italians love leather. Almost every store you'll encounter is going to have some sort of leather item on sale, be it a jacket, a handbag, or a pair of gloves. If you just can't get enough of that tanned cowhide smell, your first stop should be at **Skin** to check out its leather jackets for men and women and luxe accessories. Italian favorite **Sermoneta** has an astounding selection of shoes and gloves for women. Check out **Ibiz,** a tiny artisan shop in Campo de' Fiori, where leather goods such as wallets and briefcases are made-to-order in the adjoining workshop. If leather is more of a lifestyle than an occasional indulgence for you, pop into **Eventi,** a shop with a selection of naughtier goods—such as bustiers and chaps—geared to Rome's fashion-forward gay community. The store has a quasi–locker room theme, with tiled walls and dressing rooms designed to look like shower stalls.

Lords of the Fleas... Noisy crowds, junky *banche* (stalls), and some altogether unsavory characters are what you'll encounter at Rome's popular Sunday flea market at **Porta Portese.** Sort through tables of second-hand clothes, boxes of old postcards, racks of CDs (some counterfeit, some legit), furniture, vases, kitchen appliances, and trashy trinkets. Worthwhile finds are few and far between, even though there's at least a mile of junk to pick through. However, you may be able find a bargain in the early hours or late in the afternoon, when vendors are trying to unload their wares. A lot of these same merchants spend their weekdays at the market at **Via Sannio.** Claustrophobes and late sleepers who'd rather avoid the chaos of Porta Portese can find good deals on leather jackets, bright scarves, military goods, and soccer jerseys. A parking garage off the Via Veneto houses the **Underground,** a monthly market full of the usual schlock, as well as jewelry, silverware, and brass knobs. Find the best selection of antiquarian books (in Italian, English, French, and other languages), back issues of magazines, and art prints at the **Mercato delle Stampe,** just off Via del Corso.

How 'bout them apples?... True, some Romans have been lured away by convenient, suburban supermarkets—but, a majority of the city still does its grocery shopping in the local *alimentari* and fresh meat and produce markets. Big vats of Cerignola and other oil-cured olives, sacks of dry herbs, and ripe fruits and vegetables by the crate-full are just a few of the finds at **Campo de' Fiori,** a daily (except Sunday) market that's liable to make first-time foodie visitors faint. Although the cobblestones in the piazza were dug up and refitted during the year leading up to 2000 (causing the market to take a brief hiatus), not much has changed here since the 16th century. Everyone, from local chefs to pilgrims, rubs elbows in the Campo, eager to get their hands on some choice artichokes or an *etto* (just short of a quarter-pound) or two of the finest *porcini* mushrooms. Despite its name, the Campo de' Fiori wasn't named for the stalls of flower at the end of the square, but rather for the field of wildflowers that once grew here—before the pope paved over it during the mid-15th century, that is. Whereas a stroll in the Campo de' Fiori can make for an easygoing morning, a visit to **Piazza Vittorio** can be a nightmare. Long taken over by the large immigrant population living in the Esquiline area, this busy food market (open daily except Sunday, from about 6am until 2pm) is the place to pick up exotic spices, fresh fish, and a shawarma on the fly—but only if you can handle the maddening crowds and cutthroat lines, in which regulars often try to cut. In the middle of all of this chaos sits a once-tranquil little park that's rarely used because it's hidden by the market. City authorities have been debating for years about whether the market should be moved elsewhere so that local residents can reclaim the park, but at press time it was still operating in its longtime location. If the hustle and bustle of these markets gets you down, you can always head outside the Centro to the covered market in **Piazza Testaccio,** where locals—but very few tourists—pick up the best Roman produce (open daily except Sunday, from about 6am until 2pm) for less than elsewhere. The only tourists you'll find at the small market in **Piazza delle Coppelle** (open 6am to 2pm) are the ones who made a wrong turn at the Pantheon. The produce here is superb, and so are the quiet, medieval surroundings. Flower fiends should head to the **Mercato dei Fiori** near the Vatican (open 6am to 2pm) for a jaw-dropping selection of fresh cut flowers and potted plants. But remember: You can't take any of these items home to America. Customs regulations forbid it.

Incredible edibles... Caught at the last minute without

a gift? Wine, balsamic vinegar, olive oil, decorative pasta, and other packaged goods are guaranteed to excite anyone with a working set of tastebuds. **Castroni,** a Roman *alimentari* (deli) with several branches around the city, is where many expat locals go to get comfort foods from home. It's also a one-stop shop for Italian coffee, sweets, pasta, and liqueurs. **Buccone,** one of the city's top wine sellers (see "Divine wines" below), also carries fancy bottles of vinegar and *limoncello* (a lemon-flavored, after-dinner drink with a high alcohol content) and jars of truffles, olive spreads, and other delights. After downing a shot of some of the best espresso in the city, pick up a package of ground coffee or chocolate-covered espresso beans from **Sant'Eustachio** [see Dining]. Got a sweet tooth? Make a beeline for **Pasticceria Valzani** [see Dining], where you can choose from just about every pastry imaginable, or **La Bottega del Cioccolato,** a chocolate lover's dream. Creations here are almost too pretty to eat—think bon-bons in the shape of animals, flowers, and even St. Peter's—but that sun's hot, right? They're not gonna last long, so you might as well snarf 'em before they melt.

Divine wines... Smart tourists who find the Tridente area's road-less-traveled—the Via Ripetta—will be rewarded with finding **Buccone;** every kind of red and white wine under the Italian sun, including even some million-lira vintages of Brunello, lines its shelves. **Mr. Wine,** the favorite *enoteca* of parliamentarians (it's across the street from Rome's parliament building), stocks an equally big range of both moderately priced and expensive wines. Oenophiles shouldn't miss **Trimani,** either. Founded in 1821, it's Rome's oldest, most beloved wine vendor, with approximately 3,000 vintages in stock, including wines from every region in Italy. Wine lovers who want to keep things kosher can pick up a bottle or two from **Kasher,** a tiny shop in the Jewish quarter.

The family jewels... Rome's answer to Tiffany's is **Bulgari,** the classic designer of hauter-than-thou necklaces, bracelets, and rings, all done in plenty of gold and precious gems. The bright, beaded bracelets and unique chokers in the display window outside of **Danae** are enough to make you want to check out the modern, creative wares inside. Silver is the specialty of **Gioielli Mateul,** a small boutique in the Ghetto, Rome's traditional jeweler's district. For gold in the Ghetto, stop by **Finocchiaro,** where you can splurge on fine necklaces and bracelets in white or yellow gold or buy whimsical charms of local landmarks. Cross the river to Trastevere to find chunky, handmade jewelry; **Pandora** sells jewelry made from recycled items and large, flawed gems to girls with attitude. Or, while you're in the neighborhood, drop by **Guaytamelli,** which specializes in—get this—wearable sun dials. A sun dial watch or ring is guaranteed to be a conversation (time)piece!

Slip into something more comfortable... The display window at **Intimissimi** usually features a revolving mannequin torso outfitted in the skimpiest, butt-baring thong—enough to make most women with a hint of cellulite run in the other direction. Nevertheless, this popular lingerie store with branches all over the city has reasonably priced bras, panties, and slips for femmes who enjoy a bit of lace and a punch of color. Similarly, the nearby **Etam** shop sells colorful underwear, as well as matching sleepwear and Turkish cotton robes. **La Perla,** the luxury lingerie and swimwear manufacturer from Bologna, is one of the few stores that could inspire you to purchase an $80 silk G-string.

Shopping for the *bambini*... Even though Italy has one of the lowest birth rates in Europe, the capital city has a number of stores that will help you spoil your son, daughter, niece, or nephew. **Città del Sole** sells rocking horses, activity blankets, kites, chess sets, and bins of toys and trinkets. **Berte,** right on Piazza Navona, is packed with traditional-looking wooden toys, games, and decorations for the baby's room. Unfortunately, the shop employs a snobby look-but-don't-touch policy; come only if you know exactly what you want to buy before you get inside. At the other end of the square is the wildly popular stuffed-animal emporium **Al Sogno.** Children love the jungle and farm scenes all laid out in plush. If you really want to make sure that your kid is embarrassingly photographed wearing the most frou-frou outfit possible, check out **Lavori Artigianali Femminili (LAF),** specializing in prissy handmade dresses and cutesy clothing for kids up to eight years old. On the other hand, if the little one is more rough-and-tumble you can get good deals at **Benetton 012,** a store for babies up to 12-year-olds. Up-and-coming clothesmongers will be happy to wear the latest and greatest from **Pure** or **Raphael, Jr.** too—as long as Mommy and Daddy can afford it.

The Old and the Beautiful... Antiques hounds won't have trouble finding something to do in Rome. **Marmi Line,** on the city's main antiques artery (the Via de' Coronari), has a jumbled assortment of restored marble columns, busts, and fountains. **W Apolloni,** specializing in silver and 17th-century furniture, is one of Rome's best-known antiques stores. If you're looking for collectibles from the 20th century, including Art Deco designs, **Comics Bazar** is bound to have it. The unusual **Animalier e Oltre** deals in all things inspired by animals, from vases to jewelry. Of course, if you have a good eye for antiques, your best bet may be to simply head for one of the local flea markets like **Porta Portese,** where haggling is acceptable.

Interior motives... Travelers who are into home decorating should have no problem finding one-of-a-kind stuff in Rome. You'll have to endure grumpy old saleswomen (and a few young, jaded ones too) at **Leone Limentani** if you want a chance to buy the stores' ceramics and crystal at warehouse prices. **C.U.C.I.N.A.** is where Romans go to pick up inexpensive tableware, cooking utensils, and basic kitchen towels, tablecloths, and aprons. Yuppies are attracted to the modern restaurant and bookstore concept called **'Gusto** [see Dining]. The smallish storefront has a selection of decorative kitchen gadgets, hand-crank and electric pasta makers, and shelves of cookbooks. For homewares, Carla Fendi swears by **TAD,** which stocks everything from cherry furniture to Egyptian linens and vases made from colorful pieces of broken tile. If you're snobby enough to insist on *haute couture* bed linens and tablecloths, then **Frette** is the store for you. However, embroidered sheets and pillowcases from **Lavori Artigianali Femminili,** are lovely and much less expensive (read: a great gift for Grandma). For the rest of the trimmings, try **Crocianelli,** a fabric and interiors store packed with *passementerie*—that's French for "little things that you don't need to spend your money on, but what the hell—you're in Rome."

Holy Ornaments... If you're in the market for, say, a priest's robe, a miter (the tall, ornate, triangle-shaped cap traditionally worn by bishops), or a jewel-encrusted goblet for communion, head to Via de' Cestari, a small street just steps from the Pantheon, considered by some the Rodeo Drive of religious articles. There are no less than 10 shops here selling everything you would need to hold your own liturgical services. **Ghezzi** is a particularly good shop, selling robes in more colors than there were in Joseph's dreamcoat, as well as cozy sweaters and appropriately frowzy pajamas for nuns. **De Ritis** also sells Godly garb, including made-to-order vestments and a whole range of sacred statues. Pilgrims near the Vatican who want the latest in "pope-pourri" should peruse the wares of **Comandini.** Postcards, small pope sculptures, lighters sporting the likeness of famous saints, or Padre Pio playing cards are just a few items you may be able to pick up. Finally, for still more religious books and icons, head to **Libreria Coletti,** a friendly store across the street from San Giovanni in Laterano.

Nooks of (English) books... Ever since Keats took off for Rome in hopes of curing his consumption (sadly, it didn't work—check out the Protestant Cemetery), the city has been a hot spot for expat Brits to settle down. This Anglo presence is most obvious at **The English Bookshop,** a charming little book nook near Piazza del Popolo. Many of the city's British residents head here for the latest fiction paperbacks and fashion mags. It's also an ideal place to pick up books about Rome, including children's books—and all in the King's English. The **Libreria del Viaggiatore,** on a quiet side street just off Campo de' Fiori, is a must for travelers from the States and all over Europe. Not only does this travel bookstore stock just about every book on Rome one could hope to find (in English, Italian, German, French, and other languages too), but it also sells a wide selection of English guidebooks for other European destinations to help you plan that last-minute flight of fancy. **Bibli,** a sizable bookstore and coffee shop, is a favorite Trastevere hangout, carrying thousands of titles—some of them in English.

The Index

Al Sogno. A world of plush stuffed animals, arranged in inventive layouts.... *Tel 06/686 41 98. Piazza Navona 53, buses 46, 62, 64, 70, 81, 87, 90, 90b, 116, 186, 492.* **(see p. 145)**

Animalier e Oltre. A menagerie of animal-inspired antiques.... *Tel 06/320 82 82. Via Margutta 47, Metro Flaminio or Spagna.* **(see p. 146)**

Atelier Ritz. Monthly flea market featuring outcast clothing from Rome's elite.... *Tel 06/807 81 89, Via Frescobaldi 5 (Hotel Parco dei Principi), buses 52, 53, 910, tram 30.* **(see pp. 136, 139)**

Bata. Italian chain selling cool, comfy shoes for men and women.... *Tel 06/482 45 29. Via Nazionale, 88 A, buses 70, 71.* **(see p. 141)**

Benetton 012. Colorful, children's wear from the household name design house.... *Tel 06/687 10 08. Via del Corso 315, buses 56, 60, 62, 85, 90, 95, 492.* **(see p. 146)**

Berte. Wooden mobiles, cribs, handpainted toys, and more. A look-but-don't-touch toy store.... *Tel 06/687 50 11, Piazza Navona 107, buses 46, 62, 64, 70, 81, 87, 186, 492.* **(see p. 145)**

Bibli. A multifunction bookshop in the heart of Trastevere. Has English language titles, a tea room, and an Internet cafe. *Tel 06/588 40 97. Via dei Fienaroli 28, tram 8 to Piazza Sonnino.* **(see p. 148)**

Bottega Veneta. Leather goods and accessories for the more adventurous trendsetter.... *Tel 06/68 80 97 13, Piazza San Lorenzo in Lucina 8, buses 35, 56, 60, 85, 116.* **(see p. 139)**

Brioni. Classic suits, shirts, and accessories for men, plus expert tailoring.... *Tel 06/484 517, www.brioni.it. Via Barberini 79, Metro Barberini.* **(see p. 140)**

Bruno Magli. Favorite footwear of Italian playboys and O.J.... *Tel 06/488 43 55, Via Veneto 70, Metro Barberini.* **(see p. 141)**

Buccone. Packed to the ceiling with wine from every region, extra-virgin olive oil, balsamic vinegar, and packaged foodstuffs. Best place to find the perfect gift for the foodie on your list.... *Tel 06/361 21 54. Via di Ripetta 19–20, Metro Flaminio.* **(see p. 144)**

Bulgari. Rome's biggest name in jewelry, a kind of Italian Tiffany's.... *Tel 06/679 38 76. Via Condotti 10, Metro Spagna.* **(see p. 144)**

C.U.C.I.N.A. Rome's 1-stop shop for kitchen appliances, cookbooks, and cookware. Small, warehouse-like environment keeps prices low.... *Tel 06/679 12 75. Via Mario de'Fiori 65, Metro Spagna.* **(see p. 146)**

Camper. Cool, casual footwear for men and women from slick Spanish retailer.... *Tel 06/69 925 678. Piazza di Spagna 72, Metro Spagna.* **(see p. 141)**

Campo de' Fiori. Famous produce market in the heart of the Centro Storico.... *No telephone. Piazza Campo de' Fiori, buses 44, 46, 56, 60, 62, 64, 70, 81, 492 and others to Largo Argentina, tram 8. Open Mon–Sat roughly 6am–2pm.* **(see p. 143)**

Carlotto Rio. Classic shoes and handbags at traditionally steep prices. Can also make shoes to order.... *Tel 06/687 23 08. Via dell'Arco della Ciambella 8, buses 64, 70, 75, 116.* **(see p. 141)**

Castroni. Ethnic foods alongside bins of Italian goodies. A Roman institution.... *Tel 06/39 72 32 79. Via Ottaviano 55, Metro Ottaviano.* **(see p. 144)**

Centro Commerciale Cinecittà Due. Rome's answer to the suburban shopping mall.... *Tel 06/722 09 10. Viale Palmiro Togliatti 2, Metro Cinecittà.* **(see p. 138)**

Città del Sole. Toys, puzzles, and games for kids of all ages.... *Tel 06/687 54 04. Via della Scrofa 65, buses 64, 70, 75, 116.* **(see p. 145)**

Coin. Italy's biggest department store chain, selling clothing for men, women, and children. Good finds in the jewelry and accessories departments. See also Coin branches at Via Mantova 1 (Porta Pia) and Via Cola di Rienzo 173 (Prati).... *Tel 06/708 00 20, www.coin.it. Piazzale Appio 7, Metro San Giovanni.* **(see p. 138)**

Comandini. Papal souvenirs and gifts. Lots of kitsch.... *Tel 06/687 50 79. Borgo Pio 151, Metro Ottaviano.* **(see p. 147)**

Comics Bazar. Bawdy furniture from the 1700s, collectibles from the 1940s, and lots of other stuff from the years in between.... *Tel 06/688 02 923. Via dei Banchi Vecchi 127, buses 23, 41, 46, 62 64, 65, 280.* **(see p. 146)**

Crocianelli. A wide variety of tassels, braids, frogs, fringes, and more for your home.... *Tel 06/687 35 92. Via dei Prefetti 37–40, buses 35, 56, 60, 85, 116.* **(see p. 147)**

Danae. Chain mail and silver bracelets, beaded necklaces, and other jewelry, all designed in-house. Unique work with gemstones.... *Tel 06/679 18 81. Via della Maddalena 40, buses 64, 70, 75, 116.* **(see p. 145)**

Davide Cenci. Classic, made-to-order outfitter of men's shirts and suits; in business since 1926.... *Tel 06/699 06 81.*

Via Campo Marzio 1–7, buses 56, 60, 116, 492.
(see p. 140)

David Saddler. Men's retail store with an especially nice selection of shirts; many larger sizes.... *Tel 06/871 98 819. Via del Corso 103, buses 35, 52, 53, 56, 58, 60, 61, 71, 85, 116.* **(see p. 140)**

De Ritis. Loads of liturgical items. But expect surly glances if you're not a man or woman of the cloth.... *Tel 06/686 58 43. Via de' Cestari 48, buses 64, 70, 75, 116.*
(see p. 147)

Diesel. For Roman teens, the ultimate jeans to have on your behind.... *Tel 06/678 66 41. Via del Corso 185, buses 35, 52, 53, 56, 58, 60, 61, 71, 85, 116.*
(see p. 140)

Dolce & Gabbana. Sex-goddess chic meets Catholic schoolgirl. A favorite of Madonna's.... *Tel 06/678 29 90. Via Borgognona 7d, Metro Spagna.* **(see p. 139)**

Dominici. Bold, youthful selection of footwear and clothing.... *Tel 06/361 05 91. Via del Corso 14, Metro Flaminio or Spagna.* **(see p. 141)**

Empresa. Hip, young men and their hip, young girlfriends visit for quality suits, the latest shirts and sweaters, and trendy shoes. Quite expensive.... *Tel 06/683 24 28. Via dei Giubbonari 25/26, buses 44, 46, 56, 60, 62, 64, 70, 81, 492, and others to Largo Argentina, tram 8.*
(see p. 141)

Energie. Assorted urban streetwear for girls and boys.... *Tel 06/687 12 58. Via del Corso 408–409, buses 35, 56, 60, 85, 116, Metro Flaminio.* **(see p. 141)**

The English Bookshop. Large selection of English-language fiction and nonfiction, as well as British and American periodicals. Great travel and children's sections.... *Tel 06/320 33 01. Via di Ripetta 248, Metro Flaminio.*
(see p. 147)

Ermenegildo Zegna. Master men's couture tailor. Easy urban suits to elegant tuxedos, plus a wide range of ties, belts, and casual wear.... *Tel 06/678 91 43, www.ezegna.com. Via Borgognona 7E, Metro Spagna.* **(see p. 140)**

Etam. Wide range of bright lingerie and comfortable sleepwear.... *Tel 06/69 29 31 95. Via del Corso 170/171, buses 35, 52, 53, 56, 58, 60, 61, 71, 85, 116.* **(see p. 145)**

Ethic. Funky duds you can wear from work to the wine bar without changing.... *Tel 06/68 30 10 63. Piazza Benedetto Cairoli 11/12, buses 44, 46, 56, 60, 62, 64, 70, 81, 492, and others to Largo Argentina, tram 8.* **(see p. 141)**

Etro. Funky, distinctive clothing and accessories for men and women. Especially bright ties.... *Tel 06/678 82 57. Via del Babuino 102, Metro Spagna.* **(see p. 140)**

Eventi. Cheeky shop for club kids. The perfect place to pick up some suede chaps, a studded belt—or a stud.... *Tel 06/36 00 25 33. Via della Fontanella 8, Metro Flaminio.* **(see p. 142)**

Fendi. Now and forever the "it" brand for Rome's ladies who power-lunch.... *Tel 06/679 76 41. Via Borgognona 36A/39, Metro Spagna.* **(see p. 139)**

Fendissime. Younger, hipper line of clothing from the 3rd-generation of the Fendi fashion family.... *Tel 06/69 66 66 54. Via Fontanella di Borghese 56A, buses 35, 56, 60, 85, 116.* **(see p. 139)**

Finocchiaro. Ghetto area goldsmith with wide selection of costume jewelry, plus some interesting handcrafted gifts.... *Tel 06/686 11 77. Via Falegnami 18, buses 23, 44, 56, 60, 65, 75, 170, 710, 774, 780.* **(see p. 145)**

Fiorucci. Lots of midriff-bearing shirts, dyed and studded denim, and over-the-top teen wear. Looking trashy costs more than you'd expect.... *Tel 06/686 54 00. Piazza Benedetto Cairoli 106, buses 44, 46, 56, 60, 62, 64, 70, 81, 492, and others to Largo Argentina, tram 8.* **(see p. 140)**

Frette. Think 300-thread-count linens. Now decide whether you've got $750 to burn on sheets.... *Tel 06/678 68 62. Via del Corso 381, Metro Spagna.* **(see p. 146)**

Furla. Super-slick handbags and accessories.... *Tel 06/36 00 36 19. Via del Corso 481, Metro Spagna.* **(see p. 139)**

Gente. Up-to-date selection from a variety of *alta moda* designers.... *Tel 06/320 76 71. Via del Babuino 81, Metro Spagna.* **(see p. 139)**

Ghezzi. Clothing and gift shop serving the needs of Rome's ecclesiastical community, but anyone else is welcome too.... *Tel 06/686 97 44. Via de'Cestari 32/33, buses 64, 70, 75, 116.* **(see p. 147)**

Gioielli Mateul. Superb silver bracelets and brooches, along with unique, Ming dynasty–inspired jewelry.... *No telephone. Via dei Pettinari 80, buses 23, 65, 280.* **(see p. 145)**

Giorgio Armani. Minimalist chic at maximum prices.... *Tel 06/699 14 61. Via Condotti 77, Metro Spagna.* **(see p. 139)**

Guaytamelli. Sun dials you can wear, plus hourglasses and handcrafted jewelry with an ancient look.... *Tel 06/588 07 04. Via del Moro 59, buses 56, 60, 75, 170, 280, trams 8, 30.* **(see p. 145)**

Gucci. Clothing for all the beautiful people, designed by Texas pretty boy Tom Ford.... *Tel 06/678 93 40. Via Condotti 8, Metro Spagna.* **(see p. 139)**

'Gusto. Got a request to bring home a ravioli maker? This is the place. Also features cookbooks (in Italian and English), kitchen gadgets, and a top-notch restaurant next door.... *Tel 06/322 62 73. Piazza Augusto Imperatore 9, Metro Flaminio.* **(see p. 146)**

Ibiz. Stop in to smell a whiff of leather, then take home a handcrafted briefcase, wallet, or belt and inhale in private. All items crafted in the workshop next door.... *Tel 06/68 30 72 97. Via del Chiavari 39, buses 44, 46, 56, 60,*

62, 64, 70, 81, 492 and others to Largo Argentina, tram 8. **(see p. 142)**

Intimissimi. Classy, lacy skivvies at surprisingly moderate prices.... *Tel [TK ??]. Via del Corso, 167–167/A, buses 35, 52, 53, 56, 58, 60, 61, 71, 85, 116.* **(see p. 145)**

Kasher. Kosher red and white wines.... *No telephone. Via Santa Maria dei Calderari 25, buses 23, 44, 56, 60, 65, 75, 170, 710, 774, 780.* **(see p. 144)**

La Bottega del Cioccolato. Too pretty to eat. Chocolate bon-bons in the shapes of animals, flowers, and even St. Peter's.... *Tel 06/482 14 73. Via Leonina, 82, buses 70, 71.* **(see p. 144)**

La Cravatta su Misura. Choose from dozens of ties in all styles and colors, or have one custom-made in 3 to 5 days.... *Tel 06/699 42 199. Via Seminario 93, buses 64, 70, 75, 116.* **(see p. 140)**

La Perla. The sexiest, laciest bras, panties, and corsets.... *Tel 06/699 41 934. Via Condotti 79, Metro Spagna.* **(see p. 145)**

Lavori Artigianali Femminili (LAF). Fine, handmade children's clothing and linens of silk, lace, and wool, plus yarns and fabrics, too.... *Tel 06/679 29 92. Via Capo le Case 6, Metro Barberini.* **(see pp. 146, 147)**

Leone Limentani. Take a look, then take a number if you want to buy china or crystal from Villeroy Boch, Baccarat, Wedgwood, and other names. Wide selection of pasta bowls and espresso sets also make good gifts.... *Tel 06/68 80 66 86. Via Portico d'Ottavia, buses 47, 23, 44, 56, 60, 65, 75, 170, 710, 774, 780.* **(see p. 146)**

Libreria Coletti. Books, notecards, rosaries, and other Catholic paraphernalia. Most titles are in Italian.... *Tel 06/70 47 54 53. Piazza di San Giovanni in Laterano 38/38A, San Giovanni.* **(see p. 147)**

Libreria del Viaggiatore. Travel bookstore with numerous titles in English. Also sells Roman travelogues by Goethe, Stendhal, and others—in the original languages.... *Tel 06/688 01 048. Via del Pellegrino 78, buses 44, 46, 56, 60, 62, 64, 70, 81, 492, and others to Largo Argentina, tram 8.* **(see p. 147)**

Loco. One-of-a-kind shoes for women who don't have enough.... *Tel 06/688 08 216. Via dei Baullari 22, buses 44, 46, 56, 60, 62, 64, 70, 81, 492, and others to Largo Argentina, tram 8.* **(see p. 141)**

Marmi Line. Wide selection of restored marble antiques. Will ship anywhere in the world.... *Tel 06/689 37 95. Via de' Coronari 113–141/145, buses 41, 280.* **(see p. 146)**

Max & Co. Younger, hipper line of MaxMara. Affordable suits, unique sweaters, and shoes.... *Tel 06/678 79 46. Via Condotti 46, Metro Spagna.* **(see p. 137)**

MaxMara. Work and resort wear for women.... *Tel 06/69 92 21 04. Via Condotti 17–19A, Metro Spagna.* **(see p. 137)**

Mercato dei Fiori. Indoor market with 2 floors of flowers near the Vatican.... *No telephone. Via Trionfale 45, buses 23, 70, Metro Ottaviano. Open Mon–Sat roughly 6am–2pm.* **(see p. 143)**

Mercato delle Stampe. Market of used and antiquarian books, prints, and magazines. Open Mon–Sat 7:30am–noon (approximately).... *No telephone. Largo della Fontanella di Borghese, bus 119.* **(see p. 142)**

Missoni. The originator of colorful Italian knitwear.... *Tel 06/679 25 55. Piazza di Spagna 78, Metro Spagna.* **(see p. 139)**

Mr. Wine. The preferred wine seller of Rome's parliamentarians; across street from the parliament building.... *Tel 06/68 13 41 41. Piazza del Parlamento 7, buses 119, 913.* **(see p. 144)**

Onyx. Hippie/techno wear for junior-high girls.... *Tel 06/679 15*

09. Via del Corso 132/Via Frattina 91, buses 35, 56, 60, 85, 116, Metro Spagna. **(see p. 141)**

Oviesse. Combo dime/department store, occasionally with good copies of the season's accessories. Perfume and toiletries section is sizable; the baby clothes are cheap and unique.... *Tel 06/589 53 42. Viale Trastevere 62/64, tram 8.* **(see p. 137)**

Pandora. Trastevere's funky Bohemian set look to this tiny shop for handmade rings, bracelets, scarves, and other knick-knacks. Look for the door decorated with recycled mirrors and glass.... *Tel 06/581 71 45. Piazza Santa Maria in Trastevere 6, buses 56, 60, 75, 170, 280, trams 8, 30.* **(see p. 145)**

Piazza delle Coppelle. Quaint produce market on a medieval street near the Pantheon.... *No telephone. Piazza delle Coppelle, buses 64, 70, 75, 116. Open Mon–Sat roughly 6am–2pm.* **(see p. 143)**

Piazza Testaccio. Covered produce market in a neighborhood off the tourist track.... *No telephone. Piazza Testaccio, Metro Piramide. Open Mon–Sat roughly 6am–2pm.* **(see p. 143)**

Piazza Vittorio. Rome's largest meat and produce market. Large selection of ethnic foods.... *No telephone. Piazza Vittorio Emanuele, Metro Vittorio Emanuele. Open Mon–Sat roughly 6am–2pm.* **(see p. 143)**

Porta Portese. From personal treasures to guilty pleasures, vendors at Rome's biggest open-air flea market sell everything: African wood carvings, secondhand clothes, bicycles, and loads more.... *No telephone. Between Via Portuense and Via Ippolito Nievo, buses 170, 280, 718, 719, tram 30, Metro Piramide. Open Sun roughly 6am–3pm.* **(see pp. 135, 136, 142, 146)**

Prada. Hipper-than-thou Italian design house catering to wealthy waifs and wallflowers. Great view of the Spanish Steps from the balcony—if you can sneak past security.... *Tel 06/679 08 97. Via Condotti 92–5, Metro Spagna.* **(see p. 139)**

Pure. The place to outfit little tykes in Armani and other designer duds. Window display is always whimsical; also sells some toys and accessories.... *Tel 06/679 45 55. Via Frattina 111, Metro Spagna.* **(see p. 146)**

Raphael, Jr. Designer clothes for stylish kids.... *No telephone. Via Veneto 98, Metro Barberini.* **(see p. 146)**

Rinascente. Rome's main department store specializing in men and women's ready-to-wear. No shoe, luggage, or children's departments, however.... *Tel 06/679 76 91, www.rinascente.it. Largo Chigi 20, buses 35, 52, 53, 56, 58, 60, 61, 71, 85, 116.* **(see p. 138)**

Romy Shop. Perhaps Rome's largest selection of shoes and boots, mostly knock-offs of the season's hot styles.... *Tel 06/683 27 69. Via del Corso 404, buses 35, 56, 60, 85, 116.* **(see p. 141)**

Salvatore Ferragamo. Long a trusted name in women's heels and boots.... *Tel 06/679 15 65. Via Condotti 73–74, Metro Spagna.* **(see p. 141)**

Sermoneta. Trendy bags, shoes, and accessories that both mothers and daughters can agree on.... *Tel 06/679 46 89. Corso Vittorio Emanuele 43, buses 44, 46, 56, 60, 62, 64, 70, 81, 492, and others to Largo Argentina, tram 8.* **(see p. 142)**

Sisley. Trendy men's and women's casual wear and denim; part of the Benetton label since 1974.... *Tel 06/684 19 5. Via Condotti 19B, Metro Spagna.* **(see p. 137)**

Skin. Sumptuous leather jackets and handbags at steep prices.... *Tel 06/678 55 31. Via Capo la Case 41, Metro Spagna.* **(see p. 142)**

TAD. Italian and imported furniture, decorative mirrors and frames, vases, boxes, baskets, and accoutrements for the home. Friendly and (relatively) affordable.... *Tel 06/321 67 52. Via di S. Giacomo 5, Metro Spagna.* **(see p. 146)**

Testa. Modern suits, colorful ties, and hip leather goods for men.... *Tel 06/679 06 60. Via Frattina 42, Metro Spagna.* **(see p. 140)**

Trimani. Opened in 1821, this place knows wine. More than 3,000 varieties, plus a wine bar next door.... *Tel 06/446 96 61. Via Goito 20, Metro Termini.* **(see p. 144)**

T'Store. Trussardi's younger, yet hardly less-expensive, clothing line.... *No telephone. Via del Corso 477/478, Metro Spagna.* **(see p. 141)**

Underground. Once-monthly market held in parking lot near the Spanish Steps. Lots of vintage jewelry, political and religious knick-knacks like buttons, signs, and decorative plates, and everyday junk.... *Tel 06/36 00 53 45. Via Francesco Crispi 96, bus 95, Metro Spagna or Barberini.* **(see p. 142)**

United Colors of Benetton. Superstore branch often has overstock of men's and women's clothing, thus good sales.... *Tel 06/699 24 010. Via Cesare Battisti 129–131 (Piazza Venezia), buses 44, 94, 710, 718, 719.* **(see p. 137)**

Upim. Low-cost department store ideal for toiletries, inexpensive tools, and kitchen items.... *Tel 06/446 55 79. Piazza di Santa Maria Maggiore, buses 16, 27, 70, 71.* **(see p. 137)**

Valentino Uomo/Donna. The Roman couturier's flagship store.... *Tel 06/678 36 56. Via Condotti 13, Metro Spagna.* **(see p. 139)**

Versace. Flamboyant, sexy line designed by the late Gianni's sister Donatella.... *Tel 06/678 05 21. Via Bocca di Leone 26, Metro Spagna.* **(see p. 139)**

VestiAStock. Culls from overstocked menswear from top international and Italian brands. Hit or miss.... *Tel 06/322 43 91. Via Germanico 170A, Metro Ottaviano.* **(see p. 140)**

Via Sannio. Daily market (Mon–Sat) selling both new and used items. Best buys are leather jackets, vintage cocktail dresses, and soccer jerseys.... *No telephone. Metro SanGiovanni.* **(see pp. 135, 136, 142)**

W Apolloni. Antiques vendor of art and furniture from the 17th century, rare sculpture, and jewelry from various eras. One of Rome's most exclusive antiquarians.... *Tel 06/679 24 29. Via del Babuino 132, Metro Flaminio or Spagna.* **(see p. 146)**

high

6 tlife

A night out in Rome can be as raucous or relaxed as you want it to be. That's the good news; the flip side is that you'll need a lot of energy—and even more cash—to participate. And watch out for those doormen. Even though the *Dolce Vita* was largely a myth, Romans—especially those in charge of the velvet rope at nightclubs—act as though it still exists. At the trendier *discoteche,* a veritable catwalk of characters queue up for entry, all at the mercy of the almighty velvet rope. Even if staff does deign to let you in, you'll instantly be hit for cover charges of as much as 40,000L (about $20)—and that often doesn't even include a drink! Clubs are curiously cliquish, too: Don't be surprised if you're asked to fill out a membership card (*tessera*) when you arrive before gaining entry. Venues that feature live music and/or DJs are required by law to issue these membership cards to guests, but they seem like a complete rip-off, especially when you find yourself buying a monthly or yearly membership to a club that you'll only visit once. Luckily, some places waive the card fee or apply it to the price of your first drink. Once you're inside a *locale* (club), however, you'll also realize just how utterly cheesy the local scene can be. Roman DJs have a tendency to run pop songs into the ground, be they remixed Cher anthems, revved-up Backstreet Boys ballads, or yet *another* rendition of *I Will Survive.* And, more than likely, the most requested songs will be ones that you're already sick of. The "meat market" factor is also present in full force, which means Roman men will be completely unafraid to try their best pick-up lines on the visiting *Americana*; a *Night at the Roxbury* scenario—suave guys double-teaming unsuspecting women on the dance floor—is not uncommon. Gals, bring your patience and your best scowl. Guys will have just as much "fun" trying to attract the dolled-up Italian girls, who are mighty jaded from lifetimes of fending off advances from the opposite sex. Not unlike Paris or New York, some of Rome's best music and dancing is in its gay clubs or on *serate gay* (gay nights) at established discos. Both Testaccio—a regular working-class neighborhood by day—and the Ostiense area adjacent to it set the scene for some of the most exciting gay or occasionally gay venues. Warehouse-style discotheques have popped up all over this area in recycled slaughterhouses and abandoned factories, the most popular of the moment being **L'Alibi.** Meanwhile, **Qube** is the site of the infamous gay/drag queen scene each Friday night called *Muccassassina* (once located at the straight club **Alpheus**). The "killer cow" (not to be confused with mad cow disease) is simultaneously the name of a raucous, all-night dance party *and* the team of DJs from the Circolo Mario Mieli di Cultura Omosessuale

(Mario Mieli Gay Cultural Association) that keep the beats flowing. So, what else is there to do in Rome if you're not a club kid? Plenty, actually. The popularity of Latin music here is at an all-time high right now, not just because of Ricky and Quique but also because of the city's buoyant Caribbean and Latino contingent. More and more Latin-flavored clubs are making the scene, and a number of discos regularly feature salsa, meringue, and Cuban nights, among others. Jazz and blues have long been the nighttime choice of both young and old bohemians, who count on Via Veneto's easy-going **Alexanderplatz Jazz Club** and Trastevere's welcoming **Big Mama** to deliver the goods. Probably the most frustrating thing about going out in Rome is figuring out how to get home. Most of the really cool clubs and discos are far from the city center (hey, at least that ensures a locals-only crowd), and most don't really get going until well after midnight—when public transportation has shut down for the night. Try to arrange for a taxi to pick you up later in the night; a few places have taxi stands right outside them, but most don't. Also, be suspicious of those who claim they're cab drivers but whose cars don't say so. They're likely to take you for a *real* ride, both literally and financially.

Sources

To find information on concerts and club goings-on, pick up ***TimeOut Roma*** at any kiosk (4,000L). The monthly magazine has listings for pubs, discotheques, social clubs, and restaurants—though in Italian only. ***Roma C'è*** (2,000L) comes out each Thursday and includes nightlife listings categorized by neighborhood and genre. It also has a short English-language section called "This Week in Rome," but this is written in broken English and often contains the same listings from week to week. At least you can view it long-distance on the Internet (*www.romace.it*). Newspapers *La Repubblica* and *Il Manifesto* print a weekly listing of Rome venues, usually on Wednesday or Thursday. Also, be on the lookout for fliers advertising raves, dance parties, and other special events in record stores or on pub bulletin boards.

Drinking Prices and Practices

If you're looking for a cheap night out, you might want to stick with wine. Beer prices generally start at 8,000L, and prices for mixed drinks can range anywhere between 8,000 and 16,000L (about $4 to $8), depending on where you go. Another thing to keep in mind is that Italians, in general, don't drink to get drunk. Unlike in, say, Madrid or Edinburgh—where the nightly bar crawl tends to be a spectacle of wobbly-kneed, vomiting students—public drunkenness in Rome is a major *faux pas*. (There are, of course, exceptions at so-called American-style pubs like **Sloppy Sam's** or **The Drunken Ship**; at these places, however, the clientele is mainly foreigners.) That's not to say that Romans don't have fun, they just know their limit. Know yours.

The Lowdown

Livin' *la dolce vita*... The epitome of the oft-superficial glamour that passes for Rome's "sweet life" is **Jackie O,** a legendary club right off the Via Veneto that has been revamped and is making a comeback among the wealthy set. Walk through the imposing wrought-iron gate to the piano bar or discotheque and be...well, pretty unimpressed, to tell the truth. The sterile interior is full of beautiful people who don't know what it means to sweat. **Gilda,** just a couple paces from the Spanish Steps, is likewise all style and no substance. Aging Rita Hayworths with boob jobs and sleazy politicos hobnob here to show off their newest Fendi furs or flaunt their fortunes. A younger generation frequents **Alien,** a full-on disco with a (usually) dance-worthy mix of house and pop music. Most of the rich kids who come here mingle with the peons, but there's an obnoxious VIP room for them if all that slumming gets to be just a bit too much. For the *Pariolini* (due north of Villa Borghese and Via Veneto) who don't want to bother coming all the way into the *Centro Storico,* there's **Max,** a see-and-be-scene that seems to have dropped right out of a Fellini film. Note that if you're actually into this scene, and you're visiting Rome during the heat of summer, you can follow the glamour trail all the way down to the beach: Both Gilda and Alien set up their discos in the coastal town of Fregene when the weather gets too hot to shake it in town.

Making like John Travolta... Of all the discos in Rome, **Ex-Magazzini** certainly gets the most points for coolness. The top floor of this trendy *discoteca* has trippy glass paneling so you can watch the crowd bump and grind below you. **Piper** has lost much of its glossy appeal since it was first opened by Italian pop star Patty Pravo in the

'70s, but it has still managed to hang on to a mixed-age crowd with its diverse music (anything from New Wave to house to electronica) and special parties, fashion shows, and gigs. At **Goa,** you're never sure what kind of crowd you're going to run into. The tribal atmosphere, faintly reminiscent of a desert retreat, is replete with incense and ethnic-inspired decor (which changes every several months) and attracts gay, straight, and transgender dancers for some serious trance and electronica. When not playing host to *Muccassassina,* Rome's most happening gay dance party, **Qube** is a popular student haunt with nightly DJs playing a blend of soul, funk, techno, and electronic music. Meanwhile, **Alpheus,** once the home of *Muccassassina,* still packs in throngs of teens and 20-somethings who writhe to the pop, house, and retro tunes. **Chic & Kitsch** is new on the disco scene in name only. Formerly known as Ciak Dance, this super-stylish club—with all the gold fixtures, marble accents, and tiger/leopard print furniture, a better name might be Chic and Chicer—gets its groove on with heaps of house music, '70s disco, and Top 40 dance tracks.

See-and-be-scene bars... The "triangle of fun" near Piazza Navona holds claim to some of the choicest watering holes in the city. **Bar della Pace** is one of those places that you'll either love or hate. If you're showing off the proper designer labels, the twig-thin waitresses will flash you an ingenuine smile as they serve you your overpriced cocktail. The slightly less self-conscious crowd at **Bar del Fico** sip their drinks under the stars and a gnarly bunch of fig trees, lest they catch glimpses of themselves in the well-placed mirrors indoors. (The play-on-words name, by the way, means both "the bar of the fig" and "the bar of cool.") The most pretentious person you'll encounter at **Jonathan's Angels** will probably be the Italian owner himself. An ex-circus acrobat, owner Nino Madras has decorated his bar with a number of exalted, tongue-in-cheek portraits of himself; the ego has landed—Nino's ego, that is. The rest is inch-upon-inch of pop culture kitsch. The art continues in the restroom, easily one of the most spectacular toilets in all of Europe. Other cool dives in the city include **Bar Taruga,** said to be where Gwyneth, Jude, and Matt hung out while shooting *The Talented Mr. Ripley*—its eclectic, Indian-inspired decor is done up in brights and pastels—and **RipArte**

Café, a minimalist sushi bar where black-clad art snobs go to chill out from their obviously stressful lives. **Le Bain Art Gallery,** a restaurant-slash-lounge with sparse (but sleek) furnishings and pouty waitresses, offers luxe for less (there's no cover) near the Ghetto.

Painting the town pink... Fabulous queens, muscle men, transvestites, and straight-acting gays all flock to Rome's premier gay disco, **L'Alibi,** which has two of the most happening dance floors in the city—even after 25 years in the biz. The interior is a bit decrepit, and the darker nooks even more squalid, but the rooftop terrace and third dance floor create a rather playful atmosphere in the summer for boozing and cruising. American-owned **Hangar** has also been around for quite some time and attracts a considerably more attractive selection of fashionable young gays and lesbians despite (or perhaps because of) its proximity to Termini. The most notorious gay event in town is the *Muccassassina* ("killer cow"), which lasts well into Saturday morning at **Qube** under the artistic direction of drag queen and party promoter Vladimir Luxuria. Another popular gay night at a straight venue is "Stomp," a wild scene at **Piper** every Saturday night where you're sure to find oodles of queens and transgressives (think modern-day Marquis de Sades) in the most outrageous of costumes. **K Men's Club** is the place to find leather-clad studs. Lesbians have fewer nightlife options, but the number is growing; for now, most make due with **New Jolie Coeur,** a private club near the seedy Termini area which hosts a women-only night on Saturdays. **The Jazz Hole,** a laid-back cocktail bar/disco pub, also hosts a *serata lesbica* called "Go Fish" on Tuesdays and Thursdays. Those looking for less of a pick-up scene should head for **Shelter,** a cafe/bar that welcomes gay men and women and eschews the usual meat-market mentality. There are also a lot of one-off events in and around Rome for gay men, women, and transsexuals sponsored by the **Mario Mieli Gay Cultural Association** (tel 06/541 39 85, www.mariomieli.org). **ArciGay** (tel 06/855 55 22, www.arcigay.it) and **ArciLesbica** (tel 06/418 03 69) are also important names to know when exploring Rome's queer scene. Consult these organizations directly for further events information.

All that jazz (and blues)... Like no other musical genre steeped in American traditions, jazz is the one that Europeans, and especially Italians, have embraced. Rome is more than capable of quelling the appetite of its resident jazz fans with a handful of clubs. If you're searching for that commercialized, tweed jacket kind of jazz, then the **Alexanderplatz Jazz Club** is for you. This venue near the Vatican regularly hosts the biggest names in American and Italian jazz and blues and is one of the most respected nightspots in the city. **Big Mama,** a blues haunt in Trastevere, is down and dirtier, with a regular clientele of bohemians and daily performances from mostly local artists, some of whom are starving artists from the States. If you can ever figure out exactly when **Stardust** is open—some nights it opens at 6pm, some nights at 9pm, some nights it decides not to open at all—you'll be treated to lively doses of jazz, funk, and blues. The bare-bones Trastevere club is a musician favorite because of its impromptu jam sessions. If jazz on a Sunday afternoon is more your pace, check out the **New Mississippi Jazz Club,** which, despite the name, has been a fixture in the Vatican/Borgo area for many years.

A good band is hard to find... When it comes to seeing live acts from the pop, rock, and alternative music worlds, Rome is severely lacking. Blame it on laziness—most major bands touring Europe only hop down as far "south" as Milan during their tours, figuring that Rome is too far out of the way. What you often instead get are the leftovers: ridiculous Italian cover bands, rock "discos," and the occasional big budget, megastar shows. Your best bet for live music is at **Brancaleone,** a *centro sociale* that regularly hosts international and domestic alternative and punk bands, home-grown DJs, and drum-and-bass nights known as "Agatha." The DJs at **Villagio Globale,** a left-wing hangout located in one of Testaccio's former slaughterhouses, mix it up with reggae grooves, punk, and political rock. (However, the bathrooms are squalid.) In the summer, there are a number of outdoor concerts here as well. Hard kids with mohawks and tattoos squat at **Forte Prenestino** until a good show comes around, which is fairly often: Big names in the hardcore, punk, and power pop scenes, like Fugazi and the Buzzcocks, have played here. **Black Out** and **Radio Londra** are, for the most part, alternative discos, but they also occasionally feature live rock, hip hop, and alternative acts from around Italy, the United States, and the United Kingdom. For the really big shows—from bands like The Cure or U2—check out the listings for **PalaEUR** and **PalaCisalfa,** two huge sports complexes in the EUR district sometimes tapped for arena-rock concerts [see Entertainment].

Latin spice... Music from Latin America has been popular in Rome for quite some time, but only now are mainstream clubs like **Alpheus** and **Piper** hosting salsa, samba, and rumba nights (check weekly listings in *Roma C'è* or *TimeOut* for info). However, for the time being, Brazilian music seems to be the main musical genre that's drawing crowds, and Trastevere is where you'll find it. For live samba and some of the tastiest *caipirinhas* (Brazilian drinks containing *cachaca*—a Brazilian sugar cane brandy—plus lime juice and more sugar) in the city, head to **Yes Brazil,** a wildly popular dive where you had better know how to dance. Get out your sexiest clothes for a trip to **Berimbau,** a Brazilian club with both a disco and live music that's very popular with Rome's local and international jet sets. Neither the monitors showing cheesy brochure scenes of Rio nor the inevitable cover of *The Girl from Ipanema* should spoil your fun at **Bossa Nova,** though the steep drink prices will surely disappoint. Meanwhile, pop over to Testaccio for the sultry sounds of Brazil, Jamaican reggae, and Cuban salsa at **Caffè Caruso,** a trendy *locale* that's generally jam-packed on weekends.

Tapping the local pub scene... Walk into almost any pub in Rome, and you might as well be in some hole-in-the-wall in England or Ireland. The decor is the same (Guinness memorabilia, soccer pennants, scratched-up, wood-paneled bars), and the stench is that same unforgettable mélange of beer, piss, and smoke you've come to know and love back home; more often than not, the bartenders don't even speak a lick of Italian. Fitting the mold perfectly is **Trinity College,** an Irish dive off of Via del Corso where you can enjoy a pint, some fish and chips, and a satellite feed of your favorite soccer team's game on the weekends. Rome's first Irish pub, the **Flann O'Brien,**

was practically dismantled in Ireland and rebuilt on the Via Nazionale with all the typical tchotchke. Old Italian men in houndstooth caps come to the **John Bull Pub** each afternoon to drink their troubles away; by night, the English-style bar welcomes a DJ and a *much* younger clientele. The **Abbey Theatre,** an Irish bar named after the national theater of Ireland located near Piazza Navona, similarly hops with young Roman kids and expats at night, and it also offers several computers for surfing the Net. **Ned Kelly,** an Australian pub, has been coasting on the Outback craze for quite some time now, drawing in a crowd of Italians, Aussies, Americans, and Brits for rugby talk (yes, Italy fields a rugby team!). Alternatively, for that *Oktoberfest*-type of atmosphere head to **Löwenhaus,** a pub with a Bavarian-clad waitstaff, or to **Birreria Viennese,** which keeps a variety of German, Austrian, and Czech beers on tap and also serves a menu replete with *würstel* and similarly rib-sticking fare.

Pour me a shot and leave me the bottle... The residential neighborhood of San Giovanni has little in the way of cool, modern bars, the exception being **The Dome,** a Goth-style locale with an extensive drink menu. Suffused lighting, black accents, and crumbling brick walls give the place a medieval feeling. Order up a pricey gin fizz, a tequila sunrise, or from a long list of liquor drinks—if you can get the bartender's attention, that is. A number of *Brickskeller*-type places are also good to try if you feel like knocking back a few. **Pub 64** in Trastevere is hardly the balls-out sort of place to enjoy a pint (Renato Zero, Italy's answer to early Bowie, is a fan), but you can choose from more than 100 kinds of beer. A better choice is Testaccio's **L'Oasi della Birra,** which boasts approximately 500 brands of brew, including a number of Italian microbrews if you're so inclined.

We're an American band... Hard drinking is even more special when you're among countrymen, and you won't have to go far to find them: Campo de' Fiori is home to two obnoxious, American-style bars. **The Drunken Ship** has bottles of Bud, kamikaze shooters, and an omnipresent crew of misplaced frat boys and bottled blondes. No different is **Sloppy Sam's,** run (not surprisingly) by the same people who own the Drunken Ship.

The jury is still out on which of the two is sloppier; call it a tie for now. Ask Claudio, the longtime bartender at the **Rock Castle Café,** for a whiskey Coke, then get set for a musical trip down memory lane. Almost all the DJs at Rock Castle are American, and they routinely spin sets of hits from the likes of Bon Jovi, the Clash, Nirvana, and the Red Hot Chili Peppers to appease a decidedly collegiate crowd. Admit it—you love this stuff.

Where to get wasted for less... A happening night out in the Eternal City doesn't have to mean excessive cover charges or long-distance taxi treks. **Fonclea,** a British-style, Vatican-area mainstay for more than 20 years, has nightly jazz, funk, and rock shows and a Happy Hour from 7 to 8pm. A 30-something crowd piles into **Escopazzo,** a laid-back bar in the *Centro Storico,* throughout the week to listen to free live music, including jam sessions on Mondays and Tuesdays and acoustic sets too. One of Trastevere's newest spaces is adjacent to and part of the English-language Pasquino cinema, **Nuovo Pasquino.** It offers two floors of dancing, lounging, and—if you must—late night Net chatting.

Sex in the city... By night, the otherwise dull neighborhood of San Giovanni becomes a haven for perverts of all orientations at **Gender.** Live sex shows, spanking parties, and S&M demos are not uncommon on the main floor, and there are also private rooms for the *really* serious fetishists; check your inhibitions at the door. Sleazy **Apeiron,** in the Termini area, is a gay fetish bar where you can watch male strip shows or hard porn flicks. Hetero males with idle hands and hefty wallets tend to head for **Boite Pigalle,** a seedy slice of Paris transported to the *Centro Storico* where local and international erotic dancers let it all hang out.

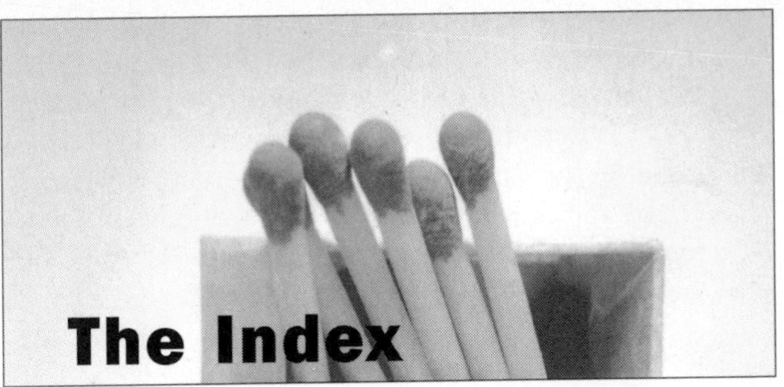

The Index

Abbey Theatre. Two-floor Irish pub near Piazza Navona popular with Roman and foreign students. Internet access available downstairs.... *Tel 06/686 13 41, www.abbeyrome.com. Via del Governo Vecchio 51–53, buses 46, 64, 70, 81, 492. Open daily. No cover.* **(see p. 169)**

Alexanderplatz Jazz Club. One of Italy's renowned jazz clubs. In the summer (June or July), the club sponsors an outdoor jazz event at Villa Celimontana.... *Tel 06/397 42 171, www.alexanderplatzjazz.com. Via Ostia 9, Metro Ottaviano. Closed Sun. Cover charge 10,000–15,000L.* **(see p. 167)**

Alien. Via Veneto–area disco playing techno-pop and house and sometimes hosting fashion shows and art exhibits. Currently, the place where all the beautiful people go; relocates to the Fregene beach in the summer (tel 06/665 64 761, Piazzale Fregene 5).... *Tel 06/841 22 12. Via Velletri 13–19, bus 63. Open Tue–Sun 10:30pm–4am. Cover charge 35,000L. Women sometimes admitted free before midnight.* **(see p. 164)**

Alpheus. Four floors of music and "Magic" parties every Friday night in conjunction with the local music video station. Expect to hear everything from rock to house to "black" (soul, R&B, rap) music. Students free on Thur.... *Tel 06/574 78 26. Via del Commercio 36, bus 75, Metro Piramide. Open Tue–Sun 10pm–4:30am. Cover charge 10,000–20,000L.* **(see pp. 162, 165, 168)**

Apeiron. Discreet meeting place for Rome's gay men. Porn movies and private dark rooms located on lower level.... *Tel 06/482 88 20. Via dei Quattro Cantoni 5, Metro Cavour. Open Mon–Sat 10:30pm–3am. Cover charge 20,000L.* **(see p. 170)**

Bar del Fico. Stylish cocktail bar with a mixed-age crowd.... *Tel 06/686 52 05. Piazza del Fico 26–28, buses 46, 64, 70, 81, 492. Open daily. No cover.* **(see p. 165)**

Bar della Pace. By day, this bar would likely have been a favorite of Kerouac's. By night, it's a very cool bar for the squeaky clean.... *Tel 06/686 12 16. Via della Pace 3–7, buses 46, 64, 70, 81, 492. Open daily. No cover.* **(see p. 165)**

Bar Taruga. Secluded, Ghetto-neighborhood bar named after the "turtle fountain" that it faces. A favorite with local fashion plates.... *Tel 06/689 22 99. Piazza Mattei 9, buses 56, 60, 65, 170, 710, 718, 719. Open Tue–Sun 10pm–2am. No cover.* **(see p. 165)**

Berimbau. Newly moneyed locals sway to the sounds of Brazil. Live music and a disco.... *Tel 06/581 32 49. Via dei Fienaroli 30b, tram 8. Open Wed–Sun 10:30pm–3am, closed July and Aug. Cover charge 10,000–20,000L.* **(see p. 168)**

Big Mama. Big Mama is Rome's blues scene, with nightly performances by Italian and international blues and jazz acts. Monthly membership card 10,000L, yearly card 20,000L; Fri and Sat night shows are for members only. Even with a membership, you'll still have to reserve tickets for big names in advance.... *Tel 06/581 25 51. Via San Francesco a Ripa 18, tram 8. Open daily, closed July–Oct.* **(see pp. 163, 167)**

Birreria Viennese. Austro-German-style pub with German and Czech beers on tap. Popular with center-city business types and roving students.... *Tel 06/679 55 69. Via della Croce 21, Metro Spagna. Open daily. No cover.* **(see p. 169)**

Black Out. Live punk, garage, and indie music, sometimes by artists from the U.S. and the U.K. Also a disco where resident DJs with names like Scratchy, Shark, and Diego spin underground hits.... *Tel 06/704 96 791. Via Saturnia 18, Metro Re di Roma. Open Thur–Sat 10:30pm–4am, closed in the summer. Cover charge 10,000–15,000L.* **(see p. 167)**

Boite Pigalle. High-profile strip club off of Via del Corso....

Tel 06/678 54 75. Via dell'Umiltà 77, buses 56, 60, 62, 85, 90, 95, 492. Open daily from 10pm until late (times vary). Cover charge 10,000–20,000L. **(see p. 170)**

Bossa Nova. A carnival-like atmosphere year-round, with hip-shaking music and a genuinely friendly clientele.... *Tel 06/581 61 21. Via degli Orti di Trastevere 43, trams 8, 30. Open Tue–Sun 10pm–3am, closed Aug. No cover charge, but first drink obligatory.* **(see p. 168)**

Brancaleone. A *centro sociale* that boasts a cinema, a disco, and a recording studio. Friday "Agatha" nights have been known to attract crowds of more than a thousand during summer.... *Tel 06/820 00 959, www.brancaleone.it. Via Levanna 11, Metro Piazza Bologna. Open Thur–Sun 10:30pm–5am. Cover charge (donation) 5,000L.* **(see p. 167)**

Caffè Caruso. *Legit* locale in Testaccio, with live Latin American and Caribbean musicians about twice each week. Disco Sundays include a dance menu of Latin, hip hop, and salsa.... *Tel 06/574 50 19. Via di Monte Testaccio 36, bus 75, Metro Piramide. Open Tue–Sun 10pm–3am, Thur–Sat in the summer. Cover 10,000–15,000L.* **(see p. 168)**

Chic & Kitsch. House, techno, and pop music; formerly known as Ciak Dance. Cliché furnishings, maybe, but they sure look good.... *Tel 06/578 20 22. Via di Santa Saba 11a, Metro Piramide. Open Wed–Sun 11:30pm–4am. Cover charge 20,000L for women, 25,000L for men.* **(see p. 165)**

The Dome. By far the best bar in San Giovanni. Medieval feel comes from suffused lighting, black accents, and crumbling brick walls; cool and casual mixed-age crowd don't mind occasional covers or perpetually steep drink prices.... *Tel 06/704 52 436. Via Domenico Fontana 18, buses 16, 85, 87, 117, trams 13, 30, Metro Manzoni. Open daily 10pm–3am, closed July and Aug. Occasional cover charge 2,500–5,000L is good for first drink purchase.* **(see p. 169)**

The Drunken Ship. American-style bar popular with the student/backpacker crowd. Sister bar is Sloppy Sam's, also on the Campo.... *Tel 06/683 00 535. Campo de' Fiori 20–21, buses 44, 46, 56, 60, 62, 64. Open daily 5pm–2am. No cover.* **(see pp. 164, 169)**

Escopazzo. In the shadow of the Vittoriano monument, this lively bar hosts local acts (mostly rock) nightly.... *Tel 06/692 00 422. Via d'Aracoeli 41, bus 44, 46, 56, 57, 60, 64, 65, 70, 75, 90, 170. Open daily 8:30pm–2:30am. No cover.* **(see p. 170)**

Ex-Magazzini. One of Rome's trendiest discos, with a see-through disco floor on the upper level. Almost all dance genres, from electronica to industrial and rock, are given ample play.... *Tel 0/575 80 40. Via Magazzini Generali 8, Metro Piramide. Open daily 9pm–4:30am. Cover charge 10,000–15,000L.* **(see p. 164)**

Flann O'Brien. Rome's original Irish bar. Guinness and Harp on tap, plus soccer matches on TV you pay a cover charge to watch.... *Tel 06/488 04 18. Via Napoli 29, Metro Repubblica. Open daily. No cover.* **(see p. 168)**

Fonclea. Vatican venue with nightly happy hours (7–8pm) and live music most nights. Expect to hear soul, funk, jazz, and rock.... *Tel 06/689 63 02. Via Crescenzio 82a, Metro Ottaviano. Open daily. No cover.* **(see p. 170)**

Forte Prenestino. An old prison yard retooled into a *centro sociale* for fans of the punk rock scene. Regular concerts from renowned international bands, and the yearly "Festa del Non Lavoro" (non–Labor Day) take place here.... *Tel 06/218 07 855, www.ecn.org/forte. Via Delpino, tram 5. Opening times vary.* **(see p. 167)**

Gender. Intimate, erotic lesbian/gay/transsexual club in San Giovanni with strip shows, private cabins, and equal opportunity for exhibitionists and voyeurs alike.... *Tel 06/704 97 638. Via Faleria 9, Metro San Giovanni. Open Tue–Sun 11pm—3am. Cover charge 20,000–60,000L.* **(see p. 170)**

Gilda. Expensive club near the Spanish Steps frequented by local celebrities and high rollers. Beware the velvet rope.... *Tel 06/678 48 38. Via Mario de' Fiori 97, Metro Spagna. Open daily 10pm–4am. Cover charge 40,000L. Gilda-on-the-beach takes place each summer, Tue–Sun in Fregene.... Tel 06/665 60 649, Lungomare di Ponente 11.* **(see p. 164)**

Goa. Cavernous club that gets pumping with ambient, trance, electronic, and techno music by owner/DJ Giancarlino. Ethnic feel, and a gay and straight mix. Keep an eye out for transvestite prostitutes lurking near the entrance.... *Tel 06/574 82 77. Via Libetta 13, Metro Garbatella. Open Tue, Thur–Sat 11pm–3am. Cover charge 15,000–30,000L.* **(see p. 165)**

Hangar. Rome's first gay bar, opened in 1983 and still a very popular hangout on weekends. Mon night is porn night; Thurs features amateur striptease performances.... *Tel 06/488 13 97. Via In Selci 69a, Metro Cavour. Open nightly 11:30pm–2am. Cover charge 5,000–20,000L.* **(see p. 166)**

Jackie O. The fab '60s disco of legend has been revamped, meaning you'll need more than a little grace to get into this posh pit. Piano bar and disco for aging members of the glitterati.... *Tel 06/428 85 457. Via Boncompagni 11, Metro Barberini. Open Thur–Sun 9pm–3am. Cover charge 20,000–35,000L.* **(see p. 164)**

The Jazz Hole. Intimate jazz bar with lesbian nights Tue and Thur; live jazz from local artists Thur–Sun.... *Tel 06/709 60 31. Via Umberto Biancamano 80, Metro San Giovanni. Open nightly 7pm–2am. Cover charge 10,000L for live music (otherwise, free).* **(see p. 166)**

John Bull Pub. Smelly but charming English-style pub. Cheap beers, a mixed international and local crowd, central location, and DJs most nights.... *Tel 06/687 15 37. Corso Vittorio Emanuele II 107a, buses 46, 62, 64. Open daily 9pm–3am. No cover.* **(see p. 169)**

Jonathan's Angels. Fantastic, fresco-like paintings of Jonathan surrounded by angels and his Harley motorcycle decorate this trendy cocktail bar near Piazza Navona. Restrooms have some of the most spectacular toilets in all of Europe.... *Tel 06/689 34 26. Via della Fossa 16, buses 46, 64, 70, 81, 492. Open daily 4pm–2am. No cover.* **(see p. 165)**

K Men's Club. The place where leather men go to meet leather boys. Hardcore S&M/leather venue and occasional naked nights. Don't say we didn't warn you.... *No telephone. Via Amato Amati 6–8, bus 105. Open Mon–Thur 11pm–3am, Fri and Sun until 4am, and Sat until 5am. Cover charge 10,000–20,000L.* **(see p. 166)**

L'Alibi. Notorious gay disco playing a prerequisite mix of house and techno. Fantastic rooftop terrace and 2 dance floors (3 in summer) on Monte Testaccio. Heavy, though casual, pick-up scene.... *Tel 06/574 34 48. Via di Monte Testaccio 40–47, bus 75. Open Wed–Sun 11pm–4am. Cover charge 20,000L, Sat only (otherwise, free).* **(see pp. 162, 166)**

Le Bain Art Gallery. Art/cocktail bar for the Eurotrash set. Hip lounge-style music.... *No telephone. Via delle Botteghe Oscure 32a–33, buses 64, 492. Open Tue–Sun 8pm–2am. No cover.* **(see p. 166)**

L'Oasi della Birra. Just what the name says—an oasis of beer in the middle of Testaccio. Choose from more than 500 brands, including Belgian Trappist brews, German white beers, and a typical menu of Irish and American labels.... *Tel 06/574 61 22. Piazza Testaccio 41, buses 23, 57, 95, 716, Metro Piramide. Open daily 7:30pm–1am, closed Aug. No cover.* **(see pp. 162, 169)**

Löwenhaus. Bavarian-style pub with German and Irish beers on tap. Live music on weekends.... *Tel 06/323 04 10. Via della Fontanella 16d, Metro Spagna or Flaminio. Open Tue–Sun noon–2am, Mon 6pm–2am. No cover.* **(see p. 169)**

Max. Stylish restaurant/bar with high-tech look tucked away in the tony Parioli district. Don't dare let anyone know you took public transport.... *Tel 06/842 41 630. Viale Liegi 64, buses 3, 4, 52, 53, 57. Open Tue–Sun 8pm–3am. No cover.* **(see p. 164)**

Ned Kelly. Where Roman (and other) rugby fans come together for a Foster's. Major sporting events shown daily via satellite and Happy Hour weekdays from 6:30–9pm.... *Tel 06/683 22 20. Via delle Coppelle 13, buses 64, 70, 75, 116. Open daily 12:30pm–3am. No cover.* **(see p. 169)**

New Jolie Coeur. Rome's main lesbian venue, where it's women-only on Saturday nights. Music is mainly New Wave and retro rock.... *Tel 06/862 15 827. Via Sirte 5, buses 3, 4, 52, 53, 57. Open Sat 11pm–3am. Cover charge 15,000–20,000L.* **(see p. 166)**

New Mississippi Jazz Club. Vatican area landmark with nightly jazz concerts. Jazz brunches on Sundays.... *Tel 06/688 06 348. Borgo Angelico 18a, Metro Ottaviano. Closed Sun night, Mon, and Tue. Annual membership is 15,000L.* **(see p. 167)**

Nuovo Pasquino. Don't know what to do after the movies? A space adjacent to the Pasquino movie theater has been transformed into a bar and Internet cafe. Thurs through Sun, the lower level becomes a disco. Mostly rock and pop music.... *Tel 06/580 36 22. Piazza S. Egidio 9, tram 8, 30. Open daily 4pm–2:30am. No cover. Small charge for Internet usage.* **(see p. 170)**

Piper. Historic disco venue where many Italian pop stars got their start and still a happening dance club for young schmoozers. Bring your best pick-up line. Sat nights are gay.... *Tel 06/855 53 98. Via Tagliamento 9, bus 63. Open Tue–Sun 11pm–4am. Also hosts teen dance parties Sat–Sun 4–8pm. Cover charge 15,000–35,000L.* **(see pp. 164, 166, 168)**

Pub 64. Trastevere bar with more than 100 different brands of beer and at least as many vintages. Occasional jazz, blues, or rock concerts.... *Tel 06/580 38 89. Piazza Trilussa 64, buses 23, 65, 280, tram 8. Open 8pm–3am. No cover.* **(see p. 169)**

Qube. A raver's haven in a rough neighborhood, now also the host of Rome's most famous gay night, *Mucca Assassina*.... *Tel 06/438 10 05. Via Portonaccio 212, tram 5. Open Thur–Sun*

11pm–4am. Cover charge 10,000– 25,000L.
(see pp. 162, 165, 166)

Radio Londra. Live rock and alternative music in a military-themed venue.... *Tel 06/575 00 44. Via di Monte Testaccio 57, bus 75. Closed Tue and Wed. Cover charge 10,000–20,000L.* **(see p. 167)**

RipArte Café. Get here early for sushi [see Dining], then stay for the DJs. Lounge, groove, and ambient music featured nightly after 11pm.... *Tel 06/586 18 52. Via Orti di Trastevere 7, bus 63, 75, tram 8. Closed Sun. Cover charge up to 30,000L.* **(see p. 165)**

Rock Castle Café. Subterranean dance bar gets rocking after 11, mostly with American and British rock 'n' roll. Huge expat scene.... *Tel 06/688 07 999. Via B. Cenci 8, bus 63, tram 8. Open daily 9pm–3am. Cover charge 10,000L Sat only.* **(see p. 170)**

Shelter. Unlikely mingling of gays, lesbians, and friends in a relaxed, loungey atmosphere.... *No telephone. Via dei Vascellari 35, tram 8, 30. Open daily 9pm–3am. No cover.* **(see p. 166)**

Sloppy Sam's. American bartenders and chatty co-eds create the spectacle. Cheap drinks make it easier to wash down.... *Tel 06/688 02 637. Campo de' Fiori 9–10, buses 44, 46, 56, 60, 62, 64. Open daily 5pm–2am. No cover.* **(see pp. 164, 169)**

Stardust. Small jazz joint in Trastevere, where jam sessions are liable to last until dawn.... *Tel 06/583 20 875. Vicolo de' Renzi 4, tram 8. Opening times vary. Cover 10,000–20,000L.* **(see p. 167)**

Trinity College. High school hangout with Irish beers on tap and the usual pub food. A cozy stop during Rome's rare cold days.... *Tel 06/678 64 72. Via del Collegio Romano 6, buses 63, 492. Open daily 11am–3am. No cover.*
(see p. 168)

Villagio Globale. Left-wing student venue located in an old slaughterhouse that now houses concerts, disco parties, and art installations. Normally open during the school year (Sept–May) only.... *Tel 06/573 00 329. Lungotevere Testaccio, bus 170. Opening times vary. Cover charge 5,000L.* **(see p. 167)**

Yes Brasil. The place where serious *sambistas* go to shake their rumps. Fruit juices and *caipirinha* drinks serve as refreshments.... *Tel 06/581 62 67. Via San Francesco a Ripa 103, tram 8. Open Mon–Sat 10pm–2am. Cover charge 10,000–15,000L.* **(see p. 168)**

enterta

7

inment

The entertainment scene in Rome is highly unpredictable, and it can hardly be compared to the fancy performing arts scene in Venice and Milan, much less those in world capitals like New York, London, and Paris. The **Teatro dell'-Opera** has long been a source of embarrassment for opera enthusiasts in Rome, as it has seen numerous strikes, walkouts, and lackluster performances. (This is changing, but slowly.) Classical music can be relatively reliable, with top-notch concerts from the **Accademia Nazionale di Santa Cecilia** and the **Accademia Filarmonica Romana** stealing the scene. Theaters are plentiful, but many of them specialize in staid, Italian standards and tacky, cabaret-type shows—not always the best choice for non-Italian speakers. Otherwise, Rome's entertainment landscape is tailored to the masses. Cinemas continue to rake in big bucks, and the American-style **Warner Village** multiplex in the suburbs is bringing in the crowds (though all films are dubbed into Italian). And, of course, *calcio* (soccer) remains the biggest draw for the plebeians. Including the weekly games from the two soccer teams, **AS Roma** and **SS Lazio**—plus World Cup, UEFA, and other friendly matches—you've got a season that lasts almost all year. *Roma C'è* and *TimeOut Roma* have extensive listings in Italian for the city's film, theater, and musical performances. The tourist office also puts out the monthly *L' Evento,* which highlights up-and-coming performances in Italian and English (for some listings). There's really no single source for reserving tickets, so you'll have to go to the individual cinema, theater, or music hall to secure your seats. And, to add to the hassle, credit cards are not always accepted. Make sure you have cash.

The Lowdown

Classical gas... Entertaining Romans since the 16th century, the **Accademia Nazionale di Santa Cecilia** has set the standard for the classical music scene in Rome, if not in the world. Steeped in tradition (its name comes from the patron saint of music), even the Accademia is bending a bit, hiring on Korean-born Myung-Whun Chung as director in 1997. Until the symphony's new (and elaborate) performing hall is complete, most concerts can be heard in the **Auditorio Pio.** Summer performances take place in the *nymphaem* at Villa Giulia (north of the Pincio Gardens in Villa Borghese). Playing in the **Teatro Olimpico** is Rome's other major classical troupe: the **Accademia Filarmonica Romana.** With a lineage going back to Verdi and Rossini, the Roman Philharmonic's musical recipe is generally choral and chamber music. However, these days they're tempered with a pinch of blues, jazz, or experimental music every now and then.

What's opera, doc?... You would think that the city that was the setting for *Tosca* and the capital of the country that Pavarotti calls home would be an opera powerhouse—but you would be sadly mistaken. (Do not pass Go; do not collect $200.) In fact, the opera scene in Rome has long been a joke, especially when compared to the grand spectacles at La Fenice and La Scala. There's nothing particularly striking about the **Teatro dell'Opera,** for example: From the outside, the building is dwarfed by the surrounding hotels and business offices, and the potted plants surrounding the entrance give no clues to the fact that this is an opera house and not a recreation center. All criticism aside, the Teatro dell'Opera does put on some beautiful performances and is beginning to attract well-known singers and patrons now that its management is stable. What kept the Teatro dell'Opera going for so many years were its summer performances at the Baths of Caracalla. Unfortunately, those performances are no longer permitted, as the music and the singing began to wreak havoc on the ruins. The summer season is now held in the **Stadio Olimpico.**

Front stage story... The Teatro di Roma lays claim to two of the city's finest venues for the performing arts. You can't miss the **Teatro di Roma—Argentina,** which sits prominently on Largo Argentina, across from the Area Sacra and a few blocks from Campo de' Fiori. Built in the 19th century, the Argentina—which is today Rome's best-known theater—has seen world-famous operas, theater productions, and dance troupes come and go. On the other hand, the new **Teatro di Roma—India,** fashioned out of an old soap factory and opened in September 1999, features more experimental performances, including contemporary dramas and recitals. For cheaper seats, try the privately owned **Teatro Eliseo,** which handles Italian classics and foreign works (adapted in Italian) with flair. The **Teatro**

Flaiano is also a good option for innovative plays on largely controversial subjects. Had it with trying to decipher foreign dialogue? Rome's large expat and tourist population has spurred the popularity of English-language theater in the city. Touring American and English theater groups often play in the **Teatro Olimpico,** which also attracts internationally acclaimed dance and musical troupes, and the **Teatro Sistina,** which occasionally gets off-Broadway productions. Additionally, a number of English speakers from the States, England, Scotland, and Australia have formed English theater groups; the most well-received seems to be the **Off-Night Repertory Company,** led by American Gaby Ford. The group usually puts on two plays a year, each very professional if not a bit quirky. Rather new on the scene (sometimes a characteristic that is sadly apparent) are the **Miracle Players,** who stage free or cheap plays in and around the ruins of the Forum area. Mostly, the performances are a bit amateurish—but talk about a great set!

Silver screen dreams... Cinecittà—a dream of Mussolini and the production studio for such epics as *Ben Hur* and *Dolce Vita*—no longer holds the mythic status it held during the 1950s when it was referred to as "Hollywood on the Tiber." These days, the studio still churns out some winners, including Benigni's *Life is Beautiful* and Minghella's *The Talented Mr. Ripley,* but mostly the lots have given way to campy variety shows, bad soap operas, and Italian slapstick duds. Oh yeah—Stallone's dreadful tunnel thriller *Daylight* was also shot here. There's not really too much to see here, but if you've got some time to kill, you can take a tour of some of the lots at the suburban studio. Elaborate sets depicting the Old West, Ancient Rome, and Venice are on view, and there's even a reconstruction of the Trevi Fountain, complete with a statue of Anita Ekberg, the blonde bombshell star of *La Dolce Vita*. You may also get a glimpse of Martin Scorsese's set of 19th-century New York for *The Gangs of New York,* one of the most recent big-budget Hollywood films shot here.

Cinema Paradiso... Romans' appetite for film is still as strong as it ever was. Unfortunately for non-Italian speakers, however, all film imports to Italy are dubbed. So, it's not really Mel Gibson's voice that you're hearing—that's Claudio Sorrentino. There isn't a shortage of screens, at least—if you don't mind dubbed Hollywood flicks and first-run Italian films, that is. The all-too-familiar Warner Brothers have invaded Rome with two Warner Village outposts. **Warner Village—Esedra** has five screens, while the suburban **Warner Village—EUR** has an unfathomable 18 screens; you can easily find either, but bear in mind that this is Italy and even the most familiar Hollywood tripe will have been dubbed into Italian, with no English subtitles in sight. Learn to lip-read. **Barberini** (right at the base of the Via Veneto) has the "latest" (three months too late, usually) box office hits. And, not far from here, the **Quattro Fontane** shows mostly artistic, independent films from Italian studios. **Pasquino,** Rome's famous English-language film house named after the "talking statue" in the square of the same name (curiously on the other side of town in Trastevere; see Diversions is one of the best places to see first-run flicks from the U.S. and the U.K. in their *lingua originale* (original language). Likewise, single-screen houses **Alcazar** and **Nuovo Sacher,** both in Trastevere, dedicate their screens to English, and often French, films. For English movies in the *Centro Storico,* try the **Quirinetta. Palazzo delle Esposizioni** also shows English and other foreign language movies, including documentaries from France, artsy-fartsy dramas from the Czech Republic, and whathave-you. Since 1995, PalaExpo has hosted the **MedFilm Festival** (www.mediatecaroma.it/medfilm) each June, which focuses primarily on dozens of short films and features from Mediterranean Europe. PalaExpo is also the site of a varying schedule of lectures, concerts and others events (see Diversions).

Rock 'n' Roll, Part 1... Rome generally suffers when it comes to getting big-name pop and rock tours, mostly because it lies too far outside the usual European circuit. The few big names who do make it past Milan now play at one of two venues in out-of-the-way EUR (though it is accessible by the Metro and other public transit.) The **PalaCisalfa** is a relatively new venue with good acoustics and adequate views from almost all its seats; hope that your act is playing here. You may also be able to catch some popular music at the **PalaEUR,** but it won't be as much fun—no wonder the activity here has tailed off in recent years. Built for the 1960 Olympics, the aging stadium and its notoriously poor sound system have fallen out of favor with musicians and music lovers alike. Don't feel like getting out to EUR? Though smaller, more intimate clubs and other venues don't exactly abound, there are a few and decent musical acts do pass through occasionally. (See Nightlife for more details.)

Kidding around... Romans, like all Italians, adore kids; they either leave them in the capable hands of extended families or else bring them along for whatever they happen to be doing. If you're a tourist with kids to entertain, however, this can be a bit of a problem: Since children are such an integrated part of everyday Italian life, there aren't really very many special events or facilities geared to the tykes beyond, well, school. Blame it on cultural differences and deal with it. There are a few options, though. If all the ruins, fountains, and unclothed statues don't drive the little ones wild, for instance, try taking them up to the **Teatro Verde** way up on the Janiculum hill. This puppet theater presents lively *Punch and Judy* (in Italian, *Pulcinella*) style shows every afternoon except Wednesday and also on weekend mornings. Another option for the wee ones is the **Cinema dei Piccoli** in Villa Borghese, which usually features classic Disney cartoons dubbed in Italian—not really a big deal if your kids have already seen *Fantasia* 20 times already.

Getting it out in the open... To capitalize on the throngs of summer tourists, Rome abounds with open-air festivals. The city gets it right with **Estate Romana,** a summer-long event that runs the gamut from outdoor classical and pops concerts to films and impromptu plays in picturesque *piazze.* Summer also brings the terrific **RomaEuropa Festival,** one of Italy's biggest and best, which takes place at the Villa Medici (on the grounds of Villa Borghese) and is organized by a number of international cultural associations; its slate includes everything from chamber music concerts to acid jazz performances, dance recitals, and films. Note that the festival lasts from June through July, takes a break in August, and then picks up again from September through mid-November. Many philharmonic troupes and classical orchestras also take their music outdoors during the summer. The scenic **Villa Giulia,** a small park north of Villa Borghese, plays host to summer concerts for the **Accademia Nazionale di Santa Cecilia,** while **Villa Celimontana** (see Getting Outside) sets the scene for the cool **Jazz and Image Festival** (tel 06/397 42 171). One of Europe's largest jazz festivals, lasting from June through August, this shindig has hosted such internationally renowned artists as Tito Puente, B.B. King, and Herbie Hancock. If you're looking for art among the ruins, check entertainment listings for information on classical concerts at the **Teatro di Marcello** (see Diversions). There's also talk of staging at least one future summer production of a Greek or Roman classic at the **Colosseum.** In the meantime, travel to **Ostia** (see Getting Outside) where, in July and August, you can watch the **Teatro Romana di Ostia Antica** perform classics in an ancient amphitheater.

A kick in the balls (and other sports)... Rome is home to two major soccer teams—**AS Roma** and **SS Lazio**—and during the fall season, one or the other will be playing on any given Sunday in the **Stadio Olimpico.** Traditionally, Roma fans sit in the Curva Sud, while Lazio fans occupy the Curva Nord. (It's probably no coincidence that these seating arrangements jibe geographically and politically with each team's fan base: Roma fans are largely a working-class bunch, whereas Lazio fans are more often moneyed—a reflection of Italy's long-standing North/South cultural divide.) If you're lucky, you'll be in town during the Roma-Lazio derby—it usually takes place in April—which pits these soccer rivals in a veritable fight to the death. Tensions on and off the field are incredibly high during the derby, making for one of the most authentic Roman moments you are likely to encounter. Also be on the lookout for UEFA and Champions League qualifiers, more common these days since both teams have stepped up their programs. Usually held on Wednesdays, cup-qualifying matches are your chance to see Rome's teams battle the best in Europe. (The smaller, adjacent Stadio dei Marmi is a laugh, too, as it features huge Fascist-style statues in a variety of sporty poses—many with fig leaves carefully covering their genitals.) Soccer isn't the only big sporting event in Rome, though it's certainly the most fanatically followed. Tennis is mighty big, too; the Italian Open, held each May at **Foro Italico** in the same Stadio Olimpico complex, is a big draw and brings the world's top players to town for an important clay-court event. It's the largest tournament before the (also-clay) French Open and Wimbledon Grand Slams begin. And, believe it or not, Italy even fields a rugby team that competes in the Six Nations Championship; the other five—in case you were wondering—are England, France, Ireland, Scotland, and Wales. Home rugby games are played in the **Stadio Flaminio,** and Six Nations scrums are held each year from February through April.

The Index

Alcazar. Small, *lingua originale* cinema in Trastevere. Often shows films *senza intervallo* (without intermissions).... *Tel 06/588 00 99. Via Merry del Val 14. Ticket prices range from 8,000–13,000L.* **(see p. 185)**

Accademia Nazionale di Santa Cecilia. Founded by Palestrina in the 16th century, this is Rome's foremost symphony orchestra.... *Tel 06/328 171, www.santacecilia.it. Via Vittoria 6. Tickets range from 25,000–75,000L per performance.* **(see pp. 182, 187)**

Accademia Filarmonica Romana. Founded in 1821, the Roman Philharmonic's fall season includes performances of chamber and choral music and dance. Concerts are held in the Teatro Olimpico (see below).... *Tel 06/320 17 52, vivaldi.nuovo.nexus.it/filarmonica/. Via Flaminia 118. Tickets start at 30,000L per performance.* **(see p. 183)**

AS Roma. One of Rome's Serie A soccer squads. Its colors are crimson and gold (*giallorosso*).... *Tel 06/506 02 00, www.asromacalcio.it. Tickets can be purchased at the Stadio Olimpico on game day or at the Official AS Roma store at Via Colonna 360, tel 39/06 678 65 14.* **(see pp. 182, 187)**

Auditorio Pio. Temporary home of the Accademia Nazionale di Santa Cecilia.... *Tel 06/688 01 044. Via della Conciliazione 4, buses 64, 492, Metro Ottaviano.* **(see p. 182)**

Barberini. Five-screen, Via Veneto multiplex showing mainstream films—mostly dubbed Hollywood flicks. Weekday matinees, occasional morning showings, and late-night films on Saturdays.... *Tel 06/482 77 07. Piazza Barberini 24–26, Metro Barberini. Tickets range from 8,000–13,000L.* **(see p. 185)**

Cinecittà. Rome's major film studios, where *Dolce Vita* was born. Not quite up to its former glories, but it still offers tours. Out in the suburbs.... *Tel 06/722 931, fax 06/722 21 55, cinec@tin.it. Cinecittà, Metro Cinecittà.* **(see p. 184)**

Cinema dei Piccoli. Small cinema in Villa Borghese featuring cartoon classics and family films.... *Tel 06/855 34 85. Via della Pineta 15. Tickets range from 5,000–8,000L.* **(see p. 186)**

Estate Romana. Rome's summertime cultural festival, featuring art exhibitions, dance, music, theater, and children's programs. Varying locations.... *Tel 06/488 991, www.caltanet.estateromana.it. June–Sept. Ticket prices vary, many events are free.* **(see p. 186)**

Foro Italico. Huge sports and tennis complex, home to the annual Italian Open tennis tournament.... *Tel 06/368 58 218. Viale dei Gladiatori 31. Ticket prices vary.* **(see p. 188)**

Miracle Players. New English-language theater group putting on plays in some of Rome's most historic tourist venues, including the Forum.... *Tel 06/446 98 67, www.miracleplayers.org. Piazza Confienza 3.* **(see p. 184)**

Nuovo Sacher. Trastevere cinema screening films in their original languages (usually French and English).... *Tel 06/581 81 16. Largo Ascianghi 1, trams 8, 30. Tickets range from 8,000–13,000L.* **(see p. 185)**

Off-Night Repertory Company. Expat Gaby Ford's theater group focuses on original plays, often comedic and always enjoyable. Venues may change from season to season.... *Tel 06/444 13 75, email gabyford@hotmail.com. Via di Castelfiardo 31 Int. 11.* **(see p. 184)**

PalaCisalfa. Rome's premier venue for large-scale concerts and sports tournaments.... *Tel 06/474 76 68. Viale dell'Oceano Atlantico 271, buses 76, 772, 775, 777, Metro EUR Fermi. Ticket prices vary depending on event.* **(see p. 185)**

PalaEUR. Once Rome's largest music and sports arena, this massive colosseum is now overshadowed by the newer, more technically advanced PalaCisalfa.... *Tel 06/397 60 420. Piazzale dello Sport, Metro EUR Palasport.* **(see p. 186)**

Palazzo delle Esposizioni. Films, lectures, and other cultural events at the Sala Multimediale (multimedia room) each week.... *Tel 06/474 59 03. Via Nazionale 194, buses 64, 65, 70, 71, 75, 117, 170. Open Wed–Mon 10am–9pm (last admission at 8:30pm). Closed Jan 1, May 1, and Dec 25. Admission charged.* **(see p. 185)**

Pasquino. The premier English-language cinema in Trastevere, showing general releases and the occasional indie film.... *Tel 06/580 36 22. Piazza Sant'Egidio 10. Tickets range from 8,000–10,000L.* **(see p. 185)**

Quattro Fontane. Small multiplex with regular showings of Italian indie and art films. Open for matinees Mon–Fri.... *Tel 06/474 15 15. Via Quattro Fontane 23, buses 56, 64, 65, 70, 75, Metro Barberini. Tickets range from 8,000–13,000L.* **(see p. 185)**

Quirinetta. Attractive, old-fashioned cinema owned by the Cecchi-Gori film group. First-run, English-language films screened weekly.... *Tel 06/679 00 12. Via M. Minghetti*

4, buses 52, 53, 58, 61, 71, 85, J2, J7. Tickets range from 8,000–10,000L. **(see p. 185)**

RomaEuropa Festival. One of Italy's biggest and best performing arts festivals, with a season lasting from June through July and Sept through mid-Nov. Offerings include everything from chamber music concerts to acid jazz, dance and film.... *Tel 06/474 22 86, www.roma europa.net. Venues and ticket prices vary.* **(see p. 186)**

SS Lazio. Rome's other big-deal soccer team, and AS Roma's fierce intercity rival. The team's colors are baby blue and white.... *Tel 06/323 73 33, www.sslazio.it. Tickets can be purchased at the Stadio Olimpico on game day or at the Lazio Point on Via Farini 34, tel 06/482 67 68.* **(see pp. 182, 187)**

Stadio Flaminio. Small stadium north of Piazza del Popolo where the Italian rugby squad and minor city sports leagues play.... *Tel 06/368 57 832. Via Flaminia. Ticket prices vary by event.* **(see p. 188)**

Stadio Olimpico. Site of the 1960 Olympic games, and current home of the AS Roma and SS Lazio soccer squads on alternating Sundays. Also home to opera performances.... *Tel 06/323 73 33 (ticket office). Viale dello Stadio Olimpico. Soccer tickets range from 30,000–150,000L.* **(see pp. 183, 187)**

Teatro dell'Opera. The opera house's lavish, 19th-century interior clashes with its ugly, Mussolini-era facade. Summer season takes place in the Villa Giulia.... *Tel 06/481 601, www.opera.roma.it. Via Firenze 72, Metro Repubblica. Ticket prices start at 40,000L.* **(see pp. 182, 183)**

Teatro di Roma—Argentina. A theater with a past, the Argentina was where Rossini's *Barber of Seville* debuted—to jeers and boos. Today, look for first-rate dance, musical, and theater productions.... *Tel 06/688 04 601, www.teatrodiroma.com. Largo Argentina 52, buses 64, 492.* **(see p. 183)**

Teatro di Roma—India. The Teatro di Roma's secondary venue is one of the newest performing arts spaces in town. Features a largely alternative repertoire.... *Tel 06/684 00 008, www.teatrodiroma.com. Lungotevere Papareschi.* **(see p. 183)**

Teatro Eliseo. Terrific for Italian speakers, this large theater regularly features mainstream dramatic productions on the cheap—but, no, there are no subtitles, so you're on your own.... *Tel 06/488 08 311. Via Nazionale 183e, Metro Repubblica.* **(see p. 183)**

Teatro Flaiano. Decked out in blue velvet, the private Teatro Flaiano is known for its serious dramas.... *Tel 06/679 64 96. Via San Stefano del Cacco 15, buses 64, 492. Tickets start at L15,000.* **(see p. 183)**

Teatro Olimpico. Offers a wide range of alternative and classic theater, as well as dance. Some English-language plays and musicals end up here. Home auditorium of the Roman Philharmonic.... *Tel 06/326 59 91. Piazza Gentile da Fabriano. Box office open daily 11am–7pm.* **(see pp. 182, 184)**

Teatro Romana di Ostia Antica. Ancient classics and modern-day comedies are each performed among the ruins. Performances usually begin at approximately 8:30pm.... *Tel 06/688 04 601. Ostia Antica. Box office open July–Aug daily 10am–2pm and 3–6pm.* **(see p. 187)**

Teatro Sistina. Theater hosting English-language plays and musicals, as well as Italian adaptations of shows like *Hello Dolly* and *Some Like It Hot*.... *Tel 06/482 68 41, www.ilsistina.com. Via Sistina 129, Metro Spagna or Barberini. Ticket prices start from 20,000L.* **(see p. 184)**

Teatro Verde. Home of Rome's *Punch and Judy* puppet shows and other Italian-language plays for children. Performances Oct–April, Sat and Sun only at 5pm.... *Tel 06/588 20 34. Circonvallazione Gianicolense, train to Stazione Trastevere. Ticket prices range from 8,000–12,000L.* **(see p. 186)**

Warner Village—Esedra. Big releases from the United States (dubbed over in Italian, and thus hard to follow) plus current Italian movies. No intermission.... *Tel 06/477 79 202. Piazza della Repubblica 45, Metro Repubblica. Ticket prices range from 10,000–14,000L.* **(see p. 185)**

Warner Village—EUR. With 15 screens to choose from, there's something for everyone at this behemoth—if you speak Italian, that is. The on-site pizzeria and restaurant are accessible to all. One bonus: Films are shown without intermissions.... *Tel 06/658 55 111. Viale Parco dei Medici, Metro EUR Magliana. Ticket prices range from 10,000–14,000L.* **(see p. 185)**

25
10
5
1
ABC 2
DEF 3
GHI 4
JKL 5
MNO 6
PRS 7
TUV 8
WXY 9
*
0
#
PUSH
(401)555-1212
COIN RETURN
PULL

hotlines & other basics

Airport... **Fiumicino Airport,** also known as Leonardo da Vinci, is Rome's main airport and is open 24 hours. Before the Jubilee, it wasn't so easy getting around the airport. However, some superficial updates, such as improved signage in English, have made it easier for travelers to find their way to ground transportation and to trains into the city (located one flight up from the International Arrivals Hall, Terminal C). Other notable improvements include a new satellite wing with duty-free shops and restaurants and the Hilton Rome Airport, accessible via walkway from all terminals (see Accommodations). If your bags do not arrive at the same time you do, try the Left Luggage desk just beyond baggage claim in the Arrivals Hall, open 24 hours (tel 06/659 54 25 267). There is a 4,100L charge per day for each piece of luggage left at the desk. Rome's other airport, **Ciampino,** is mainly a hub for military flights, but it sometimes handles charter flights from within Europe. Only bus transportation is available from Ciampino into town. For more information on Rome's airports, call Fiumicino at 06/65 951 or Ciampino at 06/794 941.

Airport transportation to downtown... Two train services run directly from Fiumicino into the city. The express service to Termini station costs 15,000L and runs about every half hour between 7am and 10pm. Local service is 8,000L, runs about every 15 minutes, and also makes stops at Trastevere, Ostiense, Tuscolana, and Tiburtina stations. If you're lugging around a couple suitcases, you'll definitely want to take a taxi; a ride to or from Fiumicino costs at least 70,000L, plus additional surcharges (12,000–14,000L, plus approximately 2,000L per bag). If you're taking a cab from the airport, make sure the taxi is licensed and has a meter; rip-off artists posing as taxicab drivers often prey on non-Italian speakers, offering them a ride into town in an air-conditioned Mercedes or similarly flashy car. Sure, they may give you a comfortable ride—but they'll then charge you upwards of 150,000L or more.

Babysitters... Most hotels do not provide childcare. If you're in a bind, call **United Babies,** (tel 06/589 94 81, Piazza Nicoloso da Recco 9) a licensed daytime playgroup run by American Lucy Gardner. The service is open from 8am until 2:30pm, and babysitting is available until 6pm. Americans who plan to be in Rome for a longer period of time may want to contact the United States Embassy, which can provide you a list of other English-speaking babysitters in the city.

Banks and currency exchange offices... Banks are open Mon–Fri 9am–1pm and 3–5pm, and Sat from 9am–1pm. Most will handle currency exchanges and credit card cash advances at a nominal fee, but bear in mind that you may need to wait in a line—and Roman lines are a little chaotic. Currency exchange offices are also located throughout the *Centro Storico,* as well as in Fiumicino Airport and Termini train station, though fees here can be steep. ATMs are plentiful around the city and are the cheapest and best option—by far—for getting cash, most charging little or no fee for the service.

Car rentals... Hertz (Via Veneto 156, tel 06/321 68 31) and **Avis** (Via Sardegna 38a, tel 06/428 24 728) have offices in the city center. Many rental companies have offices at Fiumicino Airport, including **Avis** (tel 06/650 11 531), **Thrifty** (tel 06/793 40 137), and **Hertz** (tel 06/650 11 553). All three open daily until midnight. **Europcar** (tel 06/488 28 54), **Avis** (tel 06/481 43 73), and Italian chain **Maggiore** (tel 06/488 00 49) operate rental offices at Termini Station, though lines are often long and chaotic.

Consulates and embassies... United States

Embassy: tel 06/467 41, Via Veneto 119A/121. **Embassy of Canada:** tel 06/445 981, Via Zara 30. **Embassy of the United Kingdom:** tel 06/482 54 41, Via XX Settembre 80A. **Embassy of Australia:** tel 06/852 721, Via Alessandria 215. **Embassy of New Zealand:** tel 06/440 29 28, Via Zara 28.

Currency... The Euro will become the official currency among European Union members—including Italy—on January 1, 2002. At that time, more than 90 percent of Italian ATMs will dispense Euro coins and bills. Italian lira will still be in circulation but will be phased out gradually. At press time, 1 Euro equaled approximately 2,000 lira.

Driving and parking... Driving in Rome in seriously impractical. Many streets are too small, usually only one lane wide; larger streets are often unmarked, leaving drivers to figure out lanes for themselves. Roman drivers are aggressive, theft is rampant, and there are many areas in the city that are off-limits to drivers. Get the drift? Not only is driving a hassle, but parking is almost impossible—as you'll witness from makeshift parking jobs on sidewalks and at crosswalks. On the other hand, if you're planning to venture outside of the city, a car is definitely your best bet. Some useful parking garages are located in the Villa Borghese (Viale del Muro Torto), the Lepanto Metro Station (Via Lepanto), and in Piazza del Popolo. The controversial Vatican Parking Garage (Via Aurelia), built atop ancient ruins for the 2000 Jubilee, was inaugurated in February 2000; it provides more than 800 spaces for buses and cars.

Electricity... Italy's electrical outlets put out 220 volts, whereas the United States system is wired for 110 volts. If you're bringing electrical appliances from the States, you'll need to buy a two-pronged adapter before leaving home; otherwise you can purchase (a more expensive) one at an appliance shop or dime store (*casalinghe*).

Emergencies and police... For general emergencies, dial 113. You can reach the **Carabinieri** by dialing 112, and the **Polizia** by dialing 06/468 61. Mind the differences between the two: *carabinieri* are military police posted throughout the country; *polizia* are a civilian force. Both are generally helpful, though mountains of paperwork can be involved for even minor claims. For fire emergencies, dial the **Vigili del Fuoco** at 115. For auto assistance, call the **Automobile Club d'Italia** at 116. It has a reciprocal agreement with AAA. The most centrally located police office is located in Piazza del Collegio Romano 3, reached by buses 56, 60, 62, 85, 90, 95, and 492.

Events information... For information on concerts, theater performances, or other types of entertainment, you can buy the weekly magazine ***Roma C'è,*** which has an English-language section, or the monthly ***TimeOut.*** Too strapped for that? Free info is available from tourist kiosks, which are scattered around the city center. Ask for ***L'Evento*** and/or ***Un Ospite a Roma.*** The latter is also available at upscale hotels.

Festivals and special events...

JANUARY: All children, naughty and nice, get a visit and gifts from **Befana** (the old witch) on Jan 6.

FEBRUARY: Pranksters don ugly masks and children dress as if it is Halloween for **Carnevale** (Feb or March). There's usually a children's parade by the Colosseum on Martedi Grasso (Fat Tuesday).

MARCH: **International Woman's Day,** on March 8, is one day when it's perfectly acceptable for women to harass men. Gangs of girls go out to dinner (or to a Chippendale's-type show) with bouquets of mimosa flowers. Non-stop religious services, hordes of pilgrims, and sweet treats are the highlights of **Settimana Santa,** the week leading up to Easter (March or April); an outdoor mass in St. Peter's Square on **Easter Sunday** draws tens of thousands. **Settimana dei Beni Culturali** (tel 06/589 93 59, March or April) is one of the best times to visit Rome, when all state-owned museums and archaeological sites are open free of charge. The third Sunday in March sees the main streets closed to traffic for the **Rome City Marathon.**

APRIL: The **Natale di Roma** (Rome's birthday), celebrated on the Campidoglio, falls on the Sunday before April 21. A sea of azaleas replaces the lounging masses on the Spanish Steps on the **Festa della Primavera** during the beginning of the month.

MAY: Rock concerts in the Piazza San Giovanni in Laterano and labor demonstrations mark **Primo Maggio** (May Day); also be on the lookout for the **Festa di Non Lavoro** (No Work Day) at Forte Prenestino on May 1. The **Italian Open,** Italy's closest thing to a Grand Slam tennis tournament, takes place at the Foro Italico in late May.

JUNE: **Estate Romana** and the **RomaEuropa** cultural festivals begin in June and last throughout the summer; a wreath-laying ceremony at the Vittoriano commemorates **Armed Forces Day** on June 2; June 23 is the **Festa di San Giovanni,** which entails huge feasts of snails and suckling pig. Rome's patron saints—Peter and Paul—are celebrated at their respective basilicas (St. Peter's and San Paolo Fuori le Mura) on **San Pietro e San Paolo** on June 29.

JULY: The **Expo Tevere** is an arts, crafts, and food fair that takes place along the Tiber at the beginning of July. Trastevere holds the **Festa de Noantri** street fair during the last two weeks of July; also in late July, **Le Donne Sotte Le Stelle,** sometimes known as **Roma Alta Moda,** is a huge fashion show at the Spanish Steps.

AUGUST: The **Festa della Madonna della Neve** at Santa Maria Maggiore on Aug 5 recalls with white flower petals a late summer snow in the fourth century, which prompted the building of the basilica. The city (and most transit) officially closes down on Aug 15 for the huge summer holiday known as **Ferragosto** and, for the most part, remains closed until the second week of Sept.

NOVEMBER: Romans remember their dead on **All Saints Day** or **Ognissanti** on Nov 1. The **Vino Novello Wine Tasting** takes place in late Nov in Campo de' Fiori.

DECEMBER: On Dec 8, the **Day of the Immaculate Conception,** the pope rides down Via Condotti to the Trinita dei Monti church, where he gives mass. Sweet treats and sundry bric-a-brac are available at the **Christmas Market** in Piazza Navona until Jan 6; and, throughout the month of December, all major basilicas and many local churches display **Nativity Scenes.**

Gay and lesbian sources... For info on the latest happenings, including nightlife, events, lectures, and counseling services for AIDS/HIV, look to the **Circolo Mario Mieli di Cultura Omosessuale** (tel 06/541 39 85, fax 06/541 39 71, www.mariomieli.org). **ArciGay** (tel 06/855 55 22, www.arcigay.it) and **ArciLesbica** (tel 06/418 03 69) offer helplines for gay men and lesbians, respectively, as well as political and social forums. **Libreria Babele,** the city's only gay and lesbian bookstore, sells the *Gay and Lesbian Map of Rome* for approximately 15,000L. Also available for purchase is the *Guida Gay,* an annual Italian/English guide that provides information on queer venues and events.

Health matters... If you have an emergency medical

problem, you can go to the *Pronto Soccorso* (emergency room) of any local hospital. The most centrally located hospitals are **Ospedale Fatabenefratelli** (tel 06/683 72 99, Isola Tiberina, buses 23, 97, 774, 780) and **Ospedale San Giacomo** (tel 06/362 61, Via Canova 29, Metro Flaminio). There's also a major hospital near San Giovanni in Laterano: **Ospedale San Giovanni** (tel 06/770 51, Via Amba Aradam 8, Metro San Giovanni). Twenty-four hour home medical service is available for residents and tourists. All doctors at the **MEDline** (tel 06/808 09 95) speak English. Most pharmacies in Rome are open from 8:30am–1pm and 4–8pm, and can fill almost any prescription. Outside of normal operating hours, pharmacies stay open on a rotating basis; most local papers print a list of these, and each pharmacy is also required to post this information on the nearest open pharmacy. There are a few 24-hour pharmacies, as well: **Farmacia della Stazione** (Piazza dei Cinquecento, near Termini, tel 06/488 00 19) and **Piram** (Via Nazionale 228, tel 06/488 07 54). If you're near Vatican City, the **Farmacia del Vaticano** (Porta Sant'Anna, tel 06/698 83 422) is open Mon–Fri 8:30am–6pm and Sat 7:30am–1pm and stocks many drugs that are hard to find in Italian pharmacies—often at cheaper prices.

Holidays... Italy observes a number of federal and religious holidays: Jan 1 (New Year's Day); Jan 6 (Epiphany); April 25 (Liberation Day); May 1 (May Day); Sun nearest June 2 (Anniversary of the Republic); Aug 15 (Assumption of the Blessed Virgin Mary); Nov 1 (All Saints Day); Sun nearest Nov 4 (World War I Victory Anniversary Day); Dec 8 (Immaculate Conception); Dec 25 (Christmas Day); Dec 26 (San Stefano/Befana).

Internet access... Far more popular than the McDonald's that occupied the same space before it, **Easy Everything** (tel 06/429 03 388, Via Barberini 2–16), open 24 hours, has three floors with approximately 350 Internet-equipped computer terminals, plus business services like faxing and photocopying. Before plopping down at one of the computers, you'll have to buy a ticket with a passcode; 3,000L will get you anywhere from 30 minutes to an hour of Internet time—far cheaper than any other net cafe in the city—and if you don't use all your minutes, your secret code will be valid for up to a month. Also centrally located is **Trevinet Pl@ce** (tel

06/699 22 320, Via in Arcione 103), which charges 9,000L per hour but also offers Internet-assisted telephone calls to the United States for five minutes at no extra cost. Student hangout **Internet Café** (tel 06/445 49 53, Via dei Marrucini 12) in San Lorenzo offers Internet access for 8,000L per hour and a small menu of drinks and snacks in case there's a wait for a terminal.

Newspapers... You can pick up the *Wall Street Journal, USA Today,* and the *Financial Times* from almost all kiosks, though they tend to be at least one day old. A local edition of the *International Herald Tribune* is edited and printed locally in Italy and includes the *Italy Daily* supplement, a good local news summary in English. As for news in Italian, the main Roman dailies are *Il Messaggero* and *La Repubblica,* whose Thursday *Trovaroma* section provides weekly info on cultural events.

Opening and closing times... Opening and closing times in Rome are highly irregular and tend to change with the season or on the whims of the owner. Most cafes and *tabacchi* bars open around 7am and stay open until 10pm. Boutiques and other shops open at 10 or 10:30am, close in the early afternoon, and reopen around 3:30pm until 7:30pm. Many stay open later in the summer, until 8 or 8:30pm. Almost all restaurants take a *riposa settimanale* (day off), usually on Sunday or Monday. All state-owned museums are closed on Mondays; private museums may or may not close during the week. To avoid any confusion, always call ahead.

Passports and visas... Citizens of the United States, Canada, Australia, and New Zealand do not need a visa to visit Italy, nor do citizens of the European Union. If you are staying for longer than three months, you are required to apply for a *permesso di soggiorno,* available from the main police station. Be prepared for the red tape.

Post office... You're far better off sending mail through the excellent, trustworthy, and often uncrowded **Poste Vaticane** if timeliness is important. Two branches of the Vatican's post office are located on either side of St. Peter's Square, and one branch is located within the Vatican Museums. Otherwise, you can go to the **Posta Centrale** (Piazza San Silvestro 18–20, tel 06/679 30 64) to buy stamps, mail packages, or send a fax—but this is the official Italian mail, so it will almost certainly travel more slowly. Other branches are located on Via Taranto

(Metro San Giovanni) and Via Terme di Diocleziano (Metro Repubblica). If you are just mailing out a few postcards, you can buy stamps (*francobolli*) from the local *tabacchi* bar.

Public transportation... Ignore the fact that the Metro and buses are slow and packed to capacity; public transportation in Rome is fairly reliable, with a number of cross-town routes (buses 46, 64, 117, and 492, among others), clean, effective tram service, and the **Metropolitana** subway, which covers many tourist sites as well as the outlying suburbs. Routes and stops are clearly marked at each bus stop, which makes using public transportation easy for out-of-towners. **ATAC** (Via Volturno 65, tel 06/469 64 444, www.atac.roma.it) runs the city's public transportation, while **COTRAL** (Via Volturno 65, tel 06/575 31) handles extra-regional transportation such as buses to Tivoli. One-way tickets (*Biglietto Integrate a Tempo—BIT*) for the bus or the Metro cost 1,500L and are available at *tabacchi* bars. Also available are daily tickets (*Biglietto Integrate Giornaliero—BIG*) for 6,000L and weekly tickets (*Carta Integrate Settimanale—IS*) for 24,000L. You must stamp your tickets on the bus or at the Metro turnstiles upon entry. (Transport inspectors rarely show up to check your tickets, but if you're caught, you risk a fine of up to 100,000L—about $50—and heaps of public humiliation.) ATAC also runs night buses (**Bus Notturno**) at major stops. These indicated on signposts with an "N" after the bus number and by the symbol of an owl—handy, huh? Times are irregular, though, so try to avoid waiting at stops if you're traveling alone. The **Archeobus** (tel 06/469 54 695) operates as a tour bus with guided tours in Italian (and sometimes in English), helping tourists get to sites along the Appia Antica. Traveling from Piazza Venezia to the Appia Antica every hour on the hour from 9am until 5pm, this bus gives tourists a stop-and-go option whereby you can hop off one bus and on a later one without buying new tickets. Archeobus tickets are available on board for 15,000L. For the Jubilee, ATAC also introduced a new fleet of buses for the **J Line,** connecting the major basilicas with pilgrim sites. The J Line buses are faster, and run every three to seven minutes (rather than the usual five to 10 minutes); get info from the same ATAC office listed above or from ticket vendors.

Religious services... Each month brings ample opportunities to see His Holiness. The last Sunday of every month, the pope gives an address—often in Italian and another language, depending on the crowd—from his apartment two stories up overlooking St. Peter's Square. You'll want to check with your local diocese or the **Vatican's** website (www.vatican.va) for info on major masses and events. Most churches post mass times outside their door. There's always at least one mass on Sunday (at approximately 9am) and often daily masses at 7am, noon, and 6pm. **Santa Susanna** (tel 06/488 27 48, Via XX Settembre 14, Metro Repubblica) is the American parish in Rome, while **San Silvestro in Capite** (tel 06/679 77 75, Piazza San Silvestro 17a) is the British parish. English-language services are held at both of these churches on a regular basis. There are a few non-Catholic places of worship in Rome—*very* few. Attend Jewish services at the **Sinagoga** (tel 06/684 00 61, Lungotevere Cenci); Muslim services at the **Moschea** (tel 06/808 21 67, Viale della Moschea); **Methodist** (tel 06/481 48 11, Via Firenze 38); Presbyterian at **St. Andrew's** (tel 06/482 76 27, Via XX Settembre 7).

Taxes and duty free... As required by the European Union, Italy imposes a sales tax or **Value Added Tax** (VAT) of 12–35 percent for all goods and services. Shops that display the "Euro Tax Free" sticker will give you a refund form for the VAT on goods worth more than 300,000L. Present this form, along with your passport, receipts, and purchases upon departure from the EU. In most instances, a check will be mailed to you later; however, if you have shopped in a store displaying the "Tax-Free Shopping for Tourists," you are entitled to a cash refund on the spot at the border customs office. Note that items that have been used in any way are *not* eligible for these rebates.

Taxis... Taking a taxi in Rome feels like a rip-off. There are surcharges for luggage (2,000L for each piece), traveling to and from the airport (12,000–14,000L), and for simply taking a cab between the hours of 10pm and 7am (5,000L). Hailing a cab is just not done in Rome; instead, go to a cab stand (located near major sites) and flag the first one in line. Watch out for car jockeys who lurk near taxi stands; if the cab name and number is not painted on a car, they are not legally sanctioned drivers and will probably gouge you. The concierge at any hotel should call a cab for you. However, if you need to call one on your own, contact **Radio Taxi** (tel 06/49 94) or **Cooperativa Samarcanda** (tel 06/55 51). Note that when you call a taxi, the meter starts running at the time of the call, *not* when the cab arrives. See? Rip-off again.

Telephones... Public pay phones are a common source of frustration for locals and tourists alike; this is why you'll never be far from the high-pitched ringing of a *telefonino* (cell phone). Most Italians own cell phones, rather than bother with pay phones that are constantly out of order. If you need to use a pay phone you must first purchase a phone card from a *tabacchi* bar; the cards come in denominations of 10,000L and higher, but they can be tricky to use when making international calls. Otherwise, if you're calling from a regular phone, and have a account with AT&T, MCI, or Sprint, you can dial its toll-free number to access an English-speaking operator and make a calling card call. For AT&T, dial 172-1011 first; for MCI, dial 172-1022 first; and, for Sprint, dial 172-1877 first.

Time... Rome is one hour ahead of Greenwich Mean Time (London) and six hours ahead of Eastern Standard Time (New York).

Tipping... Tipping is perfectly acceptable in Italy, and it's expected of tourists who are used to tipping in their home countries. However, in most cases an automatic service charge of 10 to 15 percent is already tacked onto restaurant checks—known as the *pane e coperto* (bread and cover) charge—so check first before laying down any extra cash. If you've received extraordinary service, an additional tip of approximately 10 percent is customary. You should also tip porters, cab drivers, and maids a few thousand lira for their efforts. A few coins presented at a bar while ordering your cappuccino will usually get you speedier service, too.

Travelers with disabilities... With streets of uneven cobblestones, churches with tall marble staircases, and uncertain elevator access in hotels, Rome is probably one of the worst imaginable cities for disabled travelers. However, changes are in progress to make it easier for the wheelchair-bound. **Roma Accessible,** produced by the **Consorzio Cooperative Integrate** (COIN—Via Enrico Giglioli 54a, tel 06/232 67 504), contains information on accessibility in hotels, museums, restaurants, and other sites. Information is also available 24 hours a day in English on its hotline. Check the web at www.andi.

casaccia.enea.it/hometur.htm for additional updates.

Visitor information... Tourist information kiosks are located in Fiumicino Airport and Termini Station, as well near the Spanish Steps, Piazza Navona, Trastevere, and other heavy tourist areas. The city's main **tourist office** is located at Via Parigi 5 (tel 06/488 99 253, open Mon–Fri 8:15am–7:15pm, Sat 8:15am–1:45pm). Here, you can pick up free maps and guides of the city and learn about current exhibitions, musical events, and more. Agents at the kiosks tend to be quite helpful, and most speak English well enough to get you where you're going. **Enjoy Rome** (tel 06/445 18 43, open Mon–Fri 8:30am–2pm and 3:30–6pm, Sat 8:30am–2pm) is a free service run by native English speakers. They can help you out with hotel info, dining and nightlife suggestions, and tips on touring the city.

Weather... Relatively mild year-round, the city rarely sees highs drop below 55°F in the winter or go higher than 85°F in the summer. However, you should never over- or underestimate Rome's temperate climate. Summers are dry and made even more oppressive by heavy traffic. November is the rainiest month, and the moist, raw air can be bone-chilling.

Women's Rome... Women who need gynecological care can visit **Artemide** (Via Sannio 61, tel 06/704 76 220), a private clinic that offers pap smears and pregnancy tests at moderate fees. **Telefono Rosa** (tel 06/683 26 90 or 06/683 28 20) is an emergency helpline for women who need counseling or advice in reference to sexual abuse or harassment.